P9-AQL-791

The Star, the Cross, and the Crescent

After the Empire:
The Francophone World and
Postcolonial France

Series Editor
Valérie Orlando, University of Maryland

Advisory Board
Robert Bernasconi, Memphis University; Alec Hargreaves, Florida State University; Chima Korieh, Rowan University; Mildred Mortimer, University of Colorado, Boulder; Obioma Nnaemeka, Indiana University; Kamal Salhi, University of Leeds; Tracy D. Sharpley-Whiting, Vanderbilt University; Nwachukwu Frank Ukadike, Tulane University

*See www.lexingtonbooks.com/series for the series description and
a complete list of published titles.*

Recent and Forthcoming Titles

Collective Memory: France and the Algerian War (1954–1962), by Jo McCormack

The Other Hybrid Archipelago: Introduction to the Literatures and Cultures of the Francophone Indian Ocean, by Peter Hawkins

Rethinking Marriage in Francophone African and Caribbean Literatures, by Cécile Accilien

Two Novellas by YAE: A Moroccan in New York *and* Sea Drinkers, by Youssouf Amine Elalamy, translated by John Liechty

Frankétienne and Rewriting: A Work in Progress, by Rachel Douglas

Charles Testut's Le Vieux Salomon*: Race, Religion, Socialism, and Freemasonry,* Sheri Lyn Abel

What Moroccan Cinema?: A Historical and Critical Study 1956–2006, by Sandra Carter

Voices of Exile in Contemporary Canadian Francophone Literature, by F. Elizabeth Dahab

Re-hybridizing Transnational Domesticity and Femininity: Women's Contemporary Filmmaking and Lifewriting of France, Algeria, and Tunisia, by Stacey Weber-Feve

The Star, the Cross, and the Crescent: Religions and Conflicts in Francophone Literature from the Arab World, by Carine Bourget

The Star, the Cross, and the Crescent

Religions and Conflicts in Francophone Literature from the Arab World

Carine Bourget

LEXINGTON BOOKS
A division of
ROWMAN & LITTLEFIELD PUBLISHERS, INC.
Lanham • Boulder • New York • Toronto • Plymouth, UK

Published by Lexington Books
A division of Rowman & Littlefield Publishers, Inc.
A wholly owned subsidary of The Rowman & Littlefield Publishing Group, Inc.
4501 Forbes Boulevard, Suite 200, Lanham, Maryland 20706
http://www.lexingtonbooks.com

Estover Road, Plymouth PL6 7PY, United Kingdom

British Library Cataloguing in Publication Information Available

Library of Congress Cataloging-in-Publication Data

Bourget, Carine.
  The star, the cross, and the crescent : religions and conflicts in Francophone literature from the Arab world / Carine Bourget.
      p. cm. — (After the empire: the Francophone world and)
  Includes bibliographical references and index.
  ISBN 978-0-7391-2657-8 (cloth : alk. paper)
  1. North African literature (French)—20th century—History and criticism. 2. French literature—Arab authors—History and criticism. 3. French literature—Arab countries—History and criticism. 4. French literature—20th century—history and criticism. 5. Islam in literature. 6. Social conflict in literature. 7. Politics in literature. 8. War in literature. I. Title.
  PQ3980.5.B68 2010
  840.9'892761—dc22   2009048357

Printed in the United States of America

To my husband and children

Contents

Acknowledgments

I would like to thank the following colleagues and friends for their careful reading and insightful feedback on various parts of this manuscript: Jonathan Beck, Julia Clancy-Smith, Anne Donadey, Leila Hudson, Marie-Pierre Le Hir, Maha Nassar, Valérie Orlando, and Laurence Porter. Any errors and shortcomings are of course mine.

I am grateful to my colleagues from the Department of French & Italian, the Department of Near Eastern Studies, and the Center for Middle Eastern Studies at the University of Arizona for providing a stimulating and supportive work environment. I want to single out Marie-Pierre Le Hir for her valuable guidance and encouragement throughout the years. I would also like to acknowledge Irène D'Almeida and Lise Leibacher for their thoughtful mentoring.

Although this book did not originate at Michigan State University, I wish to express my deep appreciation to Laurence Porter for introducing me to Francophone Literature during my graduate studies there. His rigorous scholarship and generous mentoring will remain models for me to emulate throughout my career. Many thanks go to Ken Harrow for introducing me to African Literature during his lively and challenging seminars.

A very special note of gratitude is owed to my husband, not only for reading and commenting on most of this manuscript. This book simply could not have been written without his constant support, confidence, and encouragement. May my oldest children read this book one day and hopefully conclude that the time spent away from them was put to good use.

All efforts have been made to obtain copyright permissions. I thank the publishers for permission to reprint from the works listed below: Citations from *Ports of Call* by Amin Maalouf, translated by Alberto Manguel, published by Harvill Press are reprinted by permission of The Random House Group Ltd. Citations from *Les versets du pardon* by Myriam Antaki, © 1999 by Actes Sud, are reprinted by permission of Editions Actes Sud. Citations from *Les croisades vues par les Arabes* by Amin Maalouf, © 1983 by Lattès, are reprinted by permission of Editions Lattès. Citations from *JuifsArabes* by Farid Boudjellal, © 2006 by Futuropolis, are reprinted by permission of Editions Futuropolis. Citations from *Dreams of Trespass* by Fatima Mernissi, © 1994 by Perseus Books, are reprinted by permission of Perseus Books. Citations from *Pillar of Salt* by

Albert Memmi, translated by Edouard Roditi, © 1955 by Criterion Books, Inc., are reprinted by permission of Beacon Press, Boston. Citations from *Juifs et Arabes*, *Portrait du décolonisé arabo-musulman et de quelques autres*, and *La statue de sel* by Albert Memmi, © by Editions Gallimard, are reprinted by permission of Editions Gallimard. Citations from *Tuez-les tous* by Salim Bachi, © by Editions Gallimard, are reprinted by permission of Editions Gallimard. Citations from *Une enfance algérienne* edited by Leïla Sebbar, © by Editions Gallimard, are reprinted by permission of Editions Gallimard. Citations from *Les échelles du Levant* by Amin Maalouf, © 1996 by Grasset & Fasquelle, are reprinted by permission of Editions Bernard Grasset. Citations from *Les identités meurtrières* by Amin Maalouf, © 1998 by Editions Grasset & Fasquelle, are reprinted by permission of Editions Bernard Grasset. Excerpts from *The Last Night of a Damned Soul* by Slimane Benaissa, © 2003 by Editions Plon, translation © 2004 by Janice and Daniel Gross, used by permission of Grove/Atlantic, Inc.

For the book cover, I thank Rémi Ochlik/IP3 PRESS for permission to reprint the photograph of the veiled girl (mentioned in chapter five), and editions Futuropolis for permission to reproduce two drawings from Farid Boudjellal's *JuifsArabes*.

Introduction

Religion, Politics, and Literature from the Francophone Arab World

The resurgence of religion in various parts of the world (including the West) and across religious traditions represents a challenge to the Western construction of modernity. It disputes the modernization theory that economic progress and modernization entail secularism. Social scientists have been tackling this for some time now, for example in studies that look at the role of religion in International Relations (Thomas, Hatzopoulos and Petito) and conflict resolution (Gopin).

Although the resurgence of religion spans different cultures, religions, and geographical areas, much focus has been put on Islam. Already back in the 1980s, Said noted the double standard that was being applied by some scholars who consider that Islam is unique in being a political religion, as if Christianity and Judaism were immune to politics. Said went on to note that "Israel is perhaps the most perfect coincidence of religion and politics in the contemporary world," a fact rarely noted and taken to question in the Western media, which routinely tout Israel as the only democratic state in the Middle East. Said added that then-president Ronald Reagan "time and again connect[s] religion and politics" ("The Essential Terrorist" 157). This last statement also applies to former American president George W. Bush. In addition, "the development of a powerful and rejectionist Zionist lobby among evangelical groups in the U.S., [...] has accented yet again the contradiction inherent in an allegedly secular U.S. support for a nation-state based in large part on Biblical promise" (Qureshi and Sells 8).

There is a debate between scholars who present contemporary Islamic fundamentalism as an answer to and a consequence of modernization in the twentieth century, and those who view it as a variant of traditional social protests that have commonly used religion as a vehicle for political demands (Volpi 26). Olivier Roy points out the inadequacy of the culturalist approach that consists in simply resorting to Islam as an explanation for everything that goes on in the Muslim world. According to him, "we should take Islamisation as a contemporary phenomenon that expresses the globalization and westernization

1

of the Muslim world" (15). Likewise, comparative political theorist Roxanne Euben insists on the failure of both models to render the complexity of Islamic fundamentalism, which she sees as a "combination of the failure of ideological alternatives, the unavailability of competing political channels, and the authenticity that accrues to religious, and specifically Islamic, identifications in the Middle East" (48). The fall of pan-Arabism following the 1967 Arab defeat and the failure of Western-oriented policies to improve the lot of the people made Islamist movements the only viable and credible source of opposition for corrupt and authoritarian Western-supported regimes. This is a key reason why such movements have been gaining popularity in various countries.

Salman Sayyid remarks that "the political turn of Islam cannot be understood outside the very complex ways in which it relates to the project of Western hegemony" (xxii). Accordingly, this religious revivalism can be traced back to colonialism and neocolonialism, as evidenced by Western-backed authoritarian regimes (Esposito 21). As John Esposito points out, "When governments, faced with a viable opposition, use the charge of religious extremism to justify curtailment of political liberalization and the use of repression, the result—as we are witnessing in Algeria—is the radicalization of moderate religious voices, the creation of new, violent revolutionary groups, the polarization of society, and the ravages of civil war" (21). In other words, repression is only backfiring as it pushes moderate voices into extremism.

In addition, Western leaders privilege regimes who present themselves in terms the West is accustomed to as the agents of stability and modernity; however, such regimes "serve to arouse Islamist fervour both by their continuing repressive policies at home and by directing such fervour towards U.S./West when domestic pressures become acute" (Entelis 213). Scholars also emphasize the cleavage that has been growing between the ruling elite and the people. According to John Entelis,

> Islamist politics is first and foremost about politics—who gets what, when and how—and only secondarily about Islam. In the Islamic world, politics is controlled by the unelected few ruling over the alienated, disenfranchised many. This condition of oppression is reinforced objectively and perceptually by the alliances such regimes have made with outside powers, especially the United States, with the latter then being viewed by the masses as an additional instrument in the oppressive mechanism put in place by the *mukhabarat* state to keep civil society in check. (212)

The popularity of Islamic movements and the violent tactics some of them have adopted stem from the political illegitimacy of Arab states.

Robert Fernea points out the West's hypocrisy when it denounces authoritarian regimes that it supports: "it is our responsibility to understand what is happening rather than negatively labeling as 'Islamic fundamentalism' this new discourse, and in opposition blindly supporting sectarian governments that use familiar terms and make comfortable promises to Western governments" (x). Fatima Mernissi persuasively argues that Western democracies have promoted and profited from Islamic and particularly Saudi fundamentalism, with petrodollars funding authoritarian regimes whose massive arms purchases benefit Western companies. Indeed, "the symbiotic relationship between Western liberal democracies and the palace fundamentalisms of the Gulf states (along with the popular street fundamentalisms they fund outside their borders) puts into question the supposition of a rational, democratic, liberal West facing an irrational and fundamentalist East" (Qureshi and Sells 17).

Esposito reminds us that while the elite minority is secular, "a majority in non-western societies continues to live or to be influenced by religiously informed cultures" (20). Faced with the complete failure of the modern state to improve the living conditions that are worsening for the majority while the elite is getting wealthier, "Religious revivalisms (or fundamentalisms) often represent the voices of those who, amidst the failures of their societies, claim both to ameliorate the problems and to offer a more authentic, religiously-based society" (Esposito 21). One reason why Islamic movements have gained popularity in various countries is that they have provided basic services such as health clinics and schools, where the state had failed to meet its obligation (Esposito 21), a fact they rarely receive credit for in the Western media.

9/11 has given new impetus to the theory of the clash of civilizations, although that theory has been debunked by several studies. As Emran Qureshi and Michael Sells point out, the assertion that there is a clash of civilization "has become an ideological agent that may help generate the conflict that it posits" (3). The binary opposition between the West and the rest asserted by the theory of the clash of civilizations does not hold. As Euben points out, the contrast often made between the West as a secular humanist and the Islamic East "does not easily map onto, for example, the sociological religiosity of American culture, the growth of religious revivalism in American politics," nor does it take into account the influence of Western thought on Islamic thinkers such as Sayyid Qutb, whose writings are said to inspire fundamentalists of various calibers (166). Philosopher Jacques Derrida sees the opposition not between the West and the East, but between the US and a Europe that he sees as "the only secular actor on the world stage" (Borradori 170). Similarly, Charles Kaplan states that the "coming clash of civilizations will be not between the West and the rest but within a West divided against itself" (qtd. in Majid, *Freedom* 198). One could add and within an East divided against itself. Commenting on recent conflicts such as the genocide in Rwanda and the first Gulf War, Andreas Hasenclever and Volker Rittberger note that, "What these conflicts, together with many others, have in common is the fierce competition between domestic elites who are ready to do almost anything to keep or get political power" (112).

International relations theorists have proposed a third alternative to the Primordialists (proponents of the clash of civilizations, who see the source of conflict as rooted in cultural differences), and Instrumentalists (who see the source of conflict as based on socioeconomic grievances). The moderate constructivists, like the Instrumentalists, see the source of conflict grounded in socio-economic and political disparities, but see religion playing a role in the manner the conflict is handled. They "propose to view religion as an intervening variable, i.e., a causal factor intervening between a given conflict and the choice of conflict behavior" (Hasenclever and Rittberger 115).

While the resurgence of religion has been studied extensively in the social sciences, 9/11 acted as a watershed event that prompted scholars in the humanities to give religion more attention (although some writers and scholars were already engaged with the issue). Since the last decades of the twentieth century, Francophone writers from the Arab world have been grappling anew with Islam's resurgence, as it became increasingly associated with sensational headlines in a variety of contexts.[1] In the 1990s, prompted by contemporary socio-political events, canonical Maghrebian writers such as Driss Chraïbi and Assia Djebar wrote fictional historical accounts of Islam's beginnings.[2] As noted by Edward Said in Covering Islam, "it is not difficult to imagine that a Muslim might be made uncomfortable by the relentless insistence—even if it is put in terms of a debate—that her or his faith, culture, and people are seen as a source of threat, and that she or he has been deterministically associated with terrorism, violence, and 'fundamentalism'" (xxi). A new introduction to the 1997 revised edition ascertains that nothing has really changed in the more than twenty-five years that have passed since the book first came out in 1981. Given the amalgam that is commonplace between Muslims and Arabs in Western popular culture,[3] one can extend Said's statement about Muslims to Arabs regardless of their faith: in other words, Arabs might be uncomfortable that their ethnicity is seen as a source of threat.

With Islam (and the Arab world often conflated with it) taking center stage as the post-Cold War enemy, and the much controversial thesis of the clash of civilizations regaining notoriety after 9/11, how have writers from the Arab world represented various conflicts, which have been framed in religious (Islam/Christianity), civilizational (Islam/Christendom), and imperialist (East/West) terms? What are the paths mapped by literary texts out of the political turmoil that sparks new national constructions and allegiances?

Francophone writers from the Arab world are often cast in an uneasy position of intermediaries between their culture and country of origin on one side, and their mostly French readership on the other, as many of these writers reside in France and publish their work there. These writers, who hail from parts of the former French empire, often find themselves in a delicate situation between the colonial legacy of their language of literary expression and the conflation in the media and (popular) culture between the Arab and Muslim world and fundamentalism and terrorism. Yet, given that they occupy a liminal space between two worlds that are often posited in antagonistic terms, they seem to be in an ideal position to foster cross-cultural understanding, and to map the future coexistence of diverse groups in their communities.

However, it is not certain that they are always successful in providing insights into the complexity of the resurgence of religion, and particularly when Islam is involved. Postcolonial theory has been noted as deficient when it comes to specific issues linked to the Arab-Muslim world (Majid, Unveiling 19-21; see also Hassan in chapter one). In French and Francophone Studies, the term Islamic fundamentalism is, with rare exceptions, used indiscriminately as an unquestioned blanket term to refer to all aspects of the resurgence of religion. Anouar Majid already noted a decade ago in a brief article that, "Their [intellectuals and writers in the Islamic world today] uncomplicated, one-dimensional reading of the Islamic resurgence, makes them, unwittingly or not, accomplices of the West and the ruling elites in almost all Arab and Islamic countries" ("Islam" 87). Although he does not focus on Francophone literature, several of the examples he gives of writers whom he denounces for giving monolithic representations of Islam are Francophone (Ben Jelloun, Accad, Mimouni), and are closely examined in this study.

Focusing on the intersection of Islam, politics, history, and Francophone literature, this book examines how French and Francophone writers from the Maghreb (Morocco, Algeria, Tunisia) and the Near East (Lebanon, Syria) grapple with the intertwining of religion and politics in various conflicting contexts. To this end, this study analyzes various means of cultural production, including essays, novels, films, and comic books by Francophone Arab writers and filmmakers whose Christian (Evelyne Accad, Myriam Antaki, Andrée Chédid, Amin Maalouf), Jewish (Karin Albou, Albert Bensoussan, Hélène Cixous, Edmond Amran El Maleh, Albert Memmi), Muslim (Salim Bachi, Slimane Benaïssa, Yamina Benguigui, Tahar Ben Jelloun, Rachid Boudjedra, Farid Boudjellal, Abdelwahab Meddeb, Rachid Mimouni), and secular (Leïla Sebbar) backgrounds are emblematic of the diversity of the Francophone Arab world. It examines how these writers (dis)entangle religious, political, economic, and cultural factors, and how they articulate the past, present, and future of religious minorities in the Arab world, against the backdrop of the current international political context of Islamic fundamentalism and the persistence of Western prejudices against Islam. At a time when Islamic fundamentalism is making regular headlines, the book focuses on texts that deal with disputes commonly framed in religious terms (with Islam as the common denominator for all) in order to describe how the Francophone Arab world has responded to the discourse that pits Islam against the West.

While the cultural production of countries constituting the Francophone world is expressed in many languages, there is a disproportionate attention given to the one in French. By virtue of their publications' location and through translation of their work, these writers shape the French (and other) public's (mis)understanding of various conflicts allegedly stemming from Islamic resurgence. Their influence extends beyond hexagonal borders through translation of their work, and thanks to the rise of Francophone Studies, in the U.S. and the U.K. in particular. This book builds on Richard Serrano's assertion that the Francophone Studies model skews our understanding of those regions (6-7), a fact already noted by social scientists such as François Burgat who points out that "a French-speaking Maghreb . . . has masked the emergence of an impertinent new Maghreb, which today wants to use a new language" (5). Many writers who have been trained in the French secular tradition fail to understand and give insights into what has been broadly labeled as the Islamic Revival that has been taking place in the Muslim world in the past decades. As we will see in the case of the Algerian and Lebanese civil wars, Francophone writers are not always able to render the complexity of some events. In cases involving the complexity of the resurgence of religion, there is a remarkable downplay of the role and impact of European colonialism in shaping current events in parts of the Arab world, and this under the pen of writers who had vigorously denounced colonialism in the past. Following the failure of secular ideologies such as pan-Arabism and Marxism, these writers are for the most part unable to see the resurgence of Islam divorced from political claims. In other words, when Islamic rhetoric is linked to political issues, they point out the political events and their effects, but they fall into the trap of thinking that Islam can only be a means to achieving certain political goals. They fail to portray the fact that for many, Islam is not just a cultural background but also offers spiritual guidance. This shortcoming could be due to some degree of anxiety about maintaining their status as privileged interpreters.

The book is organized thematically around a series of conflicts in the Arab world (or linked to its diaspora) that have made headlines during the second half of the twentieth century. Some conflicts are construed as internal, such as the Lebanese civil war (a Christian/Muslim Arab conflict) and the Algerian civil war (Islamic fundamentalism against secular democracy); others as external: the Arab-Israeli conflict, and Islam's advance in the West through immigration (the headscarf affair in France).

Chapter 1, the Arab-Israeli conflict, examines works that turned to the past as a way to take attention away from the discourse on terrorism and back to the root causes of the Arab-Israeli conflict. The first part of the chapter examines Maalouf's *Les croisades vues par les Arabes* [*The Crusades through Arab Eyes*], a book that challenges the clash of civilization discourses (now and then) that pit a Christian West against a Muslim East, and that also provides a commentary on contemporary politics in the Middle East. The second part analyzes representations of the conflict through a family story and contrasts the use of genealogies as conflict resolution in two novels: Maalouf's *Les échelles du Levant* [*Ports of Call*] and Antaki's *Les versets du pardon* [*Verses of Forgiveness*]. In Maalouf's book, the union between Jewish and Arab characters functions simply as a sign of hope for future conflict resolution. Antaki's recourse to the genealogical paradigm goes beyond that; it challenges stereotypes and points towards a first step to conflict resolution by revisiting the past to move towards a future beyond the ideology of separation.

Chapter 2 focuses on the geographic displacement of the Arab-Israeli conflict by analyzing the representation of its impact on Maghrebian countries and contemporary France. It first compares two Arab Jewish writers' take on the identity of the Arab Jew in essays and articles, notably Albert Memmi's *Juifs et Arabes* [*Jews and Arabs*] and *Portrait du décolonisé arabo-musulman et de quelques autres* [*Decolonization and the Decolonized*] as well as various pieces published by Edmond Amran El Maleh. The chapter also addresses the correlation between these writers' positions on the Arab-Israeli conflict, noting the relative prominence of each writer (Memmi's renown and El Maleh's obscurity). The second part of the chapter contrasts the representation of the relations between Arabs and Jews in France in Farid Boudjellal's *JuifsArabes* [JewsArabs], a comic book, and Karin Albou's film *La petite Jérusalem* [*Little Jerusalem*]. It aims to demonstrate that, contrary to Albou's film, Boudjellal's comic book participates in an endeavor to go beyond the ideology of partition and separation that has dominated approaches to the Arab-Israeli conflict.

Chapter 3, on the Lebanese civil war, examines how Francophone Lebanese writers have depicted the conflict, and more specifically how they have dealt with the religious dimension of a civil war that was summarily depicted in the West as a Muslim/Christian rift. It argues that two novels, Chédid's *La maison sans racines* [*The Return to Beirut*] and Accad's *L'excisée* [*The Excised*], reinforce the reductive view of the Lebanese civil war as a religious conflict. A close analysis of the Biblical and Qur'anic intertexts demonstrates that Accad's inscription of verses from the Qur'an provides a stereotyped view of Islam while the Biblical quotations implicitly reaffirm Christian values of sacrifice and redemption.

Chapter 4, on the Algerian civil war, starts by analyzing the representation of the rise of the FIS and the civil war in Mimouni's *De la barbarie en général et de l'intégrisme en particulier* [On barbarity in general and on fundamentalism in particular] and Boudjedra's *Le FIS de la haine* [the Islamic Salvation Front of hate]. It demonstrates that both essays do more to feed the flames of fear than to further our understanding of the events under scrutiny. The second part of the chapter analyzes how the civil war intrudes in *Une enfance algérienne* [*An Algerian Childhood*], a collection of short autobiographical narratives edited by Sebbar that features pieces by writers from diverse backgrounds who spent their childhood in colonial Algeria. It shows that the effects of colonialism are mostly erased or downplayed, while the violence that surfaces is mostly associated with the Algerian nationalist movement during the war for independence and with the rise of Islamic fundamentalism. It also draws out the implications of this shift of perpetrators of violence given the context of publication of the volume

Chapter 5 examines how Francophone Arab writers have responded to the French Muslim headscarf affair and the discourse surrounding Islam's (in)compatibility with the secular Republic in non-fiction works. It demonstrates that prominent writers such as Ben Jelloun, Maalouf, Meddeb, and Memmi, have not adequately situated the debate in light of French (post)colonial history and have failed to provide a balanced view about the so-called Islamist challenge to the secular French Republic. This chapter then contrasts the more complex representations by Sebbar and Benguigui, and draws out the implications from the absence of pictures of veiled girls in works that include text and images.

Chapter 6 looks at the representation of 9/11 in Francophone novels from the Arab world and compares the function of extensive quotations from the Qur'an in Benaïssa's *La dernière nuit d'un damné* [*The Last Night of a Damned*

Soul] and Bachi's *Tuez-les tous* [kill them all]. These two 9/11 novels imagine the itinerary of a 9/11 hijacker leading up to the attacks. I argue that the Islamic intertext of Benaïssa's novel gives fodder to proponents of the clash of civilization discourse, while Bachi's multicultural intertext accounts for the complexity of factors behind the 9/11 attacks.

The conclusion of the book underscores the impact of 9/11 on the English translation and packaging of some of the texts treated in this study. Reflecting on the spike of American interest in the literary production of the Arab and Muslim world, the book offers a critical evaluation of this trend's impact and implications in general, and for Francophone Studies in particular.

This study provides a critical examination of representations of the role of religions in conflicts from the perspective of the Arab Francophone world at a time when, in the wake of 9/11 and the rise of Islamic fundamentalism, it is most needed. Drawing on a variety of methodologies, such as cultural studies, international relations theory and conflict resolution, the study also brings heightened awareness to the impact of literature on our understanding of contemporary issues as well as on the modalities according to which a literary work can serve as a cultural mediator. Finally, the focus on the topic of religions and conflicts in Francophone literature by Arab writers is particularly useful for examining how the Francophone studies model frames current issues and for evaluating its effectiveness in giving a complete picture of religious issues involving Islam.

Notes

1. For a summary, see the new introduction to Said's revised edition of *Covering Islam*, especially pages xii-xiv, which offer an abbreviated list of events between 1983 and 1996.

2. See Chraïbi's *L'homme du livre* and Djebar's *Loin de Médine*, and my *Coran et tradition islamique dans la littérature maghrébine* for an analysis of these texts.

3. The terms Arabs and Muslims are sometimes used interchangeably, although Arabs (among whom there are Christian and Jewish minorities) comprise only about twenty percent of the Muslim population nowadays, and despite the diversity of Muslim countries (which extend from Morocco to Indonesia).

Chapter 1

The Arab-Israeli Conflict:
Amin Maalouf's *Les croisades vues par les Arabes* and *Les échelles du Levant*, Myriam Antaki's *Les versets du pardon*

The Palestinian-Israeli conflict remains one of the most intractable clashes of the twentieth century, and unfortunately shows no sign of being resolved any time soon. In the Spring of 2008, the state of Israel celebrated its sixtieth birthday, a day commemorated by one side as "Independence day" and mourned by the other as the "Nakba" (catastrophy). This chapter examines books that are focused on the past in order to take attention away from the discourse on terrorism and back to representations of the root causes of the Arab-Israeli conflict and the different contexts that shape these representations.

In a collection of articles published in the 1980s, Said and other scholars analyzed various processes by which Palestinians, victims of a mass dispossession in 1948, are turned into essentialized aggressors. Summarizing an article written by the Israeli journalist Amnon Kapeliouk in 1986, Said noted that "as Palestinian nationalism acquired regional and international credibility in the mid-1970s, Israeli officials consciously adopted the policy of characterizing it as 'terrorism.' [...] the word 'terrorism' was a political weapon designed to protect the strong (and eliminate from memory exploits of 'former' terrorists like Begin and Shamir who now run Israel) as well as to legitimize official military action against innocents" ("Introduction" 13). In the same book, Noam Chomsky detailed how U.S. and Israeli officials, along with mainstream media, routinely labeled any acts of resistance as terrorism, thereby justifying retaliation, in the context of the 1980s' Israeli invasion of Lebanon and U.S. involvement in Nicaragua, all the while occulting their own terrorism abroad. As early as the 1980s, Said pointed out that terrorism had "displaced Communism as public enemy number one" in American public discourse ("The Essential" 149). The prevalence of the term serves to put aside historical evidence ("The Essential" 149).

Commenting on a 2002 piece by Said, Stephen Morton notes that there is "a historical relationship between imperialism and the discourse of terrorism" (36). Morton recalls that the figure of the contemporary terrorist is often summoned as the reason for the American and British invasion of Afghanistan and Iraq, as well the backing of Israeli occupation of the West Bank and Lebanon (36). He goes on to state that "Such a causal logic conceals the fact that the threat of terrorism is an instance of metalepsis: an effect of colonial discourse that is presented as a cause" (36). In other words, terrorism is supplanting Orientalism as a justification for imperialism: "If orientalism provides the sovereign power of the colonial state with a discourse of otherness to justify the suspension of the rule of civil law in times of crisis, [...] the contemporary discourse of terrorism would seem to serve a similar function" (Morton 36).

The rise of Postcolonial Studies has brought to the fore the plight of most indigenous people who fell under the yoke of European imperialism. However, it has, as Salah Hassan has underscored, neglected the issue of Palestine. As Hassan points out, "Postcolonial disengagement from Palestine is especially striking when one considers the role of Edward Said in shaping the field" (33), given that Said's *Orientalism* is considered a founding text of the field. In addition to his work on literary theory and comparative literature, Said has dedicated several books to the issue of Palestine.[1] A recent issue of *PMLA* (October 2006) tangentially started to redress that neglect, when it published the proceedings of a conference entitled "The Humanities in Human Rights: Critique, Language, Politics," held in October 2005. Two contributors (Omar Barghouti and Alisa Solomon) analyzed the dehumanization of Palestinians in Israel and in U.S. media. In the following year, Gaurav Desai mentions the Palestinian-Israeli conflict as one example of the politics of indigeneity for which postcolonial studies "will have to articulate new ways of thinking" (642). Despite these brief mentions, unease remains over the issue of the Palestinian question and whether Israel can be seen as a colonial power.[2]

Postcolonial Studies triggered the growth of Francophone Studies, which is also characterized, incidentally, by a lack of interest in the Near East. Despite the expansion of the areas under the purview of the field of Francophone Studies, the Francophone production of the Levant has somewhat been neglected, in part because of the paucity of writers of French expression from that region compared to that of the Maghreb. This chapter hopes to fill a gap in both fields by focusing on a topic (Palestine) and writers (Maalouf, Antaki) that have been left at the margins. The first part examines Maalouf's *Les croisades vues par les Arabes,* a book that challenges the clash of civilization discourses (now and then) that pit a Christian West against a Muslim East. The rewriting of history in this book is grounded in and comments on events taking place in the Middle East contemporary to the time of its writing. The second part analyzes representations of the conflict through the use of a genealogical paradigm in two novels. In Maalouf's *Les échelles du Levant*, the union between a Jew and an Arab functions as a sign of hope for future conflict resolution. Antaki's *Les versets du pardon* goes beyond that; it challenges stereotypes and points towards a first step to conflict resolution by revisiting the past to move forwards into a future beyond the ideology of separation. I unpack the genealogy that portrays the Arab-Israeli issue to show the various allegorical levels that combine to entangle history, religion, politics, and terrorism. I demonstrate how Antaki's work stands out as she invokes a means to conflict resolution grounded in scriptures.

Origins: Rewriting History in Amin Maalouf's *Les croisades vues par les Arabes*[3]

Maalouf, a Lebanese writer who won the prestigious Goncourt prize in 1993 for his novel *Le rocher de Tanios*, has received little attention from scholars of Francophone literature in the United States. As a Christian Arab exiled in France since 1976, Maalouf occupies a pivot point between his country of exile and his region of origin. While examining his identity in the essay *Identités meurtrières*, Maalouf underlines the paradox of being a Christian with Arabic, the sacred language of Islam, as his native tongue (23-24). These "appartenances multiples" 'multiple belongings' (*Identités* 40) that characterize "frontaliers" 'border people' (*Identités* 46) afford him a singular vantage point from which to take a fresh look at the historical period of the Crusades from 1096 to 1291.[4]

The title of *Les croisades vues par les Arabes* problematizes the notion of objective historiography, and makes explicit Maalouf's intent: to adopt the perspective of those who suffered from the Crusades,[5] which in Western eyes are still seen as a great epic. Indeed, the term "crusade" in today's English is used, as is *croisade* in French, to refer not only to the historical military expeditions to the Near East, but also to denote any well-intentioned though possibly overzealous campaign for a worthy cause, and as such often carries a positive connotation. Maalouf's objective in his book is not simply to set the historical record straight: his rewriting of history is also intended as a commentary on contemporary politics. In this section, I explore how narrative strategies shape Maalouf's counter-history; why considerations of the problems inherent to the (re)writing of history are relegated to the background; and what motivates the rewriting of history in *Les croisades vues par les Arabes*, given that the historiographical act takes place within a specific context and can thus be politicized.

As Linda Hutcheon puts it, there is a distinction to be made between events of the past and the historical facts drawn from them: "Facts are events to which we have given meaning. Different historical perspectives therefore derive different facts from the same events" (*Politics* 57). Because Maalouf writes in French, one can assume that his target audience is a Western reader to whom he wants to show a different version of the facts conventionally derived from the events that took place in the Middle East during the twelfth and thirteenth centuries.

Again, the title of Maalouf's book places it in opposition to others written on the same topic.[6] Texts published by medievalists prior to the 1980s were mostly titled "The Crusades" or "History of the Crusades,"[7] and purported to present a global, objective picture of these historical events. In contrast, Maalouf specifies in his title that he will examine the period from a restricted point of view. Maalouf's title thus challenges the supposed unicity of history that previous historical works on the Crusades seemed to take for granted. And while some European historians by mid-twentieth century had come to a more critical appraisal of the Crusades, there remained a gap between scholarly and popular views (Constable 2). Maalouf does not explicitly situate himself vis-à-vis his subject, hiding, instead, behind the first person plural "we" of academic narrative. However, his purpose is made clear in the Foreword, and while Maalouf did not have at the time of publication of *Les croisades vues par les Arabes* the renown that he now enjoys, his name as author is easily identified as Arabic.[8] The prologue and epilogue both emphasize his intent to set forth a little-known perspective and the influence it has had on interpreting contemporary events.

Michel de Certeau and Hayden White, among others, have emphasized how the telling of the past is linked to contemporary ideological, political, or cultural factors (Hutcheon, *Poetics* 120-22). In his ground-breaking text *The Writing of History*, de Certeau argues that any return to history reflects preoccupations contemporary to its writing:

> On ne saurait supposer non plus, comme elle [l'historiographie] tend parfois à le faire croire, qu'un "commencement", plus haut dans le temps, expliquerait le présent: chaque historien situe d'ailleurs la coupure inaugurante là où s'arrête son investigation. . . . En fait, il part de déterminations présentes. L'actualité est son commencement réel. (18)
>
> Nor could anyone believe, as much as historiography might tend to have us believe, that a "beginning" situated in a former time might explain the present: each historian situates elsewhere the inaugural rupture, at the point where his or her investigations stop. . . . In fact, historians begin from present determinations. Current events are their real beginning. (Conley 11)

According to de Certeau, the outcome or end of the story (the present) determines how the beginning (the past) of the story will be told (and which beginning as well). In Maalouf's text, there is no one-way movement between past and present: they are interconnected. The chronological move from past to present is made clear by the geographical changes illustrated by the two maps that frame the narrative: the first one appears right after the cover (and before the title page) and shows the Middle East with the boundaries of the Frankish states circa 1128; the second one, at the very end of the book, shows the borders of the Middle East after 1948. However, in the foreword Maalouf states that he chose the period of the Crusades because "ces deux siècles mouvementés . . . ont façonné l'Occident et le monde arabe, et . . . déterminent aujourd'hui encore leurs rapports" 'those two centuries of turmoil . . . shaped the West and the Arab world alike, and . . . affect relations between them even today' (9, Rothschild, Foreword). Thus, the author starts from contemporary relations between the Arabs and the West as a contextual background for his research on the history of the Crusades, while in the epilogue he refers to the past he narrated as the root of contemporary tensions. The present context triggers a quest for the origin of a contemporary problem on which the past will shed light. The beginning and the end are inextricably interwoven, since the past will explain the present, which itself determines how and which part of the past is told.

Like its author, *Les croisades vues par les Arabes* is a hybrid: neither a scholarly historical book, nor a novel, nor a historical novel, although it has elements of all three. While reviewers called it a historical essay (as Maalouf did himself during an interview; see Sassine 25), the author in the foreword presents it as the "roman vrai" 'true novel' of the Crusades between quotation marks. This may be an allusion to the Goncourt brothers' preface to *Germinie Lacerteux* (1865), in which they state: "le public aime les romans faux: ce roman est un roman vrai" 'the public loves fictitious novels! This is a true novel' (5, Chestershire 5). What Maalouf's text has in common with the first naturalist novel, which featured a woman from the working class as the main character, is that both works are based on real events and purport to tell stories from a class or ethnic background previously denied the spotlight. These scare quotes also underline the oxymoron created by juxtaposing the terms novel and true, simultaneously revealing and effacing the distinction between them, and reminding us of de Certeau's definition of historiography, that "l'historiographie (c'est-à-dire "histoire" et "écriture") porte inscrit dans son nom propre le paradoxe—et quasi l'oxymoron—de la mise en relation de deux termes antinomiques: le réel et le discours" (*L'écriture* 5) 'Historiography (that is, "history" and "writing") bears within its own name the paradox—almost an oxymoron—of a relation established between two antinomic terms, between the real and discourse' (Conley xxvii). In addition to stressing the fact that historiography is itself grounded in history, scholars following in the wake of Hayden White have emphasized the commonality of features shared by historical discourse and literature. Every historical narrative is a linguistic construct that uses rhetorical devices to create a discourse of explanation and persuasion out of events or data. Narrative techniques and rhetorical figures shape the historical account and require analysis.

Maalouf's stated desire to write the "true novel" of the Crusades shows that this work is not a new history book and acknowledges the apparent contradiction between the title (the Crusades according to one perspective), and the statement that this is an accurate account. His book is about how the Arabs who lived through the Crusades narrated and transmitted that experience to future generations, since the Arab historians quoted by Maalouf are contemporary to some of the events they relate. In a preamble to the section "Notes and Sources," Maalouf offers the only commentary on his approach: "Il va de soi que leur consultation [des récits historiques] nous était indispensable pour rassembler les témoignages arabes, nécessairement fragmentaires, en un récit continu couvrant les deux siècles d'invasions franques" 'It was obviously essential to consult them [historical narratives] in weaving the Arab testimony, which is inevitably fragmentary, into a continuous account covering the two centuries of the Frankish invasions' (285, Rothschild 268). The two classic (European) works that he cites are Grousset's and Runciman's. Clearly, Maalouf relies on Western historians to piece together the Arab testimonies scattered among annals and chronicles. As Franz Rosenthal explains, Arab historians wrote annalistic historiography, which simply records bare facts under a succession of individual years, with the exception of Usamah Ibn Munqidh, who wrote a memoir of his personal experiences. However, the Western scholars Maalouf cites also relied on the Arab chroniclers.[9]

Likewise, Maalouf draws from all sources available to him, medieval Arab as well as contemporary Western historians. This underscores the fact that the same sources can yield different historical accounts, and that records are often insufficient or contradictory. As Chaim Perelman puts it, "We can know the past only from the traces of it that remain" (qtd. in Gossman 293). The overtly controlling narrator in Maalouf's text acknowledges the limitations of his project on several occasions. For example, there are two versions of the events that will push Saladin to lift the siege at Massiaf, a fortress in Syria. Maalouf adds before narrating the second version: "Mais ce qui se passe en ce mois d'août 1176 au pays des Assassins demeurera sans doute à jamais un mystère" 'Exactly what happened in the land of the Assassins that August of 1176 will probably always remain a mystery' (199, Rothschild 182). Although most of the story proceeds in the narrative present or "historical present," as it is often referred to in French and English, which gives the impression of immediacy and objectivity because narration seems to occur simultaneously with the events and thus precludes any interference from temporal distance, it alternates with passages that either anticipate or allude to future events or to the future consequences of what was just narrated. For example, the last chapter of the third part ends with these words: "L'épopée du puissant Etat fondé par Zinki semble achevée. En réalité, elle vient tout juste de commencer" 'The epic of the powerful state founded by Zangi seems over. In fact, it has only just begun' (155). This is an example of what Gérard Genette calls "repetitive prolepsis" which plays a role of announcement and creates a short-term expectation in the mind of the reader, which is fulfilled in the chapter that follows it (*Figures III*). Maalouf ends the second part by quoting an Arab historian who uses the same device:

> En évoquant, un siècle plus tard, cette période critique de l'histoire arabe, Ibn al-Athir écrira à juste titre:
>> Avec la mort de Toghtekin disparaissait le dernier homme capable de faire face aux Franj. Ceux-ci semblaient alors en mesure d'occuper la Syrie tout entière. Mais Dieu, dans son infinie bonté, eut pitié des musulmans. (122)
> Discussing this critical period of Arab history a century later, Ibn al-Athir would write with good reason:
>> With the death of Tughtigin, the last man capable of confronting the Franj was gone. The latter then seemed in a position to occupy all of Syria. But God in his infinite kindness took pity on the Muslims. (Rothschild 105)

This prolepsis within a prolepsis underlines the fact that Maalouf's narrative strategy inscribes itself in the tradition of Muslim historiography. In *Les croisades vues par les Arabes*, most chapters end with some sort of foretelling of events that maintains the reader's interest; Maalouf presents us with a retrospective view of the past and interprets each event accordingly. These prolepses remind us that the rewriting of history is grounded in the here and now of the historian, and that this applies to the medieval sources as well, which are already interpreted accounts of the events they relate. As Christopher Tyerman notes, "most medieval written primary sources were exercises in interpreting reality, not describing it" (99).

The anecdote about the crusaders' cannibalism strikingly illustrates how context affects historiography. De Certeau has argued that any writing of History takes place in History: "Il y a l'historicité de l'histoire. Elle implique le mouvement qui lie une pratique interprétative à une praxis sociale" 'There exists a historicity of history, implying the movement which links an interpretive practice to a social praxis' (L'écriture 29, Conley 21). The cannibalism that occurred at Maara is narrated in several Frankish chronicles of the time, where the army's chiefs ascribed it to hunger, as well as in European history books of the nineteenth century. However, the incident is usually occulted in the twentieth century.[10] In the "Notes and Sources," Maalouf alludes to the civilizing mission project to explain this phenomenon (287), but does not dwell on the issue. By relegating his comment to a note outside the main body of the text, Maalouf avoids the pitfall pointed out by Arif Dirlik in an essay about Eurocentrism and History: "Critics of Eurocentrism inspired by cultural studies spend more time on what Euro-American writers and theorists have had to say about the rest of the world than they do speaking of the societies at hand, which further displaces the latter from the historian's attention" (250).

That Maalouf subverts the pattern of dichotomization he himself established in the title by choosing to quote Frankish over Arab sources to tell this episode does pose a problem, however, for contrary to what the book sets out to do, it is the Franks we hear. Maalouf quotes the chronicler Raoul de Caen: "A Maara, les nôtres faisaient bouillir des païens adultes dans les marmites, ils fixaient les enfants sur des broches et les dévoraient grillés" 'In Ma'arra our troops boiled pagan adults in cooking-pots; they impaled children on spits and devoured them grilled' (55, Rothschild 39).[11] Maalouf also quotes another Frankish chronicler, Albert d'Aix, as well as an excerpt from an official letter sent by the chiefs of the army to the Pope (39-40). This is not a case in which the only remnants of the past are to be found in the Franks' chronicles (either because of extermination or destruction of documents). Although historians point out that only a few Arab accounts of the first Crusades have been preserved, one can find a brief mention of the Franks' cannibalism in an Arab source (Kemal-eddine) translated by Michaud in his Bibliothèque des croisades: "les Francs, en proie à la disette, étaient réduits à se nourrir de cadavres et des animaux qu'ils pouvaient se procurer" 'The Franks, racked by dearth, were reduced to feeding themselves from cadavers and animals they could get' (vol. 4: 7). Maalouf knew this source, since Kemal-eddine's text is listed in the "Notes and Sources." One can see two possibilities to explain Maalouf's choice: the quotations attributed to the Frankish chronicles contain more gruesome details, which accentuate the barbarism of the perpetrators, thus contributing to Maalouf's reversal of civilized and barbarian. Second, reliance on the Franks' own writings obviates disbelief by the French reader, as if acknowledgment by the very people who committed it should attest to the veracity of such a horrendous act.

It is evident from his statement about the cannibalism episode that Maalouf, whose passion for history permeates most of his novels, is well aware of the issues involved in any writing of history, in particular the subjectivity of the historian, who weaves various sources into a coherent narrative, and the literariness of historiography. However, he uses none of the metafictional devices that disorient the reader at the level of the narrative, and which are often found in postcolonial and postmodern writings to dramatize the issue of how one can know and write the past. Maalouf does use narrative strategies that underscore the literariness of the process of writing history, but his text is not paralyzed by constant self-reflexivity, nor does it pretend to have the scientific objectivity of positivist historiography by presenting itself as a novel. Maalouf has a story to tell, and it takes priority over epistemological questions about historical discourse.

In order to tell the victims' point of view in French, the language of the crusaders' descendants, various lexical changes are required. Maalouf borrows the word *Franj*, an Arabic word still used nowadays in dialectal Arabic to designate the French, and Westerners by extension. The introduction of this Arabic word into the French language creates a feeling of strangeness for the Western reader concerning his/her own identity, thus forcing him to see himself (or herself) with the Other's eyes.[12] In commenting on the Arab chronicler Ibn al-Athir by summing up a lengthy quotation with "Ils sont fous, ces Franj, semble dire l'historien de Mossoul" 'These Franj are crazy, the Mosul historian seems to be saying' (89, Rothschild 73), Maalouf alludes to the popular *Astérix* series, where the phrase "these Romans are crazy" is frequently put in the mouths of resisting Gauls (who have been construed as the ancestors of the French), referring to the Roman assailants. In addition to grounding Maalouf's analyses in twentieth-century popular culture, this appropriation ironically underlines the position of the Franks as invaders.

Perhaps more radically, Maalouf repeatedly presents the point of view of the victims excluded from official French history by reversing the referents of the dichotomy "civilized/uncivilized." In a chapter entitled "Un émir chez les barbares" 'An Emir among Barbarians' (Rothschild), Maalouf turns generally accepted ideas upside down by calling the crusaders non-civilized beings compared to the Arabs. He does justice to the advance of the Arab civilization over the Frankish one in areas ranging from hygiene to law, and quotes at length the Damascene chronicler Usamah Ibn Munqidh, who is shocked by the Franks' backwardness. Maalouf quotes a long exerpt from Ibn Munqidh in which two Frankish doctors are shown to be more effective at killing their patients than curing them (147-48), but makes no mention of two other cases of successful Frankish treatment that Ibn Munqidh reports right after the passage quoted by Maalouf (Ibn Munqidh 162-63). While both sides recognized the superior medical skills of Arab physicians (Hallam 86), Maalouf's selection presents a more uniform view of the Franks than the source he draws from. Derrida argued that a phase of reversal is necessary to deconstruct an imposed hierarchy:

> I strongly insist on the necessity of the phase of reversal, which people have perhaps too swiftly attempted to discredit. . . . To neglect this phase of reversal

is to forget that the structure of the opposition is one of conflict and subordination and thus to pass too swiftly, without gaining any purchase against the former opposition, to a *neutralization* which *in practice* leaves things in their former state. (qtd. in Culler 165)

As Derrida makes clear, it is a necessary step to show the Franks as barbarians to deconstruct the Western image of the Crusades as a heroic, glamorous time before these two centuries can be evaluated in a balanced manner. Thus the sensitivity and humanity of some Muslim leaders are emphasized in contrast to the crusaders' savagery. Maalouf relates how in similar situations the Arab leaders were magnanimous while the crusaders were cruel. For instance, he contrasts the brutality of Renaud de Châtillon, who tortures the patriarch of Antioch and mutilates the Greek priests of Cyprus (156), to the humanitarian response of Saladin, who, moved to pity by the cries of a Frankish woman whose daughter was kidnapped, orders that the latter be found and restored to her mother. On another occasion, Saladin's generosity and magnanimity when he liberates the Frankish poor without asking for a ransom, and frees King Guy in exchange for a promise (on which the latter will renege) contrasts with the lies of the Franks, who resort to false religious propaganda to obtain reinforcements, and to Richard the Lion Hearted's cruelty when he massacres prisoners while in a similar situation Saladin had had Franks released (210-11). Other exactions by the Franks include the pillage of Constantinople, during which they killed priests and monks and looted churches, and the sack of Jerusalem's holy places in 1099, during which the Eastern Christians were evicted, the Jews burned in the synagogue, and the Muslims massacred. To this day, Arabs contrast the brutal taking of Jerusalem by the Franks in 1099 to the peaceful seizure of Jerusalem by Omar Ibn al-Khattab in 638 (51). However, Maalouf does not portray only magnanimous Muslim leaders facing cruel crusaders. Although Frederic II is considered an exception, Maalouf lingers on this emperor, king of Germany and Sicily, who spoke Arabic, admired Muslim civilization, respected the Islamic religion, despised the barbarous West, and who carried on an intellectual correspondence with the Emir of Cairo (226-30). The figure of Frederic II implicitly provides a model for positive East-West interaction.

Les croisades vues par les Arabes ends with a word whose import is immense in Arab culture: "l'on ne peut douter que la cassure entre ces deux mondes date des croisades, ressenties par les Arabes, aujourd'hui encore, comme un viol" 'there can be no doubt that the schism between these two worlds dates from the Crusades, deeply felt by the Arabs, even today, as an act of rape' (283, Rothschild 266). Rape has become a commonplace metaphor for conquest and colonization, and by using this trope Maalouf echoes the current trend in medieval historiography of viewing the Crusades as the first wave of European imperialism in the Middle East.[13] However, one can see another reason, grounded in Arab culture, for this choice of metaphor. Although in the Middle Ages women on both sides were considered the property of their male guardians, and sexual violence against them was an attack on men's honor, in the twentieth-century Western world rape has become a woman's issue since, as Kathryn Gravdal suggests, women are no longer the property of men (144).

This, however, is not the case in parts of the Middle East, where crimes of honor continue to shed women's blood to wash away the shame brought about by their allegedly (un)willing illicit sexual conduct. Rape, a crime legally punishable by death of the perpetrator in some Arab countries, dishonors the victim's whole family. But despite the similarity in the way rape was perceived in the Middle Ages by both parties, the Franks' behavior seemed more liberal towards their womenfolk compared to the Arabs, who were baffled by the fact that Frankish men let their wives interact with men, sometimes rather intimately. Maalouf quotes Ibn Munqidh's indignation upon observing that a Frank will let his wife converse alone with another man (148). Another incident narrated by Ibn Munqidh to corroborate his point (but not included by Maalouf) tells how a Frank had his wife's pubic hair shaved by a man (165-66). These incidents show that a similar concept of honor does not translate into comparable behavior for both parties. While the French no longer tie a man's honor to the sexual behavior of his female relatives, this principle exists to this day in parts of the Middle East, and may explain the choice of the comparison between the Crusades and rape to describe the psychological impact of the invasions on Arabs.

Rape is mentioned several times in the narrative, usually as the price that women have to pay for belonging to the defeated (11, 29, 173). Once, it is alluded to in a letter by the caliph al-Adid to Noureddin asking for help: "Pour émouvoir le fils de Zinki, le souverain fatimide a joint à sa missive des mèches de cheveux: *Ce sont*, lui explique-t-il, *les cheveux de mes femmes. Elles te supplient de venir les soustraire aux outrages des Franj*" 'In an effort to move the son of Zangi, the Fatimid sovereign enclosed some locks of hair with his missive. *These,* he explained, *are locks of hair from my wives. They beseech you to come and rescue them from the outrages of the Franj*' (185, Rothschild 169). Women's voices are reduced to body parts, which are given voice by their husband who uses them as tokens to appeal for help. The word "outrage," which in a general context means a grave insult, takes on the meaning of rape in French when applied to women. It emphasizes the fact that rape is a crime that affects women specifically, and suggests that the Crusades were no exception to the fact that "In war time, rape has always been more than a rhetorical figure" (Higgins, *New Novel* 108). The metaphor of rape relegates women to a silent, victim role, whose sufferings are significant only for the consequences they entail for their husbands' honor. And while the actual crime affects women first and foremost, the specific distresses that women endured are left out of the narrative.

Rape can be linked to the process of story telling. Lynn Higgins points out that "in fiction and life, rape is a special kind of crime in relation to narrative. . . Murder is not a crime whose noncommission can be narrated. Rape, on the other hand, can be discursively transformed into another kind of story. This is exactly the sort of thing that happens when rape is rewritten retrospectively into 'persuasion,' 'seduction,' or even 'romance'" ("Screen/Memory" 307).[14] In a fascinating study, Kathryn Gravdal has shown "the cultural habit of conceptualizing male violence against women as a positive expression of love" in French medieval texts (20). Rape is also a common trope in Orientalist discourse. Said points out that "the relation between the Middle East and the West is really defined as sexual. . . .The Middle East is resistant, as any virgin would be, but the male scholar wins the prize" (*Orientalism* 309). With a similar comparison that underlines unequal power distribution, Maalouf stresses the discursive violence of narratives that have portrayed the Crusades as an epic with heroic characters carrying out a noble goal, and the influence they have had in shaping the popular Western imagination about that era. The violence has been two-fold: on a literal level, as in any war, and on the discursive level. In a case of rape, if "the question is not *who committed* the crime, but *whether a crime occurred at all*" (Higgins, "Screen/Memory" 307), the issue at stake in Maalouf's work is how the Crusades have been written into history and passed on as a glorious era despite the ideological prejudices that engineered them and the crimes committed.[15]

The rape trope used by Maalouf only emphasizes the absence of Arab women's perspective on the Crusades, for *Les croisades vues par les Arabes* is a tale told by men about men. Only two women are briefly mentioned by name in Maalouf's narrative; both seized power and belonged to the elite. The first is Alix, daughter of the King of Jerusalem, who betrayed her father after her husband's death by trying to forge an alliance with Zangi (ruler of Aleppo and Mosul) in order to stay in power in Antioch. The other is Chajarat-ad-dorr, whom Maalouf portrays as a passive pawn in the hands of the Mamelouks, but who nevertheless stands out in the history of Islam as the first woman to be a ruling queen (*Croisades* 240-41). In *Sultanes oubliées*, Fatima Mernissi gives us a completely different account of Chajarat-ad-dorr's reign, in which the latter appears as a clever decision-maker, well aware of the limitations imposed on her by her gender, yet determined to circumvent them (145-62).[16]

One could argue that Maalouf, by refraining from describing rapes and other crimes at length, does not indulge in the narrative acts of which Aram Veeser accuses New Historicists, whose historical accounts that detail atrocities are said to have obscene or pornographic intentions, and teach only obedience and despair (qtd. in Rosello, "Michèle" 5). However, Maalouf also passed over the few Arab women whose participation and resistance during the Crusades have left traces in records. Although he can be credited with having brought to light the Arab male viewpoint on this period, he shows no particular concern about the women's.[17] While the absence of women's perspectives can be attributed to the lack of written testimony by them, some women's heroic deeds stood out enough to figure in Ibn Munqidh's memoirs, whom Maalouf quotes extensively on other issues. In his memoirs, Ibn Munqidh describes a couple of Muslim women warriors, another who kills her husband who had betrayed the Muslims to the Franks, and another who captured three Franks (153-59); he also gives an account of a woman who drowned after trying to escape from the Franks who took her captive (179). Maalouf ends up repeating in part what his own book is supposed to undo: by omitting what Arab women did and thought during the Crusades, he silences them out of History. The use of rape as a metaphor for the Crusades as they impacted men subsumes women's issues under the mantle of colonization.

If we accept the view that a religious motivation was the engine of the Crusades (to take the Holy Land back from the "infidels"), one may wonder why

Maalouf did not entitle his book "The Crusades as seen by the Muslims." Maalouf, himself a descendant of the Arab Christians who were doubly discriminated against during the Crusades, does not fit in the Manichean view of a Christian West against a Muslim Orient. The fact that ethnicity is foregrounded in the title challenges the view of the Crusades as a confrontation between two religions. On the one hand, Maalouf includes the Christians of the Orient on the side of the oppressed, since they were in fact twice victimized on several occasions. The double discrimination against Arab Christians is evident in the battle of Antioch: expelled by the Muslim Arabs for fear that they would betray them to the Western Christians, they were not welcomed with open arms by the crusaders, who treated them as inferior subjects and at best suspected them of sympathizing with their Muslim compatriots (as occurred when the Oriental Christians sided with Saladin during the seizure of Jerusalem in 1187). Arab Christians in other instances, such as the Copts during the seizure of the town of Bilbeis, were massacred along with the Muslims (*Croisades* 168). However, Maalouf remains silent about instances in which Oriental Christians welcomed or helped the crusaders (see for instance Grousset, *Histoire* 117, 151, 156).

Maalouf depicts a multi-ethnic society and highlights the dynamics of power that refute the vision of one homogeneous civilization fighting another. He describes alliances between Arabs and Franks, between Byzantines disappointed by the Franks and Arab emirs: emirs made deals with Franks against other emirs. Even the Frankish princess Alix, who never knew Europe and felt "Oriental," rebelled against her father by trying to forge an alliance with Zinki in 1130 (131). The description of the alliances that are forged and broken during these two centuries shows the complexity of the political situation of the Arab world at the time, divided into numerous small kingdoms at war with each other.[18] This instability reveals personal interests of the leaders that could prevail over religious or ethnic affiliations. The first Arab historians of the Crusades reported the series of wars with the Franks as one among other events happening at the time; they used the ethnic term "Franks" to designate the invaders, thus casting the invasions neither in a religious, nor civilizational light. Indeed the term "crusader" will not appear until the mid-nineteenth century (Sivan 10). Tyerman shows that up to the end of the twelfth century there is no clear distinction between pilgrims and crusaders (20-21), nor a universally accepted term to describe crusading activity, and this was the case until modern times (49-55).

Although what came to be labeled Crusades was recorded as Frankish wars and invasions under the Arab chroniclers' quill, the latter clearly did frame the conflict as religious by identifying themselves as Muslims and calling on God. The epigraphs that introduce each of the six parts that compose the book, all quotes from Arab chroniclers or leaders fighting the Crusades, can be seen as an implicit comment on historiography. Maalouf's use of citations contrasts with Runciman's, one of his European sources, who starts all chapters of his three-volume *History of the Crusades* with quotes from the Bible chosen to establish a link between Biblical events taken out of context and medieval times.[19]

In Maalouf's text, each epigraph summarizes the content of the part. For instance, the quote from Saladin, which contrasts the fierceness of the Franks with the passivity of the Muslims, frames the part that deals with the invasion (part I). These quotes fulfill most of the four functions attributed to epigraphs by Genette: commentary and justification of the title, commentary on the text itself (whose meaning it emphasizes), support of one's text thanks to the presence of a famous author's name, and a sign of culture and filiation, linking one's text to a specific intellectual and cultural tradition (*Paratexts* 156-60). These quotes are also striking in that the authors cited are well grounded in their religion, some calling upon God for the safety of their community; they see themselves as Muslims belonging to a homogeneous community of believers and not as Arabs. However, they contrast with the content of the various sections of the book in the sense that they create the false impression of a united, homogeneous Muslim world. Thus, while the quotes do inscribe Maalouf's narrative in the Arab cultural tradition and give it legitimacy, they highlight the discrepancy between the ideology they perpetuate (a united Muslim community threatened by Christians) and the actual facts (divided Arab leaders who fail to join forces against a common threat).

In *Les croisades vues par les Arabes,* Maalouf demonstrates that civilizations are neither monolithic nor immutable by reminding his readers that Muslim culture was tolerant towards others well before the Western world was. Maalouf's text illustrates how civilizations have been in contact and have borrowed from each other well before the era of globalization, by emphasizing the Arabs' numerous (and often ignored) contributions to Western civilization.[20] He dispels the simplistic view of the Crusades as a battle between Christendom and Islam, just as nowadays many intellectuals are attempting to refute the Manichean thesis of the clash of civilizations. In fact, one can read *Les croisades vues par les Arabes* as a book proleptically countering Samuel Huntington's influential *Clash of Civilizations.* Criticized by Said for having "journalism and popular demagoguery rather than scholarship or theory [as] his main sources" ("Clash" 571), Huntington's essay, which first appeared in *Foreign Affairs* in 1993, and subsequent book, claim that non-Western civilizations (Islamic and Confucianist in the lead) are the potential enemies of the post-Cold War era, when conflicts no longer divide along ideological lines, but are determined by culture. Huntington's theory enjoyed a renewal of interest as the Western media grappled to comment on the September 11, 2001 attacks (Crépon 8-9). Said forcefully debunks Huntington's notion that civilizations are monolithic and homogeneous, and points out how Huntington's view of a rigid separation among civilizations does not stand up ("Clash" 587, see also Crépon 3-61). Whereas Huntington's not so hidden agenda, according to Said, is to maintain American dominance over the world, or, according to Marc Crépon, to trigger a fear of Islam and China in the American reader (65-66), Maalouf's work intends to make one side understand the other better, and to promote a dialogue between cultures.

While most of *Les croisades vues par les Arabes* is devoted to showing how the Arabs experienced these events, the temporal indeterminacy of the title leaves room for the perspective to broaden in the epilogue, which sets out to expose the Crusades through end-of-twentieth-century Arab eyes. Hutcheon points out that the forewords and afterwords that frame nonfictional novels underscore the "particular perspective that *transforms*" (*Politics* 82). The epilogue does not anchor the text in the narrow context of France (where Maalouf has been living) with its immigrant population and the frustrations that were to be expressed by the Arab minority in the 1983 "marche des Beurs," but in the larger international context of Middle Eastern politics.

Maalouf directs attention to the parallels that are commonly drawn in the Arab world between events of the twentieth century and the Crusades. This relationship between the barbarous Middle Ages and our so-called civilized present is commonplace in the Levant, in whose view events past and present resemble each other: thus Anwar Sadat is viewed as a traitor in the direct line of al-Kamel (who gave Jerusalem to Frederic II), and Israel as a new crusader state (265). Therefore, Maalouf's implicit goal is not only to remind the reader of what happened from the Arabs' point of view, but also why it is crucial to remember that distant past now: to emphasize that current events can be situated in a historical continuum of European involvement in the Middle East.

The historiography of the Crusades continues to be influenced by the context in which it takes place. Crusading ideology continued in the sixteenth and seventeenth centuries (Constable 6). The Crusades were then discredited in the eighteenth century for their fanaticism (Tyerman 111), but with the renewal of interest in the Middle Ages that ensued in the nineteenth century, came the beginning of scholarly research about them (Siberry, "Images" 372). Contemporary historians have linked this scholarship to the colonization taking place at the time. For instance, Michaud's interest in the Crusades in the nineteenth century seems in part to have been stimulated by his study of Napoleon's expedition to Egypt (Siberry, *New Crusaders* 8). As Elizabeth Siberry shows, historians, artists, and aristocrats established a continuity between the French colonization of Algeria, which began in 1830, and the medieval expeditions: "It was no coincidence that at the time of the Algerian campaign, Louis Philippe was commissioning paintings of the medieval crusades and crusaders for the *Salles des croisades* at Versailles" (*New Crusaders* 82, see also Tyerman 117). When war broke out between the Druze and Maronites in Lebanon in 1860, Napoleon III called for a crusade to help the Christians (Siberry, *New Crusaders* 83). The use of crusade terminology continued in the twentieth century, and was used during WWI when the Palestine campaign with the capture of Jerusalem in December 1917 by Allenby was described as a crusade (Siberry, *New Crusaders* 87). Contemporary historians acknowledge that interest in the Crusades nowadays is still influenced by political and ideological interests (Constable 2; Siberry, *New Crusaders* x; Armstrong 386), and Karen Armstrong even makes the case for the Crusades as a direct cause of today's conflict in the Middle East (xiii). Indeed, this renewed interest dates from the early 1950s and coincides with the creation of the state of Israel (Riley-Smith 5); there is even a debate among historians over whether or not in hindsight the crusader states should be regarded as colonies (Constable 20), or, as some Israeli scholars see it, as the "first European colonial society" (Tyerman 123). Emmanuel Sivan notes that all Arab scholars see a parallelism between the Crusades and current events, whether it is framed as a religious contest between Islam and Christianity, a civilization conflict of East and West, or as a first phase of Western imperialism in the Arab world (11-19).

Current events lead Maalouf to make choices open to question regarding the historical events he chooses to discuss. For instance, he does not mention the crusades that were waged as the *Reconquista* of Spain, with the fall of Cordoba in 1236 and Seville in 1248.[21] Whereas Maalouf chose the period of the Europeans' incursions in the Levant, with the sack of Jerusalem as a culminating point, Bernard Lewis (a prominent Orientalist historian) sees the last years of the seventeenth century (marked by the second siege of Vienna) as the determining moments of the relations between the Muslim world and Europe (304). Each side sees the time when it was threatened or invaded by the other as the determining point in future relations, forgetting when it was itself the attacker, and thereby putting the blame on the other by privileging certain events over others. However, to give a full account of the relationship between the Europeans and the Arabs, one should go back to the initial point of conflict (the conquest of Spain in the eighth century and the Arabs' advance up to the French town of Poitiers), and include all subsequent confrontations.

In this essay, Maalouf does not treat at length historical figures who embody the crossing of civilizations that will become central to his work.[22] The fact that *Les croisades vues par les Arabes,* his first published book, does not dwell on the implication of mixed unions during the Crusades, and the fact that "transculturation [was] common in medieval Mediterranean cultures" (Kinoshita 114)—a lot of which happened through concubine slaves—is striking in the light of his subsequent fiction, pervaded by a concern with the meeting of cultures in history, minorities, and border people. Even more puzzling is the fact that the non-Arab background of some key "Arab" leaders and heroes of the fight against the crusaders is presented in the epilogue as one of the factors in the decline of the Arab world, as a sign that the latter had lost control over its destiny.

Although in the end the crusaders were chased from the Levant, Maalouf does not present the Arabs as victors. Moreover, one can wonder, along with Mireille Rosello, about the purpose of writing the victims' history. As she points out, "if the triumphalism of official history always at least partially serves the interests of the 'oppressors,' it does not necessarily follow that (historical) justice will be served by replacing the victor's story with that of the victim" ("Michèle" 5-6). In the epilogue, he draws up a brief assessment in which the Arabs are seen as victims, since the Crusades are the starting point for the rise of Western Europe while Arab civilization, which was the most advanced at the time, begins its decline.

Maalouf brilliantly unsettled past constructions of the Crusades that informed popular perceptions of them in France without falling into the trap of simply inverting victims and villains, but his sketchy explanation of the popular view of the heritage of the Crusades in the Arab world presented in the epilogue does not do justice to the complexity of the events and politics of the twentieth century alone (admittedly, this would require another book).[23] Moreover, given that Maalouf states that the Arab world is still a prisoner of the same shackles that caused its fall (lack of democratic institutions, problems of succession), one can see it as subject to a fatality, and create a defeatist feeling, even though one of the factors mentioned is debatable.[24]

Although the history of the Crusades serves as an allegory of the present, with Arab leaders still unable to unite against a new invasion, the danger of this epilogue is that it comforts the Western reader in his/her position of superiority. As Sharon Kinoshita points out, "the Middle Ages have long served as a repository of the abject and the exotic against which modernity is constructed" (111). So while French readers will no doubt acknowledge the barbarism of their ancestors, the superiority of contemporary Western civilization will nevertheless be confirmed, as if the torch of progress had been passed from the Arabs' hands to the crusaders', as Maalouf himself insinuates (264). Although the view of history repeating itself is pessimistic, the idea that the crusaders will be expelled could provide an optimistic note. However, Maalouf quickly downplays the 1291 Arab victory over the Franks, thereby cutting short the hope that there might be another victory in sight (279).

Given the brevity of the five-page epilogue, some of its oversimplifications seem inevitable, but some are particularly regrettable. Maalouf uses an image whose swift generalization about the Muslim world could use some nuances: "Assailli de toutes parts, le monde musulman se recroqueville sur lui-même. Il est devenu frileux" 'Assaulted from all quarters, the Muslim world turned in on itself. It became over-sensitive' (282, Rothschild 264). The sensitivity-to-cold-weather metaphor reduces political and imperial moves to a natural climatological phenomenon, against which Muslims could only adopt a defensive attitude. The detailed accounts in the book that took great care to underscore the divergences and the power plays among various Muslim leaders during the times of the Crusades contrast sharply with the broad generalizations presented in the epilogue, which sweep away the complexity that characterizes the Muslim world of the end of the twentieth century.

Maalouf puts all the blame on the Muslim world by citing examples of the two extreme tendencies of forced Westernizations (such as Turkey) alternating with fundamentalism (Iran), but fails to mention how Western powers have been direct or indirect contributors to these developments. He seems to hesitate between two positions. On the one hand, by stating that "le monde arabe ne peut se résoudre à considérer les croisades comme un simple épisode d'un passé révolu" 'the Arab world cannot bring itself to consider the Crusades a mere episode in the bygone past' (283, Rothschild 265), Maalouf seems to criticize the Arab world by casting it as hopelessly unable to move forward. On the other hand, one of Maalouf's rhetorical questions poignantly underscores the parallels between then and now: "Comment distinguer le passé du présent quand il s'agit de la lutte entre Damas et Jérusalem pour le contrôle du Golan ou de la Bekaa?" 'How can one distinguish the past from the present in the struggle between Damascus and Jerusalem for control of the Golan or the Bekaa?' (283). The creation of the state of Israel has had a tremendous impact on Lebanon's already precarious internal affairs, because of the influx of Palestinian refugees and the PLO moving its headquarters to Beirut in 1970. The civil war that was still raging at the time Maalouf embarked on his project, as well as Israel's invasion of Lebanon, Maalouf's native country, the year prior to the publication of *Les croisades vues par les Arabes,* constitute the backdrop to his revision of the Crusades.

While this grounding of the author's writing corresponds to what de Certeau has termed the "repoliticization' [which] will consist in 'historicizing' historiography" ("History" 215), the epilogue undermines the project of the book by failing to insist on the continuity of Western imperial moves in the Middle East. Maalouf perpetuates uncalled-for stereotypes: after quoting the Turkish man who tried to assassinate the Pope in 1981 because the latter was "commandant suprême des croisés" 'supreme commander of the Crusades' (283, Rothschild 265), he comments: "il est clair que l'Orient arabe voit toujours en l'Occident un ennemi naturel" 'it seems clear that the Arab East still sees the West as a natural enemy' (283, Rothschild 265-66). The adjective "natural" disregards the very real political events that have fostered resentment in the Middle East and essentializes the difference between East and West. This last sentence silences the plurality of voices and aspirations that exist in the Arab world, privileging anti-Western movements whose discourse is similar, as Crépon demonstrates, to Huntington's theory of the irreducibility of conflicts between different civilizations (54).

While the first siege of Vienna by the Ottoman armies (a Muslim empire, though led by the Turks) in 1529 is mentioned as a sign (albeit deceitful) of the victory of the Muslims, there is no mention of the nineteenth-century colonization of the Maghreb, nor of the French mandates in Lebanon and Syria at the beginning of the twentieth century (and the British one over Palestine), as if there had been no continuity in the Western imperialist moves in the region. Indeed, the borders of the contemporary map that closes the book, drawn by imperial powers, are indelible traces of a colonial past. This very continuity is briefly alluded to in the phrase "Dans un monde musulman perpétuellement agressé" 'In a Muslim world under constant attack' (283, Rothschild 265), and is singled out as a probable reason why the Crusades are "deeply felt by the Arabs, *even today*, as an act of rape" (Rothschild 266, emphasis mine). The historical distance allows Maalouf to see the Crusades as the beginning of a long series of incursions of the West into the Middle East. But the consistent emphasis on the Arab world's shortcomings and euphemism to downplay the modern history of colonization of the Arab world and twentieth century conflicts undermine legitimate political grievances. This silencing of the modern colonial enterprise in the Middle East is also evident in his novel *Les échelles du Levant,* which I discuss in the second part of this chapter. I surmise that this may in part be explained by Maalouf's uneasiness regarding the rise of Islamic militancy in the region following the 1967 defeat of the Arab armies.

Genealogies as Conflict Resolution: Maalouf's *Les échelles du Levant* and Myriam Antaki's *Les versets du pardon*

Maalouf's *Les échelles du Levant*

A nameless narrator (who, like Maalouf, was a Lebanese journalist) tells the story of Ossyane, a man he met by chance in Paris in 1976. Ossyane's Turkish father and Armenian mother wed at the beginning of the twentieth century, a time when relations between the two groups were antagonistic and would later lead to the Armenian genocide. After the Adana massacre in 1909, the family moved to Lebanon, where Ossyane grew up. While studying in France during WWII, Ossyane joined the French resistance and met Clara, an Austrian Jew. After the war, Ossyane returned to Lebanon. He sees Clara again, who is accompanying her uncle, the sole Holocaust survivor of her family, who decided to immigrate to Palestine. Ossyane and Clara get married while tensions are already ripe between Arabs and Jews. Right after Ossyane leaves Clara pregnant in Haifa to see his dying father in Beirut, the declaration of the state of Israel in 1948 takes place, putting an impassable border between them. Following his father's death and a sunstroke, Ossyane loses his mind and is committed to an asylum by his brother where he spends more than twenty years. When the war breaks out in Lebanon in 1975, Ossyane escapes and invites Clara to meet him in Paris. The narrator observes their meeting from afar, staying long enough to see that Clara did come, but leaves before seeing whether Clara and Ossyane will take separate ways or leave together.

Les échelles du Levant starts by emphasizing the role of genealogy and history of the main character's destiny. When asked to start by his birth, Ossyane answers with a rhetorical question: "Etes-vous certain que la vie d'un homme commence à la naissance?" 'Are you certain that a man's life begins with his birth?' (23, Manguel 15). He then proceeds with the narration of events that took place half a century before he was born (about how his grandmother became mad) and that will have a determining effect on his life. However, contrary to Maalouf's essay on the Crusades, which looks intricately at the various motivations of rulers and their positions, this novel does not dwell on the processes of history. Although the characters live through some of the most traumatic events of the twentieth century, events that have an undeniable impact on the course of their lives, there is not much historical information in this book (contrary to some of his other novels such as *Léon l'Africain*). The following passage describes the Ottoman Empire at the eve of World War I: "à Adana, comme dans toute l'Anatolie, débutaient les massacres. La terre du Levant vivait ses moments les plus vils. Notre Empire agonisait dans la honte; au milieu de ses ruines poussait une foule de pays avortons; chacun priait son dieu de faire taire les prières des autres" 'in Adana, as in the whole of Anatolia, the massacres began. Our land lived then through its most evil hour. Our empire was dying in an agony of shame; among its ruins grew a host of aborted countries, each one praying to its own god to silence the prayers of its neighbors' (45, Manguel 32). The definite article "les" for the massacres refer to common knowledge (here, the Armenian genocide). The use of the verb "pousser" 'grow' for the countries that are being carved by Western powers naturalizes historical processes. The reference to religion in the conflict stands in contrast with the main characters. Religion is relegated to the background in the narrative. Its significance is in signaling ethnicity rather than religious belonging per se, as when Ossyane defines himself as Muslim on paper (217). Although the characters do occasionally mention providence and destiny (137, 212), Ossyane and his father care very little for religion.

History is personified and presented as a force over which people have no control: "nous n'avons rien choisi, c'est l'Histoire qui a choisi pour nous" 'We didn't choose, History had made the choice for us' (57, Manguel 42). In another passage, the creation of the state of Israel is presented as inevitable as a natural disaster by being described as a tornado (and a cyclone later on): "Une tornade allait s'abattre sur le Levant, et nous voulions faire barrage de nos mains nues! C'était exactement cela. Le monde entier était résigné à voir Arabes et Juifs s'entre-tuer pendant des décennies, des siècles peut-être, tout le monde s'était fait une raison, les Anglais et les Soviétiques, les Américains et les Turcs" 'A tornado was about to ravage my part of the world, and we wanted to stop it with our bare hands. That is exactly how it was. The entire world had resigned itself to seeing Arabs and Jews kill one another for the next tens, maybe hundreds of years; everyone had got used to it, the English and the Soviets, the Americans and the Turks' (160, Manguel 122). Western nations (including Great Britain) are described as "resigned" when they were actually considerably implicated in the politics of Palestine. The same holds regarding the end of the British mandate: "le mandat britannique sur la Palestine avait pris fin" 'the British mandate in Palestine had come to an end' (177, Manguel 136), with the passive voice of the sentence silencing the fact that Great Britain decided to end its mandate because it could not cope with a situation that its contradictory agreements had created.

Another passage brings attention to the role Europe played in shaping the relations between Arabs and Jews: "au lendemain même de la défaite du nazisme, deux peuples détestés par Hitler se dressent l'un contre l'autre" 'soon after the fall of the Nazis, two groups detested by Hitler should take up arms against one another' (134, Manguel 102-3). Commenting the paragraph in which this sentence appears, Gil Hochberg points out that the reference to Hitler "emphasizes the *racial* affiliation between Jews and Arabs as (detested) Semites" and notes that "Europe, as the 'third party,' appears then as the 'real' enemy of both Jews and Arabs, who are too quick to forget their shared destiny by becoming enemies of each other" (120). However, I would stress that by referring only to Nazism and Hitler, and forgetting about the long history of European colonialism in the Middle East, this sentence presents the role played by Europe as an aberration of history.[25]

The title of the book emphasizes that the place in which the story unfolds is as much a part of the story as the characters. As indicated on the back cover, the title refers to the cities that were meeting points between cultures and civilizations in the Mediterranean Levant. There is a mention by Ossyane as to whether longing for these multicultural societies is to be seen as nostalgic or futuristic (49). The mixing of peoples, a constant theme in Maalouf's work, serves as a stark opposition to the nationalist stances of various movements that promote so-called authentic and pure identities, such as pan-Arabism, Zionism, and Phoenicianism. Indeed, the history of Lebanon, succinctly summarized when the narrator recalls the material in his history book, underscores the multitude of layers that various civilizations have brought: "l'Antiquité glorieuse, des cités phéniciennes aux conquêtes d'Alexandre; puis les Romains, les Byzantins, les Arabes, les croisés, les Mamelouks; ensuite les quatre siècles de domination ottomane; enfin les deux guerres mondiales, le mandat français, l'indépendance" 'the glories of Antiquity, from the Phoenician cities to the conquests of Alexander; then the Romans, Byzantium, the Arabs, the Crusades, the Mameluk rule; later the four centuries of Ottoman domination; finally the two Worlds Wars, the French mandate, independance' (10, Manguel 4). Occupation is seen as an inevitable part of history: "Je viens d'une région du monde où il n'y a eu, tout au long de l'histoire, que des occupations successives, et mes propres ancêtres ont occupé pendant des siècles une bonne moitié du bassin méditerranéen" 'I come from a part of the world where, throughout history, there has been one occupation after another, and my own ancestors occupied for centuries a good half of the Mediterranean' (79, Manguel 60).

Inter-ethnic marriages are recurrent in the novel, and more specifically unions between groups that are on the brink of fighting each other at particular times in history. These unions function as a common trope that symbolizes hope for possible reconciliation. Ossyane's father grew up in a cosmopolitan environment, embodied by his own genealogy: his maternal grandmother was the daughter of a fallen Turkish monarch, his grandfather's family was of Persian origin. He was educated by tutors of diverse backgrounds. The Adana massacre (which foreshadows the Armenian genocide) prompts Noubar, an Armenian, to give his daughter's hand to Ossyane's father, his best friend. Thus, the massacre is the trigger for the cement of the union between both groups. Like his father, Ossyane marries a woman who belongs to an antagonist group. Although their love story takes place against the backdrop of the violence triggered by the proposition of the partition of Palestine, Clara and Ossyane's wedding is symbolic of a possible reconciliation between Arabs and Jews (163). More than just the marriage is the attitude of both characters that is lauded when they talk about the conflict: "chacun se mettait spontanément à la place de l'autre" 'we put ourselves, each of us, in the other's place' (169, Manguel 130). So is Clara's assessment of the conflict as a misunderstanding between the victims of the Holocaust and those who are paying the price for Europe's crime (134). This possible coexistence is also forecast with the emphasis on the cordial meeting between Ossyane's brother-in-law, Mahmoud, a Palestinian who had to leave Haifa because of the tensions, and Clara's uncle, Stefan, a European Jew and the only member of her family who survived the concentration camp. Stephan has recently arrived in Haifa, the very city which Mahmoud already predicts he will never see again (152). Nadia, Clara and Ossyane's daughter, becomes the synthesis of the different communities: she is Muslim on her father's side, Jewish on her mother's, and she claims both identities (217). However, Nadia leaves the Middle East to go and settle with her husband in Brazil, thus signifying that there is no place for people who claim multiple belongings (as Maalouf will term them in a subsequent book) in the Middle East (at least not yet).

The narrator mentions in passing that the notes he took while Ossyane was telling him his story were left in a folder for twenty years, but there is no other indication about what prompted the narrator to write Ossyane's story after such a long time. Since his encounter with Ossyane took place in 1976, the narrator is writing the story in 1996. I surmise that the euphoria that followed the Oslo Accords in 1993 played a role in bringing back to memory the story of an Arab and a Jew, and most importantly in enabling the possibility of this couple finally having a future together. However, the fact that the narrator refuses to stay to see if the couple will remain together shows a level of skepticism.

Myriam Antaki's *Les versets du pardon*

Antaki, a Syrian writer from a Christian background who lives in Aleppo, published *Les versets du pardon*, her third novel, in Paris in 1999. Set against the backdrop of the Arab-Israeli conflict, the main character, Ahmed, is a Palestinian Muslim orphan. He is a self-proclaimed terrorist whose mother (Marie) and father (David) turn out to be Christian and Jewish, respectively. For the most part, the story is narrated in the second-person singular by Ahmed from prison, addressing in turn his father and mother. We learn that David, a French Jew whose parents were victims of the Holocaust, immigrated illegally to Palestine, had a relationship with Marie (a Christian Palestinian), joined the Irgoun (a Zionist terrorist organization), and helped in the making of the Israeli state by participating in events such as the King David hotel bombing. Marie, who becomes a refugee in Lebanon following the creation of Israel, gives birth to a boy (unbeknownst to his father). The newborn is abandoned in front of a mosque in a Palestinian refugee camp, where he is raised as a Muslim by a sheikh. This boy, Ahmed, eventually escapes the orphanage, and joins a combat training camp. His mother finds him and gives him his father's journal as well as a letter that she wrote to David, but never sent. The whole narrative is framed as a lyrical letter from Ahmed to his parents, written in prison where he has been tortured after he committed a bombing in Israel. The storyline is reconstructed by the son based on his parents' writings, from his prison cell where he is dying, and where he finally discovers his parents' identity.

With the obvious onomastics of the three main characters representing the three monotheist faiths that lay claim to the Holy Land, Ahmed's family tree looks simple, yet needs to be unpacked. What seems at first a straightforward allegory features several layers, and represents the complexity and intertwining of history, religion, politics, and terrorism in the Arab-Israeli conflict. In the first part of this section, I analyze the genealogy that portrays the Arab-Israeli issue to show the various allegorical levels that combine to entangle history, religion, politics and terrorism. In the second part, I examine how *Les versets du pardon* challenges stereotypes and points towards a first step to conflict resolution. Hassan has persuasively argued that "Just as the Peace Process is founded on the legacy of partition, postcolonial studies has reproduced the First World/Third World cultural opposition. To break with this cartography of difference and inaugurate a new international politics, it will be necessary to find a critical language that can speak of the past without reiterating it" (42). I examine how Antaki's genealogy revisits the past to move towards a future beyond the ideology of separation that dominates the peace process.

In postcolonial studies, the parent-child relationship is a common metaphor for the rapport between colonized and colonizer. As John Thieme points out, "problematic parentage becomes a major trope in postcolonial con-texts, where the genealogical bloodlines of transmission are frequently delegitimized by multiple ancestral legacies, usually but not always initiated by imperialism" (8). Thieme also notes that orphans and bastards, as a result of these problematic parentages, are plentiful in postcolonial texts.[26] In *Les versets du pardon*, Ahmed is considered as an orphan; he is also an illegitimate child whose parents belong to communities with antagonist claims on the brink of fighting each other. His family tree can be read as an allegory of a sketchy history of Palestine. Ahmed's father, David, a French Jew, is the European colonizer who intrudes in the native Palestinian Christian and Muslim family tree. When David arrives in Palestine, the religious sounds that dot the landscape belong to the Christian and Muslim traditions: "Les muezzins chantent aux lueurs roses de l'aube. Les clochers des églises, des couvents, carillonnent la naissance du jour" 'the muezzins chant in the pink light of dawn. Bells of churches and convents ring in the new day' (83, de Jager 68). Since David enters Palestine in the early 1940s, by which time the Jewish population had risen to 30 percent of the population (Smith 151), one could expect to find signs of their sizable presence. By choosing to detail the sounds, Antaki can erase the presence of native Jews in Palestine without seeming to deliberately do so, since there is no sound originating in a religious building that is meant to be heard from outside in the Jewish tradition. David is representative of the fact that, by the end of WWII, the majority of the Jewish population in Palestine had immigrated there (Smith 151). The note on religious sounds emphasizes that the majority of the native population in Palestine was Christian and Muslim.

Postcolonial studies have taken on various conceptual models to render the complexity of relationships engendered by colonialism. One is the difference between filiation (a given) and affiliation (a choice). These terms were brought to critical attention by Said, who draws a distinction between filiation (associated with biological descent) and affiliations (defined as cultural and social bonds) in his introduction to *The World, the Text, and the Critic* (16-25). Contrary to what is commonly retained from Said's discussion, that is, that these are mutually exclusive terms,[27] Said does recognize "the verbal echo we hear between the words 'filiation' and 'affiliation'" (*The World* 23). Said recommends that critics not be complicit with this pattern (the transfer of legitimacy from filiation to affiliation) but on the contrary "recognize the difference between instinctual filiation and social affiliation, and to show how affiliation sometimes reproduces filiation, sometimes makes its own forms" (*The World* 24).

Although Said was discussing literary relationship when he made his distinction between filiation and affiliation, and the impact literature has on society and the role texts play in the socio-political context that produces them, it has found relevance in postcolonial studies. As noted by Ashcroft et al., "the concept of affiliation is useful for describing the ways in which colonized societies replace filiative connections to indigenous cultural traditions with affiliations to the social, political and cultural institutions of empire" (106). At the very beginning in *Les versets du pardon*, Ahmed states that he was "une cire molle qu'il fallait durcir" 'soft wax that had to harden' (11, de Jager 3). This metaphor highlights that one's identity is not innate, but made, thus giving precedence to affiliation over filiation. Filiative terms abound in the novel, however, they are used to express affiliations, and more specifically, religious and territorial affiliations. Both Ahmed's territorial and religious affiliations (to the land of Palestine and to Islam) are expressed in filiative terms. Ahmed claims to be "fils du Coran" 'son of the Koran' (20, de Jager 11), thereby denying his filial Christian and Jewish heritage for affiliative identification with the sheikh who found him abandoned at the mosque's doorstep (15) and Islam. The sheikh also functions as a surrogate father, since Ahmed owes his life and identity to the sheikh who gave him a Muslim name (194). His Muslim affiliation is stronger than his Jewish filiation; indeed Ahmed denies his biological father upon discovering that he is a Jew when he exclaims in an apostrophe to his father: "ce bonheur de te découvrir et soudain te perdre" 'the joy of finding you and then suddenly losing you' (32, de Jager 21). Antaki inverses the pattern noted by Ashcroft et al. of replacing the filiative relationship to indigenous culture with affiliation to the empire: in her novel, affiliation to the native Muslim Palestinians takes precedence over his paternal connection to a European Jewish settler. This is a context in which politics (or affiliation) makes you reject biological link (filiation). Ahmed's rejection of his father is emblematic of a refusal by some Arab countries to recognize the state of Israel.

Filiative terms are also used to express an organic link between the Arab people and the land. Ahmed also identifies himself as a "fils de Palestine" 'Palestine's son' (15, de Jager 7). All we know about his years in the orphanage is that he was taught by the sheikh to "venger sa terre, sa mère" 'avenge [his] land, [his] mother' (15, de Jager 7). The land has become a surrogate mother to the boy who is raised as an orphan. After the UN's vote to partition Palestine, the Palestinians' dispossession is expressed in filiative terms: "La terre des Arabes se déchire et hurle, comme une mère qui perd son enfant" 'The land of the Arabs is dismembered and howls like a mother losing her child' (149, de Jager 131). In addition to the mother/child relationship, the text resorts to botanical images. The relationship between Abdel Qader al-Hussayni, the Palestinian resistance leader who was killed in 1948, and the land is expressed as follows: "C'est Abdel Kader qui aime sa Palestine, elle est sa sève, sa mère" 'It is Abdel Kader, who loves his Palestine which is his lifeblood [sap], his mother' (168, de Jager

149). Here the juxtaposition puts the filiative and botanical images on equal footing to describe the relationship between the Palestinian people and the land.

The botanical image evokes another model that has gained popularity in postcolonial studies: Gilles Deleuze and Félix Guattari's rhizome (a root system that spreads across the ground and grows from several points) to counter the representation of thought and knowledge as a tree with a single tap root. As Deleuze and Guattari emphasize, the figure of the tree has dominated Western thought (27). Deleuze and Guattari state that "Le rhizome est une antigénéalogie" (32) 'The rhizome is an antigenealogy.' The parallel with one of Said's terms is made explicit further on: "L'arbre est filiation, mais le rhizome est alliance, uniquement d'alliance" (36) 'The tree is filiation, but the rhizome is alliance, uniquely alliance.' Essentially, Deleuze and Guattari's botanical metaphor parallels Said's use of two terms that come from the same etymological root: filiation is the tree coming from a single tap root, while the rhizome is a perfect metaphor for affiliation. Moreover, both terms belong to the same category: just as affiliation comes from the same root as filiation, a rhizome belongs to the same category as a root of a tree. According to François Noudelmann, "La référence à la racine est nécessairement régressive, elle ne peut qu'entériner des identités univoques, qu'elles prennent le nom de négritude, de francité, d'européanité" (*Pour en finir* 145). However, Antaki's use of the genealogical paradigm does not call for a lost purity or essential identity, but on the contrary, serves to validate a pluralistic society in historical Palestine.

In addition to its historical dimension, Ahmed's genealogy is a religious allegory of the continuity of Judaism, Christianity, and Islam. On the metaphorical level, this genealogy underscores the common ground and the connection among the three monotheist religions that lay claim to the Holy Land. This point is made several times during the course of the novel, through juxtaposition of phrases as in the following: "une si vieille terre que les juifs disent promise, où le Christ est mort pour sauver les hommes, où l'Islam s'agenouille pour prier Allah" 'such an ancient ground which the Jews call the promised land, where Christ died to save mankind, and where Islam kneels to pray to Allah' (70, de Jager 56). The importance of the city of Jerusalem for the three faiths is underlined through the mention of Prophets: "Sous un même ciel, toujours bleu, Salomon a voulu élever un temple, Jésus s'agenouiller pour souffrir et mourir, Mahomet s'élever au ciel" 'Beneath this same, always blue sky, Solomon wanted to build a temple, Jesus knelt down to suffer and die, and Mohammed wanted to ascend to heaven' (124, de Jager 107). In both examples quoted above, the religions are mentioned in their chronological order of appearance, and the focus is on the land that is central to all three, and particularly Jerusalem, whose status is one of the most contested points. Intertextual references also emphasize the common ground between the three monotheist religions. A quote from Abdelkader's poetry acknowledges the fact that Islam believes in continuity between the Jewish, Christian, and Muslim scriptures (100). Ahmed refers to "une terre où coulent le lait et le miel" 'a land where milk and honey flow' (46, de Jager 34) for Palestine: this is a recurrent image in the Bible and in the narrative, where it designates the Holy Land. It also evokes the Qur'anic verse 47:15 that describes paradise as a place where rivers of honey and milk flow.

In addition, Marie's character is the link between David and Ahmed, and as emblematic of Christianity, an intermediary between Judaism and Islam. Marie is compared by Ahmed when addressing his father to "une terre féconde où croissent nos racines" 'fertile ground in which our roots grow' (179, de Jager 159). Feminist research has shown how the allegory of woman as the land and/or as the nation is highly problematic for female citizens. As Deniz Kandiyoti put it, "women are the weakest link in national projects" (387).The allegorical gendering of Islam and Judaism as male and Christianity as female is noteworthy. Marie's role can be seen as a passive Christlike figure, sacrificed by David's nationalist aspirations. The perpetrators of terrorism are Muslim and Jewish, and also male. In light of the framing of the conflict polarized along Jewish-Muslim lines, there is no regard for the place of Christian Palestinians. Thus, a parallel can be drawn between gender and religious issues: women's and minorities' rights take second place to decolonization and nationalist projects.

Ahmed's illegitimate status frames this religious allegory in the Judeo-Christian tradition (which does not recognize Islam, whereas Islam situates itself in the lineage of Judaism and Christianity). The fact that David will never know about Ahmed's existence can be emblematic of the following: Judaic theological teachings, Zionism's blindness to the fact that Palestine was not a land without a people after all, and Israel's refusal to officially acknowledge the repercussion that its creation had on the Palestinian people.

To the historical and religious levels of this allegory, one can add a political level: that literally and figuratively, Zionist terrorism breeds Palestinian terrorism. The incipit of the novel reads "Je suis un terroriste, un rêveur" 'I am a terrorist, a dreamer' (11, de Jager 3). The juxtaposition of the words terrorist and dreamer creates an oxymoron that emphasizes the gap between one's aspirations and a reality in which political frustrations and suffering foment terrorism. The novel constructs a chain reaction between the Holocaust, Zionist terrorism,[28] and Palestinian terrorism. Cheik Al-Tahi, who teaches David about the past peaceful coexistence of the Jewish, Christian, and Muslim communities in the Holy Land, forecasts that the Palestinian people will be made to pay the price for the Holocaust. He tells David: "Le monde a persécuté les juifs, vous nous persécuterez" 'the world has persecuted the Jews, and you [will] persecute us' (97, de Jager 81); "Pour l'injustice de l'Occident envers vous, nous payerons de notre terre" 'For the injustice of the West toward you we will pay with our land' (99, de Jager 83). Indeed, Marie's suffering at the hands of Zionism is described in a way that echoes David's suffering at the hands of Nazism, when both are exiled from their birthplace and suffer from thirst: David in the train (from which he escapes) en route to the concentration camp, and Marie on a refugee boat on her way to Lebanon (183).

Violence is portrayed as the only means to draw attention to one's plight and to force recognition by the other. Ahmed says to his father: "toi et moi nous avons beaucoup souffert avant de choisir. Nous avons aimé la violence pour exister" 'you and I have suffered a great deal before making our choice. We have loved violence so that we could exist' (116, de Jager 99). Violence is shown primarily as springing from thwarted nationalist aspirations and as a consequence of rootlessness and uprooting. Marie and David's relationship is described as "un amour violent" 'a vehement [violent] love' (11, de Jager 3), this oxymoron emphasizes how politics came to affect their relationship. During an exchange between Marie and David, Marie's dream about roots, in which she dreams of being a tree, predicts her upcoming exile following the creation of Israel:

> — . . . les racines sont plus fortes que le temps.
> —Mais Marie, l'homme fort pose des racines partout. (158)
> — . . . the roots [of the country of your childhood] are stronger than time itself.
> —But a strong man puts his roots down everywhere, Marie. (de Jager 139)

The use of the adjective "fort" 'strong' in this context is an understatement that both signals and softens the violence that will accompany the creation of the state of Israel. David's settling in Palestine following his exile caused by Nazism is done by violent means and causes Palestinian dispossession and exile, which in turn sets off violence against Israel. Children in the Palestinian refugee camp are "sans racines" 'rootless' (186, de Jager 166); exile and the rootlessness that ensues are seen as a cause of their recourse to violence. Ahmed explains that "c'est dans la violence que je touche à ma terre une seule fois" 'it is in violence that just once I touch my land' (18, de Jager 9); as a Palestinian refugee in Lebanon, the only contact that is conceivable with the native land he longs for is one of violence, when he commits a bombing.

Despite incompatible agendas, David and Ahmed are paradoxically united in their affiliation with political nationalist movement resorting to terrorism to achieve their nationalist aspirations (124). Their journeys bear uncanny resemblances: they both enter Palestine clandestinely, and resort to terrorism. Ahmed's intransigence in his determination to carry out attacks mirrors his father's, who was determined to expel all Palestinians from the land that was to become Israel. These parallel itineraries paradoxically strengthen the filiations that are rejected or unacknowledged. In making Ahmed's father an illegal immigrant to Palestine, as well as a Zionist terrorist, the novel puts to the fore the plight of Palestinian refugees (Ahmed is not allowed in Palestine) and their claims, while establishing a filiation between Zionist and Palestinian terrorism.

Religious discourse is relegated to the background, but the religious dimension of the conflict is present. Statements such as "la Judée, la Samarie, la Galilée, une si vieille terre que les juifs disent promise" 'Judea, Samaria, and Galilee—such an ancient ground which the Jews call the Promised Land' (70, de Jager 56), and the banner that floats on David's boat stating that "nothing can keep us from our Jewish homeland" (73, in English in the original French text) indirectly recalls that the Zionist claim to Palestine is rooted in the Biblical scriptures. Ahmed's Christian lineage, contrary to his Jewish filiation, is not cause for sorrow when he discovers his parents' identity; this highlights that a political dispute over land is at the root of the conflict, not a religious antagonism, all the while pointing out the intertwining of politics and religions in the Arab-Israeli conflict, since some claims to the land are rooted in scriptures.

The potential for all three Abrahamic religions to incite violence or mercy is underscored: "chaque geste de violence ou de miséricorde appartient à un même cri de Yahvé, Dieu ou Allah" 'every gesture of violence or of compassion [mercy] belongs to a same cry of Yahweh, God, or Allah' (95, de Jager 79). Cheik al-Tahi symbolizes a tradition of tolerance in Islam. He teaches David about the incident when the prophet Mohammed instructed his followers to protect a church (166), and quotes from the Bible when God told the Prophet David not to build the temple of Jerusalem (109): "Ne batis pas de maison à mon Nom, car tu as été un homme de guerre et tu as versé le sang" 'Do not build a house in My Name, for you have been a man of war and you have spilled blood' (Chroniques 1, 28:3, de Jager 93). In both instances, religion wants to dissociate itself from violence. Nevertheless, the fact that religion can be manipulated to various ends is underlined by Ahmed who says that he learned violence from a sheikh (although not cast in religious terms since he is asked to "venger [sa] terre" 'avenge [his] land' (15, de Jager 7) while his father was taught tolerance by another (and yet became a terrorist). The narrative does not press the religious dimension further, since violence in this novel stems from nationalist demands.

After the partition of Palestine has been voted on by the UN, "les juifs, les chrétiens et les musulmans ne peuvent plus se réconcilier que dans l'espace clos des cimetières" 'Jews, Christians, and Muslims can only be reconciled together in the closed space of cemeteries' (152, de Jager 134), that is, once they are dead, or, as stressed in a passage in Athlit, a British clearance camp, under the colonial yoke. When David is caught and jailed with other Jewish illegal immigrants, Palestinian revolutionaries, Christian and Muslim clergy, Ahmed wonders about a picture that features several prisoners of the camp: "Père, es-tu avec eux dans cette photo parce qu'ils ont voulu fixer sur une image en noir et blanc les confessions de Yahvé, Dieu, et Allah?" 'Father, are you with them in that picture because they wanted to freeze the faiths of Yahweh, God, and Allah in one single black and white image?' (90, de Jager 75). The British mandate on Palestine, when Great Britain is "la geôlière de l'Orient" 'the prison warden of the Orient' (77, de Jager 62), seems to be the only means of preserving all communities. However, David's relationship with sheikh Ahmed Al-Tahi, whom he meets in the British prison camp and who teaches him Hebrew and Arabic, is emblematic of potential coexistence through a fruitful relationship that is expressed in filial terms. In the course of several exchanges between the two characters, the sheikh keeps calling David "mon fils" 'my son' or "mon enfant" 'my child' (91, de Jager 109); David will call him "mon cheik" 'my sheik' and at one point "mon cheik, mon père" 'my sheik, my father' (99, de Jager 83).

While the historical time frame of David and Marie's story can be easily determined, thanks to the mention of events such as the massacre of Deir Yassin, such is not the case for Ahmed's. The indeterminacy of Ahmed's historical time focuses the attention on the past as a way to map out a basis for mutual recognition. It stresses the first dispossession of the Palestinians of their land as well as the Holocaust, events that are conveniently forgotten or whose importance is routinely undermined for political purposes in Israel for the first, and in the Arab world for the second. It echoes Said's stance that "the crucial issue for any discussion of Palestine has to be 1948, or rather what happened in 1948" ("Introduction" 14). In a newspaper article that first appeared in 1997, Said urged both Palestinians and Israelis to engage in mutual recognition of one another's sufferings. According to Said, the Palestinians should not engage in minimizing the Jews' history of suffering, and specifically the Holocaust, especially given the impact of the latter on the creation of the state of Israel, and reciprocally, the Israelis need to acknowledge the dispossession that the creation of their state has entailed since 1948. Said states that

> Jewish and Palestinian experiences are historically, indeed organically, connected: to break them asunder is to falsify what is authentic about each. We must think our histories together, however difficult that may be, in order for there to be a common future. And that future must include Arabs and Jews together, free of any exclusionary, denial-based schemes for shutting out one side by the other, either theoretically or politically. That is the real challenge. (*The End* 209)

The genealogy featured in Antaki's work, emblematic of some of the historical processes that define Palestine and Israel today, is a creative embodiment of the mutual recognition that Said urges.

Antaki's use of the genealogical paradigm goes against the grain of attempts to conceptualize relations between communities outside of the family tree model. In *Pour en finir avec la généalogie*, Noudelmann points out the extent to which familial and genealogical paradigms govern, structure, and legitimize collective representations. Unlike other writers who endeavor to counter and/or give alternatives to the genealogical model, Antaki uses it to construct a common heritage among the communities that lay claim to historical Palestine, thus stressing irreversible bonds between them. According to Noudelmann, "l'affiliation rétrospective permet de souder une communauté en l'identifiant à des ancêtres communs" 'retrospective affiliation enables a community to unite by identifying common ancestors' ("Pour une pensée" 195). Antaki's novel features what seems at first a scandalous genealogy, a monstrous family tree where the men are both victims and villains, and enemies turn out to be related. The illegitimate family tree is not new in postcolonial literature; it symbolizes the irreversible hybridity that colonialism engendered. In the context of the Arab-Israeli conflict, Ahmed's genealogy is striking, because "the Partition Plan reveals the success of Zionism in establishing its program of cultural differentiation as the dominant international approach to Palestine" (Hassan 36). This ideology of separation is prevalent in the two-state solution that has the most currency to solve the conflict and posits the Arab Palestinians and the Jewish Israelis as peoples who must be kept separate. The recourse to this family tree somehow shows the irrevocability of the Jewish mark in Palestine, and the intertwining of filiation and affiliation in this text highlights that separation of the two people involved is unwarranted.

Antaki's novel anticipates a new direction taken in the field of conflict resolution as mapped out by Marc Gopin. This new course comes from the growing recognition that "there is a global resurgence of religion taking place throughout the world that is challenging our interpretation of the modern world." (Thomas 10). This resurgence challenges the modernization theory that assumes that modernization entails secularization (Thomas 2, Sayyid 4). Marc Gopin has emphasized that religions do play a role in perpetuating the Palestinian-Israeli conflict, be it Islam with the religious nationalist parties, Judaism with the settlements of occupied territories, and Christianity with the American Zionist Christians for instance (*Holy War* 6). Gopin therefore argues that it is crucial to take the various religious values into account if one is to achieve a viable peace process (*Holy War* 6).

Since forgiveness is important in Judaism, Christianity, and Islam, Gopin explores the possible recourse to forgiveness as a means to conflict resolution. He notes that forgiveness, along with patience with human failing and infinite compassion, are "basic characteristics of God in the Hebrew Bible, the New Testament, and the Qur'an" ("Forgiveness" 89). Gopin argues that forgiveness should be accompanied with justice seeking and presented as a form of empowerment (which Judaism and Islam do) in order to be a successful step to conflict resolution.

In an interview, asked about how one goes beyond suffering, Antaki stated the following:

> En travaillant sur la notion de pardon, ce que je fais tout en revendiquant ma laïcité . . . faire le deuil des tragédies est un processus lent, il faut des années et des années pour que l'oubli s'installe, que l'histoire s'enfouisse. Tandis que le pardon—à ne pas confondre avec le renoncement—est une décision, une sorte d'acte volontaire qui permet d'agir sur le présent pour envisager diversement l'avenir. (qtd. in Galesne, 159)
>
> By working on the notion of forgiveness, which I do while claiming my secularism . . . letting go of tragedies is a slow process, it takes years and years to sink into oblivion, to bury history. Whereas forgiveness—not to be confused with renouncement—is a decision, a kind of voluntary act that enables one to act on the present so as to envisage the future in various ways.

Despite the author's self-professed grounding in secularism, the title of her novel refers to forgiveness grounded in faith, since the word "verset" 'verse' refers to religious texts. At the beginning of the novel, Ahmed is motivated by hatred (18), yet after reading his parents' texts, his hatred is "morte, éteinte" 'dead, extinguished' (20, de Jager 10-11). Ahmed presents his narrative as follows: "mes dernières paroles, écrites pour vous [père et mère], sont les versets du pardon" 'written for you, my last words are verses of forgiveness' (21, de Jager 12). At the end, the parents are reunited in the son's addressing both of them as "vous" 'you' instead of separately; the narrative pieces together different stories to reconstruct the family tree and reconciles the antagonisms fostered by the creation of Israel. After closing his father's journal, Ahmed dedicates a couple of paragraphs successively granting his father forgiveness and asking for the latter's forgiveness (179-80). Once again, father and son meet through similar acts: Ahmed tells his father that "notre dernière prière est celle du pardon" 'our last prayer is the prayer of forgiveness' (180, de Jager 160), since his father ended his journal by asking for Marie's forgiveness. Towards the end of the narrative, in an apostrophe that addresses both of his parents, Ahmed states: "Je sais, à present, que je contiens dans ma violence, mon salut, le Verbe de Yahvé, de Dieu et d'Allah" 'I know now that in my violence I hold my salvation, the word of Yahweh, God, and Allah' (194, de Jager 173). Since Ahmed was born on Christmas Eve, he seems to prefigure the return of the Messiah, or function as the sacrificed son that will redeem humanity's sins.

During the course of the narrative, Ahmed comes to face and accept his Jewish filiation. Eventually, he acknowledges to his father that "aujourd'hui, ce pays est pour toi et moi" 'today this land [country] is for you and for me' (107, de Jager 91). One could object that Marie (and by extension women and/or Christians) are forgotten in that last sentence, but in the context of the novel, Marie's place in Palestine is never an issue for Ahmed. While Kandiyoti noted that "Wherever women continue to serve as boundary markers between different national, ethnic and religious collectivities, their emergence as full-fledged citizens will be jeopardized" (382), in *Les versets* Marie's character actually serves to blur such boundaries. Moreover, the emphasis on Ahmed's filiation puts the three characters on equal footing in ideal circumstances. In a passage in which Ahmed envisions a time when their family story would have a happy ending, he imagines that his parents are together in Jaffa, and that when he is born "vous me tiendrez dans vos bras. Nous vivrons ainsi, sur la terre des promesses, pour planter l'arbre de la paix, du pardon" 'you two will hold me in your arms. That is how we shall live, on the land of promises, to plant the tree of peace and forgiveness' (194, de Jager 173). Peace and forgiveness are juxtaposed to emphasize that both terms in this context are linked to one another. Ahmed presents his family tree as a metaphor for future reconciliation: "je suis né de votre amour interdit qui, pour moi, n'est pas une faute mais une lune d'espérance" 'I was born of your forbidden love that, for me, is not a flaw but a moon of expectation [hope]' (20, de Jager 11). Indeed, the novel ends by first repeating the very first paragraph of the novel, but ends with Ahmed stating that "je suis le fils de David et de Marie" 'I . . . am the son of David and Mary' (197, de Jager 176). Thus the story has come full circle when Ahmed accepts his filiation.

While certainly not a solution to the conflict, which will require efforts from both parties, Ahmed's acknowledgement is in line with what Said, who recognized that Palestinians' dispossession could not be righted by the expulsion of Israeli Jews (*Humanism* 143), wrote. Said grounds his vision of coexistence in secular terms, and points out the fact that both in history and in the present, "Palestine is an irreducibly mixed place" (*The End* 318). He advocates the establishment of a secular state in which citizens have the same rights regardless of their ethnicity (*The End* 320). Antaki's genealogy is an illustration of the potential that reading Israeli and Palestinian histories side by side, as Said recommends (*The End* 319), can yield. But while Said leaves religion out of the picture—actually saying that neither Palestinian nor Israelis "should be held hostage to religious extremists" (*The End* 320), Antaki finds in religion a basis for the first step toward reconciliation.

Conclusion

By going back to the Crusades and the events of 1948, respectively, Maalouf's and Antaki's books serve to bring the attention to the root cause of the Arab-Israeli conflict; namely, a violent occupation that is seen by Arabs as a continuum of Western imperialism, a fact that is consistently obfuscated. Both *Les versets* and *Les échelles* attempt to change the historical frame through which the conflict is viewed, by tracing it back to 1948, not just 1967 or 2000, as a way to highlight the first violence done to Palestinians.[29] Each book is tainted by its context. A pessimistic tone is evident in *Les croisades*, which was written during the Lebanese civil war and Israeli invasion of Lebanon, whereas a more optimistic tone reigns in *Les versets* and *Les échelles*, both written in the wake of the Oslo Accords and before their demise with the breakdown of the Camp David talks in 2000 and the second Intifada. The Oslo Accords constituted a moment that was at the very least touted as a possible beginning of the end of the conflict (despite serious reservations by many, including Said, who from the beginning pointed out that the flaws of the Accords were bound to set them for failure). As Ilan Pappé noted, there was a flagrant disconnect between the images of Oslo propagated by politicians and the reality on the ground, but the illusion of Oslo as a viable peace accord lasted until 1996 (245). This period of optimism influenced both novels, while at the same time the absence of happy endings expresses a reservation as to a conclusion of the conflict in sight. This reservation transpires somewhat in the choice of a couple in Maalouf's novel, which opens the possibility of separation, estrangement, and divorce, as indeed happens in the novel, although the separation at first is due to events over which the characters have no control. However, Antaki's family tree emphasizes that the destinies of Arabs and Jews in the Middle East are irreversibly intertwined. In *Les versets du pardon*, like in the literary works analyzed by Hochberg in her recent study, "the tie between 'Jew' and 'Arab' . . . challenges the separatist imagination and proves the disjointing of 'Jew' and 'Arab' to be at least partially impossible" (17). One can legitimately wonder whether such a utopian vision can truly contribute to resolving the conflict whose harsh realities on the ground have recently taken grimmer turns. I would argue that Antaki's vision constitutes a necessary first step in the sense that it opens the possibility of imagining a future together that contrasts with the dominant separatist ideologies of European colonialism, Zionism, and Arab nationalism.

Notes

1. For instance, *The Question of Palestine, After the Last Sky, The End of the Peace Process, Peace and Its Discontents, The Politics of Dispossession.*

2. Historian Ilan Pappé wrote about immigration to Palestine at the end of the nineteenth century that "Although [the Zionists'] number was small, it was in hindsight a colonizing immigration. It was not a proper colonization, as Palestine was not occupied by a European power. But like colonialism elsewhere, it was a European movement, with people entering Palestine for the sake of European interests, not local ones" (42). Ella Shohat wrote that "A series of mutually reinforcing equations between modernity, science, technology, and the West has legitimized Zionism as an extension of the civilizing mission applied first to Palestine and then to Arab Jews" ("Rupture" 64).

3. This section has appeared as "The Rewriting of History in Amin Maalouf's *The Crusades through Arab Eyes*" in *Studies in 20th and 21st Century Literature* 30.2 (Summer 2006): 263-287. It has been revised and augmented.

4. Unreferenced translations are mine.

5. In the decade that preceded the publication of *The Crusades through Arab Eyes*, more than twenty percent of the historical novels published in France were set in the Middle Ages, with the Crusades as a privileged period (Pierre 34-35). While Marc Bertrand notes that one of the innovative aspects of recent historical novels is to pay attention to the minorities marginalized or persecuted for their differences, be it ethnic, religious, racial or cultural, none of the novels about the crusades that he mentions seems to present the Arabs' perspective. Examples of novels about the crusades mentioned by Marc Bertrand in his article are: *La joie des pauvres* by Zoé Oldenbourg (Gallimard, 1970), *La dislocation* by Armand Farrachi (Stock, 1974), *La croisade des enfants* by Bernard Thomas (Fayard, 1973), and *Le maître de Hongrie* by Marcel Jullian (Table Ronde, 1975).

6. The J'ai lu edition of this book bears the subtitle *La barbarie franque en Terre sainte* 'Frankish Barbarism in the Holy Land' (Paris: J'ai lu, 1999). This subtitle does not appear in the original Lattès edition of the book. This is probably a marketing ploy from the J'ai lu editions to use such a catchy subtitle (thus fulfilling what Genette calls the temptation function of a title in *Paratexts* [93]), because it reverses the generally accepted idea of the crusades as heroic deeds.

7. See Grousset, Runciman, and Oldenbourg.

8. "The I of historiography is supposed to be that of the writer whose name appears on the book cover" (Carrard 87).

9. In their bibliography, both Zoé Oldenbourg and Steven Runciman divide their sources according to their origins: Oldenbourg categorizes them according to religious criteria ("Oriental Historians" ["Historiens orientaux"] and "Christian Historians from the Orient" ["Historiens chrétiens d'Orient"]), while Runciman divides them according to linguistic criteria ("Arabic and Persian sources").

10. Grousset's *Histoire des croisades* passes over the case of the crusaders' cannibalism in silence, Runciman's *A History of the Crusades* briefly alludes to it (vol. I: 261), and Oldenbourg's *Les croisades* treats it as a mere rumor deliberately spread by the crusaders to spread terror (131).

11. Maalouf does not give precise references to any of his quotations according to scholarly conventions, but lists his sources chapter by chapter in the "Notes et Sources" section at the end of the book. For his Frankish sources on cannibalism however, he does indicate several page numbers from Michaud's *L'histoire des croisades* and *Bibliographie des croisades* under chapter 3 in "Notes et Sources," but I have been unable to

consult these texts to verify where the citations attributed to Raoul de Caen and Albert d'Aix come from.

12. At the time of the Crusades the word "Franj" seems to be a milder equivalent of the term "sarrasin" (Saracen), which was used during the Middle Ages to designate Muslims. *La chanson de Roland* (The Song of Roland) is a representative example of the derogatory connotations conveyed by the word "sarrasin" (who represents the pagan enemy).

13. "The violation of an individual woman is the metaphor for man's forcing himself on whole nations" (Robin Morgan, qtd. in Higgins 1996: 108).

14. One could argue that murder can also be narrated into rather different kinds of story (such as premeditation, self-defense, accident, or suicide).

15. In *Orientalism*, Said quotes Chateaubriand: "The Crusades were not only about the deliverance of the Holy Sepulchre, but more about knowing which would win on the earth, a cult that was civilization's enemy, systematically favorable to ignorance [this was Islam, of course], to despotism, to slavery, or a cult that had caused to reawaken in modern people the genius of a sage antiquity, and had abolished base servitude?" (172).

16. That text was prompted by Benazir Bhutto's defeated opponent's indignation in 1988 that no Muslim state had ever been ruled by a woman. Mernissi, a Moroccan sociologist, set out to unearth women who did govern during the history of the Muslim world.

17. One could also specify that the viewpoints presented are those that were recorded by historians who were close to authorities, or to those in power, and who themselves belonged to the elite. These accounts are what shaped the current popular Arab view of the Crusades.

18. The same applies to the crusaders, who were not all Franks.

19. Runciman's negative appraisal of the Crusades was published as early as 1954, and his quotes ground his work in a Christian framework. The reason he declares the Fourth Crusade ("against Christians") the greatest crime against humanity (130) is that the Byzantine Empire had shielded Europe from Muslim advances. His conclusion that the Crusades are a "long act of intolerance in the name of God, which is the sin against the Holy Ghost" (III 480) is of course grounded in Christian theology.

20. In *Les identités meurtrières*, he writes: "ce contre quoi je me bats et me battrai toujours, c'est cette idée selon laquelle il y aurait, d'un côté, une religion—chrétienne—destinée de tout temps à véhiculer modernisme, liberté, tolérance et démocratie, et de l'autre une religion—musulmane—vouée dès l'origine au despotisme et à l'obscurantisme" 'what I am fighting against, and always will, is the idea that on the one hand there's a religion—Christianity—destined for ever to act as a vector for modernism, freedom, tolerance and democracy, and on the other hand another religion—Islam—doomed from the outset to despotism and obscurantism' (66, Bray 55). And he adds : "L'islam avait établi un « protocole de tolérance » à une époque où les sociétés chrétiennes ne toléraient rien" 'Islam established a 'protocol of tolerance' at a time when Christian societies tolerated nothing' (67-68, Bray 57).

21. Simon Lloyd mentions that Urban II urged the Catalan nobles to fulfill their crusade vows in Spain during the first crusade (39).

22. See for instance *Léon l'Africain* (1986), *Samarcande* (1988), *Les échelles du Levant* (1996), *Le périple de Baldassare* (2000).

23. The Arabs and Muslims are not romanticized. Maalouf reports the killings committed by Turks (151) and massacres committed by Muslims when the Franks are expelled (273).

24. Indeed, one can easily find fault with his sweeping statement that the Arabs were unable to create stable institutions and that the situation when civil war erupts with the death of a king is much the same nowadays. The recent examples of countries such as Morocco, Jordan, and Syria, speak to the contrary. Hassan II, Hussein, and Assad were long time kings and dictator, respectively, yet their deaths were followed by smooth successions (even in Jordan where there was a last-minute change in the constitution to replace King Hussein's brother, who held the title of crown-prince for 30 years, with one of Hussein's sons). While the preceding examples postdate the publication of Maalouf's text, I cannot think of a civil war that started as a succession dispute in the Arab world prior to 1980.

25. Hochberg reaches the same conclusion: "Focusing only on Germany and its allies in destruction, while completely ignoring the colonial history of the Middle East, *Ports of Call* ultimately locates the 1948 war and the Zionist occupation of Palestine, completely outside the context of the region's own history of continual colonial occupation and the struggles against it" (123).

26. For a discussion of the Francophone writer as a bastard and an orphan, see Marx-Scouras' article.

27. See Shumway (91) and Watt (116).

28. Chomsky states that "the record of Israeli terrorism goes back to the origins of the state" (134).

29. Alisa Solomon describes the frame coverage of the failure of the Camp David peace talks, which consisted in saying that Israel had made a generous offer that was rejected by the Palestinians, occulting the continued and accelerated developments of new settlements in the West Bank, among other things. She argues that "Through this frame, which erases the occupation, the humanity of Palestinians is thrown into question. They appear as incorrigible, unaccountably violent, preternatural Jew haters. The Palestinian escalation of suicide bombings of civilian targets inside Israel during this period is, then, seen through this frame not as a desperate weapon of resistance, morally reprehensible as it may be, but as motiveless malignancy, proof of innate Palestinian barbarism" (1589). She later adds: "Whereas stories from the first intifada set events against the background of an occupation that began in 1967, today the context line in a broadcast segment . . . marks 2000 as the beginning of relevant time" (1589).

Chapter 2

The Arab-Israeli Conflict beyond the Middle East: Albert Memmi, Edmond Amran El Maleh, Farid Boudjellal, and Karin Albou

The consequences of the Arab-Israeli conflict extend to communities beyond the Middle East, to countries such as Morocco, which used to have a considerable Jewish minority, and France. The conflict has had dire repercussions on the Jewish communities that were part of the Arab world. At the dawn of the twenty-first century, these communities have pretty much disappeared. Morocco's Jewish population, for instance, was estimated at 300,000 in 1947 (Lévy 9); it has dwindled and now numbers below 3,000; Tunisia's Jewish population, estimated at 95,000 in 1946 (Sebag 259) went down to less than 3,000 today. Though Morocco's Jewish community remains the most important of the Arab world (Lévy 49), events such as the 2003 Casablanca terrorist attacks (some of which targeted Jewish places), threaten it further.

Two seemingly distant events, be they in temporal or in spatial terms, are colluding and having repercussions in contemporary France: the Arab-Israeli conflict, and the French colonization of North Africa, and particularly Algeria. Although the French colonial presence in Africa ended over forty years ago, its aftermath is still felt today. At the dawn of the twenty-first century, France happens to be home to both the largest Muslim and Jewish communities in Western Europe, in great part due to immigration from former colonies. In recent years, various crimes have brought to the forefront with renewed urgency the question of interfaith relations between Muslims and Jews in France. These include the fabricated aggression with an anti-Semite motive blamed on Maghrebians and Blacks by Marie-Léonie Leblanc on July 9, 2004, and the February 2006 horrendous kidnapping, torture, and murder of Ilan Halimi, targeted because of his Jewish background, by a mixed-race gang headed by a nominal Muslim. These recent events follow a notable increase in anti-Semite (in a broad sense) incidents in the 1990s and 2000s. Some of these crimes can be attributed to the rise of the far right and neo-Nazis, such as the desecration of Jewish (in Carpentras

in 1990 for instance) and Muslim tombs (the Muslim section of a military ceme-
tery in 2007), and some to French people of Arab/Muslim heritage.

This chapter focuses on the geographic displacement of the Arab-Israeli
conflict by analyzing the representation of its impact on the social and cultural
fabric of Maghrebian countries and contemporary France. It first analyzes two
Arab Jewish writers' take on the Arab Jew in essays and articles, notably
Memmi's *Juifs et Arabes* [*Jews and Arabs*] and *Portrait du décolonisé arabo-
musulman et de quelques autres* [*Decolonization and the Decolonized*], and
various pieces published by El Maleh. Through such analysis, this chapter builds
on Hochberg's comparative analysis of creative works, namely Memmi's *La
statue de sel* [*The Pillar of Salt*] and El Maleh's *Mille ans, un jour* [one thousand years, one day].[1] These two Francophone Jewish Maghrebian writers have
opposite views on the issue of Arab-Jewish relations and the identity of Arab
Jews, despite similarities in their itinerary. El Maleh was born in Morocco in
1917, Memmi in Tunisia in 1920. Both writers received a French education,
studied philosophy, supported the independence movements of their respective
countries, but settled in France (Memmi right after Tunisia's independence in
1956, El Maleh in 1965 at the beginning of Hassan II's repressive regime). Contrary to Memmi, El Maleh went back to his native country in 1999 and still re-
sides there. I examine how their positions on the Arab-Israeli conflict correlate
with the relative prominence of each writer (Memmi's renown and El Maleh's
obscurity) considering the current political climate.

The second part of this chapter contrasts the representation of the relations
between Arabs and Jews in France in Boudjellal's *JuifsArabes* [JewsArabs] and
Albou's *La petite Jérusalem* [*Little Jerusalem*]. I demonstrate that, contrary to
Albou's film, Boudjellal's comic book participates in an endeavor to go beyond
the ideology of partition and separation that has dominated approaches to the
Arab-Israeli conflict.

Arab Jews from the Maghreb

Albert Memmi

Memmi published *Juifs et Arabes* in 1974. The book is a collection of essays
written for different occasions, all having to do with Arabs and Jews in the Middle East and North Africa. The term "Juif-Arabe" appears in the title of one
chapter ("Qu'est-ce qu'un Juif-Arabe?" 'What is an Arab Jew?'), originally
written for a journal that had asked Memmi to write about relations between
Jews and Arabs in Arab countries (Memmi, *Juifs* 59, note 1). This term (in the
plural form "Juifs-Arabes" 'Jews-Arabs') had just been uttered by Qadhafi during a visit to Paris, in a rhetorical question recalling the common cultural heritage shared by Arabs and Sephardic Jews (Memmi, *Juifs* 49). In the course of
this essay, Memmi privileges the term "Juifs arabes" 'Arab Jews,' and "Juifs des

pays arabes" 'Jews from Arab countries' because according to him, the notion of "Juifs-Arabes" is a myth, a condition to which Arab Jews aspired but that was denied to them by Arab Muslims (Memmi, *Juifs* 50).[2]

In his book, Memmi defines himself as a strong supporter of both Zionism and Palestinians, and sees no contradiction in his stand: "je réclame la justice pour les miens sans injustice pour les autres" 'I want justice for my people without injustice for the others' (*Juifs* 13, Levieux 13), but he does not dwell on the fact that the creation of Israel did come at the expense of Palestinians. Memmi justifies his support for the two-state solution because over the years, "il s'est produit un échange de fait des populations: une partie des Palestiniens a gagné les nations arabes, une partie des Juifs de ces nations a gagné Israël" 'a de facto exchange of populations has come about. Part of the Palestinians have gone to the Arab nations, and part of the Jews from those nations have gone to Israel' (*Juifs* 14, Levieux 14). Ella Shohat has called references to "population exchange" "propagandistic" and underlined the fact that "it elides the simple fact that neither Arab Jews nor Palestinians were ever consulted" ("Rupture" 58).[3] Shohat has eloquently demonstrated that "Ironically, the Zionist view that Arabness and Jewishness were mutually exclusive gradually came to be shared by Arab nationalist discourse, placing Arab Jews on the horns of a terrible dilemma" ("Rupture" 58). Although Memmi sees Israel as a country for Jews, he does recognize that there are non-Jewish minorities in that state, and Jewish minorities all over the world. But Memmi fails to examine the implication of his statement. He overlooks the fact that he is accepting the ethnic category of Jews unquestioningly despite the fact that this was elaborated by anti-Semites, and the fact that the state of Israel is founded on religious and exclusionary grounds. Memmi advocates the two-state solution with each state having a minority that should enjoy equal rights to the majority (*Juifs* 166). He thus indirectly admits that Arabs and Jews are indeed inseparable.

Memmi's main argument is that "ce n'est pas le sionisme qui a été à l'origine de l'antisémitisme arabe, mais l'inverse, tout comme en Europe" 'it is not Zionism that has caused Arab anti-Semitism, but the other way around, just as in Europe' (*Juifs* 12, Levieux 12). Here, Memmi dehistoricizes anti-Semitism and the various ways it has been articulated throughout history in different contexts.[4] His statement also passes over the variance of the effects of anti-Semitism in different cultures and time periods. Paul Grosser and Edwin Halperin's catalogue of anti-Semitism includes an "Islamic" catalogue, but focuses on the West. They explain that in Islam, "There was a condition of religious toleration not present under Christianity. Overt violence and anti-Semitic persecution, while not absent, were episodic and unsystematic. There were periods and places of genuinely cordial Islamic/Arab-Jewish interaction" (7).

There is no rendering in Memmi's work of the complexity of factors that pushed the Jewish Maghrebian communities to leave North Africa.[5] One common element, however, which Memmi silences, is the fact that the creation of the state of Israel on Arab land is a prominent factor. The conflict between Arab countries and the state of Israel trickles down to internal tensions where the Jewish Maghrebian communities are considered or fear they will be considered guilty by association. Zafrani underlines that the political and psychological dimensions of Moroccans' emigration to Israel after independence, despite their equal citizen status, are intertwined and due in part to the Palestinian problem created by the creation of Israel and the Arab States' solidarity with Palestinians (295).

Memmi downplays the seven-century-long Andalusian period known for the peaceful coexistence of the three monotheist religions under Moorish rule. He dismisses it as an anomaly: "Jamais, je dis bien jamais—à part peut-être deux ou trois époques très circonstancielles, comme la période andalouse et en-core—les Juifs n'ont vécu en pays arabes autrement que comme des gens di-minués" 'Never, I repeat, never—except perhaps for two or three eras with very clear boundaries in time, such as the Andalusian period, and even then—have the Jews lived in the Arab countries otherwise than as diminished people in an exposed position' (*Juifs* 51, Levieux 21-22).[6] He thus participates in what Sho-hat has thus explained: "[Zionist discourse's] historiography concerning Jews within Islam consists of a morbidly selective 'tracing the dots' from pogrom to pogrom," and while she refrains from idealizing the situation of Jews in the Muslim world, she argues that "Zionist discourse has, in a sense, hijacked Jews from their Judeo-Islamic political geography and subordinated them into the European Jewish chronicle of shtetl and pogrom" ("Rupture" 59).

Memmi's rendering of the conditions of Jews in Islam and in Christendom is partial. He credits colonization for the betterment of the Jewish condition. Even when he points out the failure of French authorities to protect the Jewish community, he mitigates their responsibility by recalling Arab hostilities: "J'ai raconté dans *La statue de sel* comment nous avons été froidement abandonnés aux Allemands par les autorités françaises. Mais il me faut ajouter que nous bai-gnions également dans une population arabe hostile. . . . C'est la raison pour laquelle très peu d'entre nous purent passer les lignes pour rejoindre les Alliés" 'In my novel, *The Pillar of Salt*, I have told how the French authorities coldly abandoned us to the Germans. But I must add that we also lived amidst a hostile Arab population. . . . That is why very few of us were able to get through the lines to join the Allies' (*Juifs* 53, Levieux 23). Memmi strikingly deflects the responsibility of the Vichy regime by stressing the hostile Arab community (something which, incidentally, in the context of WWII is not depicted in *La statue de sel*). This state of affairs, however, is not reflected in Paul Sebag's study. Sebag details the discriminatory measures implemented in Tunisia during World War II (222), but stresses that "malgré les efforts de la propagande alle-mande, l'idéologie antisémite ne réussit pas à mordre sur les autres éléments de la population" 'despite the German propaganda efforts, anti-Semitism did not catch on with the other elements of the population' (244). In Morocco, Moham-med V protected Moroccan Jews by refusing to cooperate with the Protectorate authorities under Vichy (Zafrani 293), and in Algeria, it is noted that the Muslim population, contrary to the European one, did not commit any hostile act against Jews during the WWII period (Stora, "L'impossible" 295, 303). However, the

Vichy period stimulated a growing segment of pro-Zionism in the Maghreb (Laskier 85).

Given that Memmi in his essay sees Zionism as the only solution to the Jewish problem, it is surprising that the narrator of his semi-autobiographical *Pillar of Salt* chooses Argentina as his destination, since in real life, Memmi chose neither Argentina nor Israel, but France as his new home. Because Argentina was one of the proposed sites for the establishment of the Jewish state by early Zionist leaders, this might have been a way for Memmi to reconcile some of the contradictions inherent in his support: in addition to Hochberg's analysis that Argentina not only avoid the whole polarization between Arabs and Jews that ensued from the creation of the state of Israel (23), I would add that it also eschews the religious character of Zionism's claim to the Holy Land for what Memmi supports as a purely nationalist project. Memmi's efforts (not always successful) to distance himself from religion are evident both in his essays and in his creative writing.[7]

Hochberg argues that "While Memmi recognizes the subversive political potential embedded in the figure of the Arab Jew, he explicitly wishes to disarm it, stating that the promotion of an Arab Jewish identity presents a serious threat to the creation of a new national Jewish collective" (34-35). Indeed, Hochberg points out "Europe's role in constructing both the Jew and the Arab as its others, and its role in polarizing these two identities, making them Other to each other" (35), and that Memmi failed to address the role that European colonialism has played in "creating and sustaining the animosity between Muslims/Arabs and Jews and in making the Arab Jew an 'impossible figure'" (21).

The few pages Memmi devotes to the Israeli-Palestinian conflict in his recent *Portrait du décolonisé arabo-musulman*, conceived as an update to his groundbreaking *Portrait du colonisé*, testify to the same phenomenon that Hochberg had noted: the complete lack of consideration of Europe's role in shaping the relationships between Arabs and Jews. Although Memmi recognizes the transnational dimension of the conflict, which resonates throughout the Arab world and indeed throughout the world (or at least where there are diasporic communities),[8] he refuses to see Israel as "une fondation coloniale" 'a colonial settlement' because of the absence of a "métropole" behind it to back it up (*Portrait du décolonisé* 41, Bononno 25).[9] This statement fails to take into account the very prominent role played by the pro-Israeli lobbies in the U.S. (see Mearsheimer and Walt), and the fact that Israel has ranked at the top of U.S. foreign aid recipients. Israel might not have a "métropole" in the same manner that Paris ruled Algeria and London ruled India, but it does find itself in a neo-colonial situation where ties and structures on a worldwide scale have supplanted colonial power structures, albeit in a much less obvious manner. While in 1974 Memmi acknowledged "l'apport de la Diaspora en tant que telle dans la consolidation d'Israël" 'the part that the Diaspora as such played in the consolidation of Israel' (*Juifs* 194, Levieux 195), there is no word in the 2004 essay on its role.

Memmi thereafter tries to downplay the importance of the conflict, first by engaging in dubious relativism, recalling that there have been more devastating conflicts. According to him, the conflict is in fact "une lutte assez banale entre deux petites nations en gésine, dont les deux affirmations nationales se sont trouvées par malchance en contradiction territoriale" 'a rather ordinary struggle between two small emerging nations, whose national claims unfortunately turned out to involve a territorial conflict' (*Portrait du décolonisé* 42, Bononno 26). The total oblivion regarding Europe's role in creating this "unfortunate" outcome is obvious. The role of Western powers is also completely occulted when Memmi laments the "surestimation de l'affaire palestinienne" 'overestimation of the Palestinian case' (*Portrait du décolonisé* 43),[10] which he solely blames on the Arab-Muslim world. This silences the fact that the Middle East is a region that is of geopolitical interest to the West, and not the other way around (or at least, initially, not to the same degree). One could argue that Memmi's choice of living in France, in Europe, might (un)consciously lead him to completely efface the role of the Hexagon/Europe in the genesis and perpetuation of the conflict.

Memmi always champions Israel's cause as "un fait national, qui correspond à une condition difficile à vivre et à une aspiration collective" 'a national fact, the response to an untenable condition and a collective desire' (*Portrait du décolonisé* 41, Bononno 25), yet this is obviously not an aspiration that he has chosen to act upon, as evident by his choice to live in France, not in Israel. Nor was it an inspiration for most of Algeria's Jews, whose departure from Algeria after independence had less to do with Zionism but everything with the French citizenship Algerian Jews had been granted by the colonial power in 1870. Memmi lumps all Jews together and does not acknowledge that there were differences between their conditions among and within countries.[11] This is a fact that he had noted in his semi-autobiographical novel, where social class constitutes a major factor in the alienation of its main character. The narrator of *La statue de sel*, who is from the poor working class, describes the French high school he is privileged to attend thanks to his good grades and a scholarship: "J'eus des camarades français, tunisiens, italiens, russes, maltais, et juifs aussi, mais d'un milieu si différent du mien qu'ils m'étaient des étrangers. Ces juifs riches. . . m'exaspéraient" 'I had French, Tunisian, Italian, Russian, Maltese, even Jewish classmates—but the latter were from a background so different from mine that they were as foreign to me as the others. They were rich Jews [these rich Jews . . . exasperated me]' (96, Roditi 104). This passage emphasizes that social class overrides whatever religious and ethnic traits he shares with the Tunisian Jewish middle class. Later on, the narrator states that upper-middle class Jews did not suffer as much from anti-Semitism as poor Jews during WWII (215), and the wedge between the middle class and ghetto Jews was still felt even in the strained conditions of the forced labor camp (242).

Memmi's use of the word "ghetto" throughout the book to refer to the *Hara* (Jewish quarter) assimilates a European reality to a North African one. As evident when he talks about the Jewish Tunisian bourgeoisie, the ghetto is one in which the poor are stuck, not the middle-class, and is therefore a ghetto according to social class criteria. Mohammed Kenbib emphasizes the inadequacy of the "schèmes généralement puisés dans les réalités des Stetl et Judenvierthel d'Europe centrale et orientale" 'schemas usually drawn from the realities of Central and Eastern Europe's shtetls and Judenviertel' (2) to capture the Moroccan Jewish reality.[12] One can probably extend this criticism to Tunisia. In Tunisia, each ethnic group had its quarter and the *Hara* was a "cloisonnement social volontaire" 'voluntary social partitioning' (with other groups having their own quarters, Jadla 149), although the middle class left it well before colonization (Larguèche 172).

Edmond Amran El Maleh

Whereas Memmi makes broad generalizations about Jews in his texts, El Maleh, who defines himself as a "juif oxymoron" 'oxymoron Jew' (Redonnet 85), refuses to speak for all Jews and claims the right to a plurality of being Jewish.[13] El Maleh's writings have tackled the issue of Arab Jews in the context of Morocco; as he stated, "Je l'ai abordé [l'exode des juifs du Maroc] d'un point de vue marocain" 'I addressed [the Moroccan Jews' exodus] from a Moroccan point of view' (Redonnet 74). Indeed, he has dedicated most of his work to the Jewish Moroccan community and its disappearance.

El Maleh's views of the repercussions of Israel on Jewish communities in the Arab world differ sharply from Memmi's, whom he specifically accuses of misreading history by reading the history of Jews in Arab countries as a series of persecutions (Redonnet 120). El Maleh revolts against the fact that the state of Israel pretends to speak for all Jews, and qualifies the creation of Israel as a colonial project ("Au seuil" 20). One of the reasons why he speaks so strongly against Zionism is because of its policy of erasing not only the Palestinian people but also the existence of Moroccan Jews: "On oublie que le sionisme qui conjointement à sa politique de destruction du peuple palestinien s'est acharné à effacer jusqu'au moindre signe la présence millénaire des juifs marocains" 'we forget that Zionism along with its policy of destruction of the Palestininan people hounded to erase all traces of the millennial presence of Moroccan Jews' (Redonnet 119).

Maleh's novel *Mille ans, un jour* ties the fate of the Moroccan Jewish community to French colonization and events in the Middle East. Israeli soldiers are compared to "nazis aux cheveux crépus, à l'oeil noir" 'nazis with frizzy hair and dark eyes' (121); exactions committed by Israeli settlers in Gaza recall the "choses pareilles qui se passaient pendant le protectorat" 'similar things that happened during the Protectorate' (122). Ronnie Scharfman contends that "For Nessim [the main character, a Moroccan Jew], Beirut [with the massacres of Palestinians in the refugee camps of Sabra and Chatila] is the noisy, bloody version of the silent erasure and disappearance of his people" ("The Other's" 139).

Some of these comparisons can also be found in a strong piece triggered by the 1982 Israeli invasion of Lebanon, in which several parallelisms are drawn between this invasion and well-known atrocities committed by the Nazis in France during WWII: the destroyed Lebanese cities and the village of Oradour ("Le visage" 18), Palestinian women giving birth on the beach while their refugee camps are being destroyed recall women who gave birth in the Vel d'Hiv, whose roundup was just being commemorated ("Le visage" 18), summary execution of Lebanese are compared to the same done by Germans ("Le visage" 19). In that article, El Maleh was already underlining the use and abuses of language, whereby anyone daring to use the word genocide and making comparisons between atrocities committed by the Israelis with the Nazis will be anathema, while the Israeli government routinely uses such language to qualify the PLO and Palestinians ("Le visage" 20).

Arabs and Jews in Contemporary France

From *Juif-Arabe* to *JuifsArabes*: Farid Boudjellal's Comic Books[14]

Boudjellal, a comic strip artist, has taken on the question of the relations between Arab Muslims and Jews in France. Born in Toulon in 1953 of Algerian parents, Boudjellal published his first strips in 1978 in a magazine and his first comic book in 1983 (Gaumer). Known for bringing the issue of Maghrebian immigration to the fore in comic books through the series *L'oud*,[15] his work participated in the Beur culture surge of the 1980s. His comic books have focused on the plight of the lone Maghrebian immigrant worker (in *L'oud* for instance), the problems faced by immigrant families (in *Gags à l'harissa*), and the challenges faced by Beurs. According to Mark McKinney, Boudjellal is "the most published French cartoonist of post-colonial minority origin" (180), and his work has been labeled as "une authentique (et talentueuse) BD 'beur'" 'an authentic and talented comic strip by French of Maghrebian origin' in the *Dictionnaire mondial de la bande dessinée*.

In addition to his work on the Maghrebian and Beur community in France, Boudjellal has published a series entitled *Juif-Arabe*. The original four parts were published individually in the early 1990s and were titled: *Juif-Arabe* (1990), *Juif-Arabe: Intégristes* (1990), *Juif-Arabe: Conférence internationale* (1991), *Juif-Arabe: Français* (1991). These four comic books, which address the relations between the French Jewish and Arab-Muslim communities, were compiled and reissued in 1996 as *Juif-Arabe: L'intégrale*. *JuifsArabes* is a revised and augmented edition of this compilation that appeared in 2006.[16] This part focuses on the representation of the impact of events taking place in the Middle East on contemporary France as depicted in the latest version, *JuifsArabes*. It also examines the representation of past and future genealogy between both communities, a recurrent issue in the comic book, and how a visual allusion to the *Astérix* BD series highlights the diversity of France at the turn of the twenty-first century and provides a model of coexistence for the French Jewish and Arab communities.

JuifsArabes features the characters of Ismaël and Israël, both owners of religious bookstores, their wives Ismaëlle and Israëlle, and their offspring. The eldest children, Mohamed, Ismaël's son, and Yza, Israël's daughter, turn out to be boyfriend and girlfriend. The obvious onomastics of the parents' names is reinforced by the caricatural drawings. The parents' clothing styles are meant to link them to specific communities: Orthodox Jew for Israël, always wearing a black suit and hat, and Maghrebian immigrant for Ismaël with his white djellaba and flip flops. Both fathers sport a black beard (square for Israël and rounded for Ismaël) and oversized feet (recalling Astérix and Obélix, more on that later). The stereotypical rendering of Ismaël's and Israël's appearance is inherent to the genre of the satirical comics: the characters need to be immediately and easily identifiable as Jewish and Arab, respectively, although they represent a fringe of their respective communities. Boudjellal's series is an example of how a stereotypical character can be "a successful satire if it is negotiated as a comically exaggerated portrait" (Rosello 15).

According to Jacques Tramson, the fact that these books are classified in between newspaper drawings and comic books sets this series apart from the rest of Boudjellal's work (37). *JuifsArabes* is characterized by short narratives, a focus on static characters, and a lack of elaborate background, which according to Pierre Masson are hallmarks of "intellectual" and satirical BD (77). The drawings are kept to a minimum; the backgrounds are mostly bare so as to focus all the reader's attention on the dialogues and the characters' gestures and facial expressions. Most of the pages are divided into two or three (single or double) strips of equal size; only a handful of gags take up more than one page. According to Thierry Groensteen, regularity of format confers a regular metric to the reading (61). This comic book falls under the category of ethnic humor, based on ethnic or religious or other kinds of differences, but the humor of the series is also derived from political disputes.

Boudjellal draws on stereotypes that are supposed to highlight the specificities and particularities of the Arab and Jewish communities in France to better underline how similar they actually are. Despite their profound differences on political issues of the Middle East, Ismaël and Israël are very much alike. They constantly fight about the Arab-Israeli conflict, yet they react in the same way to the same events, be it news from the Middle East or the love relationship between their children. This approach fits Rosello's definition of direct intervention, defined as the "conscious cultural reappropriation of ethnic stereotypes" (*Declining* 18-19). For instance, after they discover that their children are in love, Ismaël and Israël embrace each other, crying in despair (35). When Yza and Mohamed announce that they want to get married, the fathers offer to pay for their children's honeymoon, but are shown buying one-way tickets to Algiers and Israel. The antidote to this interfaith/interethnic marriage is envisioned as a "return" to nation states based on ethnic and religious affiliations.

The issue of genealogy (past, present, and future) between the Arab and the Jewish communities is a recurrent theme. Several references are made to the shared family tree between Arabs and Jews going back to Abraham as the founding father. The very first page, entitled "Abraham père" refers to this shared ancestral genealogy. It features several frames in which Israël enumerates commonalities between the two groups: "vous rejetez le porc, nous aussi; vous êtes circoncis, nous aussi" 'you disallow pork, so do we; you are circumcised, so are we,' etc. (5). The punch line is given by Ismaël who uses the same syntax to complete the list: "vous êtes en Palestine, nous aussi!" 'you are in Palestine, so are we!' This first set of strips sets the tone for the volume, since the last commonality is the point of contention. On another page, responding to a priest who wonders why they are always fighting despite being both children of Abraham, Ismaël and Israël answer in chorus with an idiomatic phrase that stresses their shared roots: "nous lavons notre linge sale en famille!!" 'we wash our dirty linen among the family' (meaning we do not wash our dirty linen in public) (20). In another instance, Ismaël claims this common genealogy by referring to his Semite identity as a counter to Israël's accusation that he is anti-Semite (7).

In addition to these family ties established by the Biblical tradition, the two communities' destinies seem to be interdependent because of twentieth-century politics. On a page composed of two single strips, the content of the balloons and the gestures become inverted. In the first strip, the dialogue features Israël recalling that the Jewish people had a dream and Ismaël that the Arabs had a country; the content of the speech balloons are then reversed and the tenses of the verbs changed from past to present with Israël stating that they now have a country while Ismaël retorts that the Arabs now have a dream (6). Later on, the stateless Palestinian is compared to "un juif errant" 'a wandering Jew' (60). The condition of the Wandering Jew becomes a simile to describe the Palestinians' condition of statelessness, thereby linking Zionism to the Palestinian dispossession. Boudjellal pokes fun at the deadlock in which both sides of the conflict are caught with Israeli repression and Palestinian terrorism, excused by each side as a "mal nécessaire" 'necessary evil' (24), and the impossibility of progress towards a peace process because of the manner in which preconditions to negotiations are framed (39).

Even though Israël and Ismaël are both owners of religious bookstores, their dispute over the conflict is always framed in territorial terms, never in religious ones (though the role played by religions is not erased). In fact, when religion and morals are at stake, they agree, as when they collaborate on an anti-abortion demonstration. The fathers are often at odds with French society when it comes to certain issues, as their religious commitment contrasts with French mainstream secular lifestyle. Even when their children suggest that they lend each other books to better understand one another, and they yet end up fighting once again (ending up throwing those books at each other), the issue of contention is not framed in theological terms, but in nationalistic ones. Israël tells Ismaël: "Lisez ceux-là et vous prendrez la nationalité israélienne" 'Read these and you will take the Israeli nationality' (151). When they are found throwing books at each other, they respectively shout "un cadeau pour Tsahal" 'a gift for Tsahal' and "un autre pour le Hamas" 'another one for Hamas' (152). Only when the representative of the Church comes into play does the conflict gain a full religious dimension, when the priest states that the existence of the state of Israel is necessary for Jesus' second coming (78). That politics and not religion is at stake is reinforced by the choice of the name Israël (and not Isaac as in the scriptures) for the Jewish character.

There is a clear generation gap between the fathers and the children. For one thing, the children do not understand the affiliation their fathers feel with Middle Eastern communities and question why the issue is so dear to them despite the geographical distance. When confronted about their quarrels regarding Israel and Palestine, both fathers answer in unison that Israel and Palestine represent their "maison secondaire" 'secondary home' (38). This corresponds to what Esther Benbassa refers to as a "diasporic transnationalism," defined as "a nationalism with no territorial claims, reconciling loyalty to the country of residence with strong support to external causes" (190), to explain French Arabs and Jews' affiliations with Middle Eastern causes. According to her, "today, while for a number of Arab-Moslems the support for the Palestinian cause alleviates the crumbling of their traditional identity, many Jews find in their attachment to Israel a means of counterbalancing a comparable fragility" (191).

Hope seems to lie with the mixed couple formed by Yza and Mohamed. The children are not drawn in a way that marks them as different from French mainstream society. Unlike their fathers, they are not religious: indeed, Mohamed is a self-proclaimed atheist, while Yza has an argument with her father because she claims her Jewish identity as a cultural, not a religious one. When their children suggest the establishment of one secular democratic country for both Palestinians and Israelis in historical Palestine, Ismaël and Israël are both pictured as laughing until they cried at the idea (154).

One strip does highlight the potential difficulties of being in such a union because of the events in the Middle East (37). After Yza and Mohamed's relationship is discovered by their fathers, Ismaël's dismay is obvious when he asks his son about his girlfriend and his clothing. Ismaël's conception of identity is linked to the genealogical paradigm, as evidenced when he quotes a proverb to his son emphasizing the importance of one's roots: "si tu coupes mes barreaux tu me libères si tu coupes mes racines tu me tues!" 'if you cut my bars you free me if you cut my roots you kill me' (36). Mohamed's answer demonstrates a positive view of *métissage*, when he replies to his father that his clothing and his girlfriend act as fertilizers (36).[17]

Yet this optimistic view is tempered in the very next page (the two pages face each other, as if to give two possible alternatives). Titled "L'étoile, le croissant, la capote" 'the star, the crescent, the condom,' this second page highlights the fact that relations between Muslims and Jews in France are inevitably colored by the Israeli-Palestinian conflict. When Yza introduces Mohamed to a friend whose mother is Jewish and whose father is Muslim, Mohamed takes this opportunity to ask this friend how he lives his dual identity, as Mohamed is curious to know since his future children would be in the same situation. Upon hearing that, Yza's friend runs away screaming "Me parlez pas d'Israël" 'don't talk to me about Israel' although no one has mentioned the Middle East. Boudjellal underscores that the divisiveness surrounding the conflict is the main problem for the child of a mixed Jewish-Arab union.[18] The punch line of the strip, when Mohamed goes to buy condoms, suggests that from the children's point of view, the Arab-Israeli conflict is preventing the two groups from renewing their Biblical genealogy.[19]

One of the most interesting changes in the various editions of the series is the title. Boudjellal's title has changed from *Juif-Arabe* in the 1990s to *Juifs-Arabes* in the 2006 edition. The title evokes Albert Memmi's *Juifs et Arabes*, discussed in the previous section. Memmi, himself an Arab Jew, posits the two groups side by side and separate in the title of his essay. This "erasure of the hyphen" as Shohat pointed out, was crucial to Zionist thought, since the "Arabness and the Orientalness of Jews posed a challenge to any simplistic definition of Jewish national identity, questioning the very axiom and boundaries of the Euro-Israeli national project" ("Rupture" 62).

Although the Sephardic community has a long history of coexistence with Muslims and Christians in the Maghreb and other Arab countries, this shared history barely surfaces in this comic book. The term "juif-arabe" that gives its title to the series appears only twice in the comics proper. The first time is when Israël tells Ismaël that his nephew was denied access to a night club. Upon hearing this information, Ismaël asks in disbelief whether his nephew is Jewish, to which Israël replies that his nephew is "juif-arabe" (55). This is the only statement in the album that hints to a connection between Israël, who is an Ashkenazi, with the Sephardic community, and the only use of the term "Juif-Arabe" that alludes to the existence of Jews of Arab culture, or Sephardim, Jews of Islam, African Jews, and so forth, among some of the names listed by Ella Shohat.[20] Such a connection is done in the context of highlighting discrimination on the basis of facial and physical features. The second time the term "juif-arabe" appears is when Mohamed refers to his relationship with Yza as "une union juif-arabe" (148). The "Juif-Arabe" at stake in this book is the relationship between both communities in France, and the new possibility of the "Juif-Arabe" that Mohamed and Yza's children would be.

Another page alludes to the two main Judaic families. Israël is telling a joke to Ismaël, to whom he asks: "Savez-vous ce qu'est un Ashkénaze aujourd'hui?" 'Do you know what is an Ashkenazi today?' He carries on, answering his question while laughing: "Un Séfarade qui a réussi" 'a successful Sephardi' (79). This alludes to what Solange Guénoun has called "un colonialisme intérieur" 'internal colonialism' (225), characterized by a binary opposition between the Ashkenazi and Sephardic branches of Judaism. The devalorization of the Sephardic heritage by Ashkenazim has been described as the colonization of one Judaic branch by another, linked to the European colonial project, whereby European Jews imposed their norms and culture on "Oriental" Jews, a phenomenon that occurred in France,[21] colonial Algeria,[22] and Israel.[23] The title of that page, "C'est encore un Arabe," emphasizes the disappearance of the Arab Jew's identity in a world whose politics (with Zionism and Arab nationalism playing a crucial role in that process) frame Arabs and Jews as entities that must be kept separate.

In contrast to Memmi's title, the replacement of the conjunction "et" by a hyphen (significantly "trait d'union" in French) seems to demonstrate a will to bring both communities closer. The role of the hyphen is to bring together words so that they form a unit. Boudjellal's early title thus creates a link between the words it joins, the categories of "Arab" and "Jew." This closeness is further achieved, at least on paper, through the collapsing of both substantives, which posits an organic connection between both communities from the very start. The elimination of the hyphen underscores the fact that Arabs and Jews cannot be thought of without the other, a literal rendering of what Hochberg meant when she wrote that "'Jew' and 'Arab,' rather than representing two independent identities, are in fact inevitably attached" (2). The change from singular to plural may signal a will to break from abstract categories to put the focus on the mass of actual individuals they refer to.

In the final section, both families happen to be vacationing at the same place and time. This forces them to make some concessions. Phrases such as "négociations orageuses" 'stormy negotiations' and "partager le territoire" 'splitting the territory' (157) are clear allusions to the ideology of separation inherited from the partition of historical Palestine, still prevalent in the two-state solution approach that dominates attempts to solve the conflict. Boudjellal plays here on the two possible meanings of the verb "partager," which can mean either "to share" or "to split." "Partager le territoire" indeed they do, but not in the sense of splitting. Ismaël and Israël end up vacationing together, and are shown as actually sharing the territory (or rather, in the circumstances, the beach). On the beach they are both offended and thus united by their dislike of liberal French manners, specifically topless women, and they are forced to dance on a tune they both judge obscene. This unity against some French habits[24] does not prevent them from fighting over the issue of Israel and Palestine. After a respite during the vacations, once again they start arguing over the Middle East, and therefore decide to take different routes on the way back. But news on the radio about recrudescent clashes between Israel and Palestinians awakens once again their transnational solidarities, and they find themselves on the highway en route to the Near East. The last words come from Yza and Mohamed, who are of course happy to see each other sooner than expected. The last words: "Finalement, on fait la route ensemble!" 'in the end, we travel together!' (165), stress that the French Muslim and Jewish communities can find a modus vivendi.

Some of the thorny issues of the Israeli-Palestinian conflict come up here and there throughout the strip, such as the Occupied Territories (8, 12), the Intifada (16, 19, 25), the PLO's recognition of the state of Israel (23), Israel as a colony (29), the right of return for Palestinian refugees (27), and the political deadlock between Palestinians and Israelis (39). Despite these references to Middle Eastern events and their influence on the characters, the book is grounded in the French context, thanks to cultural references specific to France, such as the issue of naming the population of Maghrebian origin (47), immigration (15, 49), racism against Arabs (47, 51), anti-Semitism by various segments of the French population (both Arabs and "Français de souche"), the debates on affirmative action (14, 51), a joke about Arab grocers open late at night (56) and about the difficulty to get permits to build mosques (119), and an allusion to Serge Gainsbourg's hit single "Sea, sex and sun," which becomes "sea, sex and jeûne (pour les ramadans d'été)" 'sea, sex and fast (for summertime ramadans)' (155).

The last drawing of the book features Ismaël and Israël dressed as Astérix and Obélix, respectively, the heroes of the renowned series by René Goscinny and Albert Uderzo. Israël, who is stout, wears Obélix's striped trademark pants and carries a menhir, while Ismaël, who is shorter and thin, wears Astérix's belt, winged helmet, and sword to the side. There is a genealogy at play here, but of a different kind: with the *bande dessinée* or BD, a genre that benefits from cultural esteem, as evidenced by state support and well-established critical traditions in France and Belgium (McQuillan 7). Indeed, in France BDs are often referred to as the ninth art, "a phrase rarely uttered in the USA or the UK" (Screech 1), and that elevates comics as an art on par with cinema and photography. Boudjellal thereby situates his series in a well-established tradition of slapstick humor.[25] *Astérix* characters have made their marks not only on comic strips and French popular culture, they have also become reference points "for politicians, journalists and intellectuals," and there is for the French a "strong identification process with our puny but clever comic strip hero" (Steel 216). By casting Ismaël and Israël as avatars of Astérix and Obélix, Boudjellal seems to agree with Screech who states in the context of the *Astérix* series' international success that Astérix is "a hero with whom almost everybody can identify, wherever they come from" (75).

This last image constitutes a counterpoint to the beginning of the book. The first drawing shows Israël and Ismaël separated by a wall that interferes with dialogue, no doubt an allusion to the wall being built by the state of Israel around the Occupied Territories. However, Israël and Ismaël are often drawn sitting down having a conversation. Indeed, they both agree that were it not for the Israeli-Palestinian conflict, they would be good friends (149). In the last drawing, Israël and Ismaël have retained their black beards (as opposed to the Gaulish characters' mustaches), they have hairy arms, Israël has kept his black hat and Ismaël his glasses, thus becoming potential new inhabitants that could blend in the famous Gaulish village while retaining some of their distinguishing features. They are shown as laughing and walking together, as if to symbolize a possible friendship such as the one that unites Astérix and Obélix, in the context of France, and the assonance between their names reinforces their portrayal as a tandem.

Although in Francophone studies the now infamous phrase "nos ancêtres les Gaulois" 'our ancestors the Gauls' is often used ironically to refer to the Eurocentric curriculum taught to children in the French colonies, I interpret

Boudjellal's reappropriation of the Gaulish genealogy of the French as a means to highlight the diversity of France at the turn of the twenty-first century as well as a model of coexistence for the French Jewish and Arab communities. J.W.T. Mitchell argues that "images are active players in the game of establishing and changing values. They are capable of introducing new values into the world and thus threatening old ones" (105). While the Biblical references do point to a shared genealogy in a long gone past, the contemporary popular culture symbolized by the quintessentially French *Astérix* series is grounded in the present. Mitchell reminds us in his latest book that "The nation, as political theorist Benedict Anderson has argued, is an 'imagined community,' a cultural construction made up of images and discourses" (273). If so, then visual representations are as important as verbal ones to build the nation. Boudjellal's image is a visual integration of Muslims and Jews in the French Republic that participates in the construction of France as a country with a diverse population.

Boudjellal's series is remarkable in its choice of comic genre and humor that rely on stereotypes to treat a highly charged and divisive topic, given the current climate that Solange Guénoun has qualified as "catastrophisme ambiant concernant l'état des relations judéo-musulmanes en France" 'surrounding catastrophism regarding the state of Jewish-Muslim relations in France' (218), and the devastation caused by many of the events that are alluded to in the strip (the Holocaust, suicide bombings, repression of the Palestinians). Humor that traces its roots to a well-established tradition, recognized and respected by all segments of the population, might indeed be the best means to envision a near future where the Jewish and Arab branches of the Semitic family might cross again, in peace, as full-fledged members of the French Republic.

Karin Albou's *La petite Jérusalem*

Boudjellal's optimistic vision contrasts sharply with Karin Albou's first full-length feature film, *La petite Jérusalem* (2004). Albou is a rising Jewish French director[26] with ties to Algeria through her paternal family. Her film focuses on a community that is rarely portrayed on the screen: the Orthodox Jewish community[27] of Sarcelles, a Parisian suburb. Fifteen per cent of Sarcelles' 57000 inhabitants are Jewish; half of them are of Tunisian origin (Podselver 275). In an interview added to the English DVD, Albou stated that she wanted to shoot in that specific suburb because it is emblematic of Jewish immigration from North Africa in the 1960s.

The film is a subtle depiction of two Jewish sisters, originally from Tunisia, who struggle with sexual desire in different ways. The family, who lives on a tight budget in a small apartment in a low-income neighborhood, is composed of Mathilde, her mother, her husband Ariel, their children, and Mathilde's younger sister Laura. Laura studies philosophy at a university in Paris and longs for life in the city. Her adoption of Kantian principles is put to the test when she gets involved in a relationship with Djamel, an Algerian. Meanwhile, Mathilde's discovery of her husband's unfaithfulness leads her to question assumptions about her faith's stand on sexual matters. Albou paints a nuanced relationship between the two sisters who choose very different itineraries, and explores complex issues linked to intimacy and faith. However, her depiction of relationships between Arab-Muslims and Jews is very grim, as is the place she reserves for an observant Jewish family in France.

Although the title of the film and the focus on the Jewish family foreground the Jewish quarter and inhabitants of Sarcelles, people in the street and the subway clearly show the multiethnic character of the neighborhood, with Africans sporting traditional boubous, and Muslim women wearing headscarves along with Jewish women with nets covering their hair. Although the Arab and Jewish communities live side by side in the film, they do not have much interaction. In contrast to daylight shots that focus on the high rise HLM buildings, the neighborhood's streets are mostly shot at night, creating a dominant feeling of isolation, despair, and drabness. The scenes during which Laura takes her daily evening walk following Kant's example, are too dark to distinguish much other than the word halal on a sign and a religious bookstore.

The French DVD cover specifies that the film takes place in "un quartier de Sarcelles appelé 'La Petite Jérusalem' car de nombreux juifs s'y sont installés" 'a quarter of Sarcelles called 'little Jerusalem' because many Jews settled there.' This nickname and the explanation that is provided are significant in two ways. First, they highlight Jewish transnational affiliations to the Israeli state. But in doing so, it silences the long history of Jews in the Maghreb. Calling this area of Sarcelles 'la petite Jérusalem' can be seen as a misnomer. It is not the same as the nickname of Chinatown for part of Paris' XIIIth arrondissement for instance, because the Jews who live there did not come from Jerusalem, but from the Maghreb. Thus the explanation provided contributes to erasing the existence of Arab Jews.

While the film does reflect that this "little Jerusalem," like the Middle Eastern city, has Arab and Jewish populations living side by side, the title as it is explained in the packaging of the film occults the fact that Jerusalem has a highly contested status since both Palestinians and Israelis claim it as their capital. In some sense, the title and the film indirectly replicate the Arab-Israeli conflict over the Holy Land in France, this time in a French suburb where each group seems to fight for its place in it. The explanation given to the suburb's nickname on the DVD cover implies that only one ethnic group can claim it as its own. Albou's film's packaging thereby perpetuates the phenomenon experienced by the actual city, which sees its "Arab character. . . continually being eroded, shriveling its links to the Levant," and this despite the fact that Jerusalem is "a complete microcosm of Levantine and Arab Jewry" (Alcalay 110). Moreover, connecting Jerusalem to the Jewish state occults the fact that "during the 1,310-year period dating from the Arab conquest in 638 until 1948, there were only 129 years in which Jerusalem was *not* under one form or another of Islamic sovereignty" (Alcalay 113). This signals the effect that the creation of Israel has had on Jewish communities in the Arab world, which is to occult their link to Arab culture.

References to some cultural traits refer to the family's Maghrebian origin: the mother and Mathilde occasionally speak Arabic, the mother talks about Tunisia and uses a hand of Fatima as a talisman to protect her daughter. When Laura writes a letter to Djamel, the mother warns her against doing so, and explains to her "je les connais ces gens-là" 'I know those people.' The reference to the family's past in Tunisia is mostly associated with the traumatic event of a precipitated departure whose complex political context is not elaborated upon, but simply emphasizes that the Jews were expelled after the country's independence.

Despite some common cultural elements, religion on both sides is an obstacle to Laura and Djamel's relationship: Laura writes to Djamel that her religious upbringing does not allow her to continue seeing him, but she later relents. Djamel's family expresses its profound displeasure upon learning that Laura is Jewish, and demands that Laura convert before Djamel can marry her (contrary to Muslim tenets that allow a Muslim man to marry Christian and Jewish women, and despite Djamel's objection that he does not care for religion). Djamel, an illegal refugee from the Algerian civil war, is at the mercy of his uncle because his illegal status prevents him from standing up to his relative. He ends up breaking up with Laura because he does not want to impose his religion on her.

Details contribute to creating a climate of insecurity: a policeman keeps watch outside the synagogue during a celebration, the loudspeaker on the subway refers to the Vigipirate plan, Ariel hides his kippah under a cap when coming home, etc. Two incidents emphasize the vulnerability of the Jewish community: the local synagogue falls prey to arson, and Ariel is attacked by thugs while playing soccer outside with children, all wearing a kippah. Nothing in the film identifies the perpetrators of these crimes. However, in the context of France at the dawn of the twenty-first century, these incidents will evoke the rise of anti-Semitism that has made headlines, and that has been attributed to the far right and youth of immigrant origins, the latter being a repercussion of the second Intifada. Given that, in the context of the film, the neighbors are Arabs, this anti-Semitism will be inferred as being caused by the Arab-Muslim population. In fact, I would argue that the failed love relationship between Laura and Djamel orients the viewer to blaming anti-Semitism solely on the Arab segment of the population.

Ariel's decision to move to Israel is never explained. One can interpret it as an escape from a hostile environment, or from the shame brought by Laura's suicide attempt. I surmise that the film and the context will orient the viewer towards the first interpretation. Ariel's announcement comes after Laura's attempt to commit suicide, and after a scene in which the *mikveh*'s attendant advised Mathilde to move. Because her advice comes right after she asked about Laura, one could infer that Laura's well-being is dependent upon getting out of this neighborhood. Indeed, a recurring aerial shot of hazy Paris in which one can barely guess the Eiffel Tower and the Montparnasse Tower can be seen as a representation of Laura's unfulfilled desire to move to the city.

While several scenes stress the diversity of the French population, the decision of the family to move to Israel seems to imply that there is no safe place in France for this religious community. Ironically, it is hinted that this move will not shelter them from Arab-Jewish tensions. When the children are shown building their imaginary home in Israel, one of them takes a helicopter toy to bomb and destroy it. This scene could also be read as emphasizing the hypocritical stance of Israeli officials who alarmingly stated that Jews were no longer safe in France and should move to Israel. Either way, this (unrealistic) threat of helicopters bombing Israel serves more to emphasize (Arab) hostility towards Jews wherever they are while occulting the specifics of the context in which they take place.

At the beginning of the movie, Laura is filmed as set aside from her community: in the scene by the river, a progressive high-angle shot emphasizes that she is standing alone at a short distance from the rest of the group. After the decision is made for the family to emigrate to Israel, Laura decides to stay in France. Her mother offers Laura her ring to give her the means to move to Paris. This forthcoming move to Paris can be seen as her integration into French society and sealing her disconnect from her tight-knit community which had already been hinted at from the beginning. The last scene shows her alone in the subway, with people passing behind her in a blur. Laura might be moving to the city, but she is even more alone than she was at the beginning of the film, since at least her community was just next to her. This film offers a pessimistic glimpse of Arab-Jewish relations in France as well as on the place of the Orthodox Jewish community in the Hexagon.

Conclusion

The now commonplace reference to the Judeo-Christian tradition overshadows the fact that, as Mohamed Talbi and others noted, there is more affinity between Judaism and Islam than between Judaism and Christianity, and this especially applies to the Maghreb not only at the level of religious tenets but also at the sociological level (47). Bernard Lewis reminds us that the term Judeo-Christian is still new (qtd. in Majid, *Unveiling* note 27, 163), a fact that prompts Majid to wonder: "If the Judeo prefix that precedes the adjective of Christian is an attempt to bury this history [of Western anti-Semitism] under the assumption of a common heritage, why would the Muslim become the Jew's Other, especially if Lewis himself states that 'Jewish and Muslim theology are far closer to each other than is either to Christianity?'" (*Unveiling* 12). The term Judeo-Christian also helps silence the historical evidence that there was an inverse situation concerning Jewish-Christian and Jewish-Muslim relations that showed that Jews fared better under Muslim rule: "le tableau est donc exactement inverse: d'un côté, intolérance avec quelques exceptions, de l'autre, tolérance avec quelques exceptions" 'the picture is thus exactly the opposite: on the one hand, intolerance with a few exceptions, on the other, tolerance with a few exceptions' (Rabi Josy Eisenberg, qtd. in Talbi 49).

While the diaspora of Jews from the Arab world is brandished as a proof of Arab Muslims' anti-Semitism, less attention is being given to the fact that the migration of Jews is not solely occurring in the Arab-Muslim world, witness the post-WWII East European migration (Valensi 56). Graham Fuller notes that "to emphasize commonality [between religions] implies a quest for coexistence and understanding, an overcoming of cultural differences, and above all attaching major value to the *very act of coexistence* and tolerance as part of a religious outlook" (205). Writers such as Memmi and film directors such as Albou minimize this shared cultural heritage, while El Maleh's and Boudjellal's works remind us of past models or prompt us to envision future ones of coexistence.

Notes

1. See Hochberg 20-43. Her chapter focuses on the question of the "status of the Arab Jew today in the context of Zionism: does this figure belong to a lost history and merely represent a current political impossibility, or does it (also) represent a futuristic antiessentialist and antinationalist cultural-political stance with direct implications for the present?" (17-18).

2. Memmi expresses his dislike of the phrase "Juifs-Arabes" used out of convenience to denote that "natifs de ces pays dits arabes, originaires de ces contrées bien avant l'arrivée des Arabes, nous en partageons, d'une manière non négligeable, les langues, les coutumes et les cultures" 'because we were born in these so-called Arab countries and had been living in those regions long before the arrival of the Arabs, we share their languages, their customs, and their cultures to an extent that is not negligible' (*Juifs* note 2, 59, Levieux 29).

3. See Shohat's "Rupture and Return" about the complex factors, including the role of Zionist activists, in forcing the departure of Iraqi Jews (55-56).

4. A search on anti-Semitism in the library catalogue will yield entries on anti-Judaism for the pre-modern period, and distinctions are made by countries (anti-Semitism in France, Germany, etc.) as well as entries on the new anti-Semitism.

5. For Tunisia, see Sebag (273-297).

6. Lévy on the other hand describes the history of Moroccan Jews as a "tradition de cohabitation tolérante dans le cadre de la législation musulmane" 'tradition of tolerant cohabitation within the framework of Muslim legislation' with some parentheses (38).

7. See for instance how the titles of *Agar* and *La statue de sel* are clear Biblical allusions although the narrator of both semi-fictional novels repudiates his religious background.

8. "Car la partie ne se joue pas seulement entre Palestiniens et Israéliens mais entre la quasi-totalité des pays arabo-musulmans et la majorité des juifs dans le monde" 'For the conflict extends beyond the Palestinians and Israelis, involving nearly all the Arab-Muslim countries and the majority of the world's Jews' (Memmi, *Portrait du décolonisé* 40, Bononno 24).

9. There is a mistranslation here: "Ne possédant pas de métropole derrière lui [Israel], pour en venir à bout il faudrait le détruire" (41) became "However, to threaten

the destruction of Israel would have catastrophic consequences" (25). Here is a more faithful rendering: "with no parent state behind it [Israel], one would have to destroy it to defeat it."

10. My translation. This sentence is part of an entire paragraph that is missing from Bononno's translation.

11. For the differences in status between the various Jewish communities in Tunisia (which at the time of independence included Jews of French, Italian, and Tunisian citizenship), see Sebag's study. These differences also account for the choice of destination once the decision to emigrate had been taken (see note 5).

12. Social class is also a factor in the choice of destination when Arab Jews decided to leave the Maghreb. El Maleh states that most Moroccan Jews went to Israel, then to Canada, and the richest to France (Redonnet 80). This is corroborated by Lévy who states that middle and upper class Jews went to France and Canada (32). Zafrani explains that the Jewish Agency recruited not only poor urban masses but also people from the South and the mountains to emigrate to Israel because they were considered "plus aptes que les citadins à fonder des colonies agricoles" 'better fitted than town-dwellers to establish agricultural colonies' (293). Sebag also notes that those who were most well-off and Westernized went to France, while the most traditional and poor segments of the population went to Israel (Sebag 301).

13. "Il y a des juifs. Cette entité de l'être juif est ce contre quoi je m'insurge" 'There are Jews. What I am rebelling against is this entity of the Jewish being' (qtd. in Redonnet 91).

14. This section has appeared as "From *Juif-Arabe* to *JuifsArabes*: Jews and Arabs in France in Boudjellal's Comic Books" in *Expressions maghrébines* 7.2 (Winter 2008): 159-171. It has been revised.

15. This series includes *L'oud, Le gourbi,* and *Ramadân.* For an analysis of Boudjellal's early work, see Douglas and Malti-Douglas (198-216).

16. Some of the pages have been eliminated, such as the ones that featured two skinhead characters, shown as beating up Israël and Ismaël (who have thus found a common enemy), and painting racist insults on walls, emblematic of the rise of the far right and racism. Other pages have been modified: mentions of the Front National and Le Pen have been erased, one of them replaced by the more general term Fascism. References to the first Gulf War and Salman Rushdie have also been taken out. The original four albums and the first compilation were drawn in colors. These multicolor albums have been reduced to three colors in the last version published in 2006: black, white and brown. The choice of color (or rather lack of a color scheme) could be interpreted as a means to better highlight the conflicting situation (as Masson has said about comic strips in black and white). When I asked Boudjellal about the factors that motivated this change, he answered that the decision to change from four colors to three was made solely on aesthetic grounds, in order to give a more polished look to the album as well as a feel of "un livre d'auteur."

17. One could object that the use of the word "engrais" betrays a sexist blind spot in Mohamed's view of *métissage*, which objectifies the woman and presents her as an instrument instead of a full partner.

18. This is in line with Boudjellal's exploration of issues raised by mixed couples in *Jambon-Beur: Les couples mixtes.* Through the contrast between the children of Arab-French and Arab-Senegalese couples, Boudjellal emphasizes that history and politics bear on how one lives such a dual heritage (see McKinney 180-184).

19. The same cannot be said about the mothers. Although the fact that the Jewish matrilineal and Muslim patrilineal transmission of religion would seem to satisfy both families, since both could claim the still hypothetical children of Yza and Mohamed as their own, it is a source of conflict and is the only time in the book when Ismaëlle and Israëlle fight with each other (86-87). Otherwise, the women have a lot in common (they both cover their hair for instance, with a headscarf for one and a wig for the other), they also band together about issues such as contraception and abortion, this time against their husbands who are joining forces on organizing a demonstration (95).

20. Shohat points out that "the very proliferation of terms suggests the difficulties of grappling with the complexities of this identity" ("Rupture" 52).

21. See articles by Guénoun and Azria.

22. Benjamin Stora has detailed how the 1870 Crémieux decree, which gave French citizenship to indigenous Jews, triggered the assimilation of the Jewish community with the European community in Algeria. He has interpreted this event as a colonization of Algerian Judaism by French Judaism (292).

23. See Shohat's 1997 article.

24. The similarities that are highlighted between the two men include the position of women in society, secularist permissiveness in general, and their relationship with a Catholic priest.

25. Goscinny and Uderzo's goal with the series was to create a "*French* strip-cartoon Laurel and Hardy in order to entertain their readership" (Steel 202).

26. Her film was nominated for the César's Best First Film award (as was its lead actress).

27. Albou has stated in an interview accompanying the DVD that she finds the Orthodox version of Judaism suffocating.

Chapter 3

The Lebanese Civil War: Andrée Chédid's *La maison sans racines* and Evelyne Accad's *L'excisée*

The 1975-1990 Lebanese civil war was a bloody conflict that was spurred by internal factors and flamed by external ones, and whose complexity is impossible to render in a couple of paragraphs. The term "civil war" is actually a misnomer, as Lebanon's domestic affairs got entangled with the politics of the region and the conflict took an international dimension, fueled by Israel's invasions, Syrian troop deployment, and U.S. Marines intervention. As Latif Abul-Husn summed it up, "the conflict revolved around three main themes: reform of the political system, the national identity of Lebanon, and Lebanon's sovereignty" (2). According to him, the tension that emerged between Christians and Muslims was due to three factors: "the rise to power of an organized Palestinian armed resistance in Lebanon that aligned itself with the Muslim bloc; a soaring Arab nationalist feeling in the wider region; and the rising expectations of the Shiites and their demands on the system for a greater share in the power structure" (2).

Beginning with the Arab conquest in the seventh century, Lebanon was part of various Islamic empires, with the exception of the period of the Crusades. Following massacres of Christian Maronites by Druze in Mount Lebanon in 1860, France intervened and Mount Lebanon was established as a privileged administrative region of the Ottoman Empire. After the collapse of the Ottoman Empire, France ceded to Maronites' demands and annexed parts of the Syrian provinces that fell under its mandate to the territory of Mount Lebanon to create present-day Lebanon. Such a separation was not acceptable from an Arab nationalist point of view (Salibi, *A House* 28). According to Kamal Salibi, the establishment of Lebanon as a state under the French Mandate in 1920 was "enthusiastically accepted by the Christians, and adamantly rejected by the Muslims" (*A House* 2).

When the French Mandate ended and Lebanon became independent in 1943, an agreement known as the National Pact was reached, primarily between Maronite and Sunni elites. According to this agreement, government positions were distributed proportionally amongst the recognized confessional groups based on the data provided by the 1932 census. The census showed a slight majority of Christians and served as the basis for allocating a Christian/Muslim ratio of 6 to 5 for offices in Parliament, civil service, the army, and the judiciary.[1] Maronites kept key positions, including the Presidency and the command of the army. Part of the agreement entailed that Muslims recognize Lebanese sovereignty and independence while Maronites affirm its Arab heritage and forego Western protection. Lebanese law required that every citizen's religious affiliation be clearly indicated on their identity cards.

The National Pact solidified the sectarian social structure and Maronite hegemony. It did not anticipate the uneven population growth that would in time create further disparity to be added to economic inequities between various groups. The struggle for a redistribution of power to mirror Lebanon's demographic changes and economic disparities were major factors in the 1975-1990 conflict. Maronites opposed demands for a new census for fear of losing power. Religious sectarianism was also exacerbated by an educational system that followed confessional lines, with the teaching of history becoming a highly politicized issue (Salibi, *A House* 201-04). According to Salibi, Muslim and Christian Lebanese have fundamental differences about the historicity of their country, with Christians favoring Lebanese particularism while Muslims tend to situate it within a broader Arab-Muslim history. These opposite views of Lebanese history between Lebanism and Arabism underlie the ongoing political conflict (Salibi, *A House* 3).

In addition to the problems due to Lebanon's confessional system, there were fundamental differences among Lebanese over issues involving the rest of the Arab world, most notably the Palestinian issue and the rise of Arab nationalism following Nasser's call for pan-Arab unity and the subsequent and brief merger of his country with Syria (1958-1961). After the creation of Israel in 1948 and the Israeli occupation of the West Bank in 1967, the influx of Palestinian refugees into Lebanon further complicated its internal situation. In general, Maronites were opposed to the presence of Palestinians, who in 1968 constituted 14 percent of Lebanon's population (Smith 315), as such presence compromised the fragile population equilibrium (since most Palestinians were Muslim). Thus, Palestinians were not allowed to integrate into Lebanese society and remained confined to refugee camps. Maronites also opposed Palestinian military operations against Israel from Lebanon, as it resulted in disproportionate Israeli retaliation, culminating with the 1982 Israeli invasion of Lebanon, a watershed event. In contrast, Muslims and leftists were more sympathetic with the Palestinian cause.

It is crucial to emphasize that alliances kept changing as the Lebanese conflict evolved: "At different stages of the conflict the antagonism was greatest between the Christian and Muslim divisions, while at other stages the dividing line was between left and right, and so on, depending on the ebb and flow of the issue in dispute" (Abul-Husn 3). Thus, in the period from 1977 to 1982, "the Syrians who entered ostensibly in defense of the Christians were now engaged in battle with them; the Christian forces were entwined in internal warfare with each other; and the Palestinians and Shiites who fought side by side in the early war years were now engaged in prolonged combat" (Salem 124).[2]

This chapter examines how two Francophone Lebanese writers have depicted the conflict, and more specifically how they have dealt with the religious dimension of a civil war that was summarily elucidated as a Muslim/Christian rift in the West. Charles Smith has noted that the complexity of allegiances that characterized the Lebanon political landscape could not be delineated according to religious lines; yet, "the Maronite leadership continued to present the question as one of Muslim-Christian strife, all the better to depict the issue as a religious clash to the outside world, as they had done since 1958" (356). I demonstrate that two books published by Lebanese writers, Chédid's *La maison sans racines* and Accad's *L'excisée*, can be seen as perpetuating such a reductive view of the Lebanese civil war as a religious conflict. In addition, a close analysis of the Biblical and Qur'anic intertext of Accad's novel shows that the inscription of verses from the Qur'an provides a stereotyped view of Islam while the Biblical references implicitly reaffirm Christian values of sacrifice and redemption.

Andrée Chédid's *La maison sans racines*

Chédid's novel is characterized by a complex narrative structure that intertwines three different time frames, each being clearly indicated through the use of different numerals and font setting. It starts with a day in August 1975, when two young women, Muslim Ammal and Christian Myriam, who have been friends since childhood, are marching towards each other with the hope of sparking a march of reconciliation. That day's tragic ending is prefigured at the very beginning though its outcome will only be divulged at the end. The other time frame is July-August 1975, which is a flashback about the reasons why Kalya meets her granddaughter Sybil in Lebanon for the first time (Kalya lives in Paris and Sybil in the U.S.). This time frame eventually catches up with Ammal and Myriam's march. The third time frame is 1932, when Kalya recalls the vacation she spent in Lebanon with her own grandmother, Nouza, a situation that parallels hers and Sybil's.

There are very clear references to European historical events, including the Great Depression, which began in 1929 and facilitated the rise of fascism, specific references to Hitler and Mussolini (81), and the events of WWII (83). However, all allusions to Lebanese history and current events are deliberately vague. For instance, when the taxi is stopped for an identity check before entering the city, Kalya reflects that "Après les brefs événements d'il y a quelques années, elle pensait que tout était redevenu calme" 'After the brief events of a few years ago, she thought that everything had settled down again' (19, Schwartz 19), but never hints at what those events consisted of. Further on, the mention of "la flambée meurtrière" 'the fatal outburst' that took place fifteen years prior probably alludes to the mini-civil war of 1958, but that has to be inferred (38, Schwartz 43). During their ride from the airport, during which they pass by luxury hotels and villas, Sybil inquires about something that contrasts sharply with the rest of the landscape, and that is described as follows: "au bas des falaises, s'emboîtant les unes dans les autres, des cabanes en fer-blanc s'entassent, suivies d'un amoncellement de tentes brunâtres" 'at the foot of the cliffs, lies a tight cluster of tin huts and a mass of brownish tents' (18, Schwartz 17). The driver at first does not answer and speeds up, but after Sybil insists, wondering whether people live there, he retorts: "C'est provisoire" 'It's temporary' (18, Schwartz 17). There is no mention of Palestinians in the novel, but this description and the driver's statement undoubtedly evoke their refugee camps.

Chédid's novel tends to pass over historical events with few allusions to the issues that triggered them. For instance, in the following paragraph, which appears in the July-August 1975 time frame, one can easily recognize the events that sparked the beginning of the civil war:

> Ammal et Myriam venaient d'apprendre qu'en pleine ville des hommes armés avaient stoppé un autocar, abattu une dizaine de passagers. Le même jour, dans la proche campagne, d'autres avaient découvert les cadavres mutilés de cinq jeunes gens jetés au bas d'un talus.
> Qui avait commencé? Quel acte avait précédé l'autre? Déjà les fils s'enchevêtraient. (71)
> Ammal and Myriam had just learned that armed men had held up a bus in the middle of the city and murdered ten passengers. The same day, in the surrounding countryside, others had discovered at the foot of an embankment the mutilated corpses of five young people.
> Who had started it? Which act had come first? The threads were already becoming tangled. (Schwartz 83)

Although there is some inaccuracy regarding the date, the first allusion is to the incident that occurred on April 13, 1975, when Christian Phalanges gunmen killed 27 Palestinian passengers on a bus, and that is commonly considered the event that marked the start of the war.[3] The author purposefully avoids mentioning any of the various parties involved in the conflict, thereby refusing to blame any group, and stressing the fact that the cause and beginning of the conflict are difficult to pinpoint.

The recollection of events that happened in 1932 is triggered by what is happening in 1975, with the numerous parallelisms that brings the two time frames closer. This choice of year may be an indirect reference to the census of 1932, and the consequences it had on the political structure of Lebanon. Anne-Marie Miraglia has shown that the narrative technique of intertwining three different time periods, along with lexical and thematic resonances "facilitent l'enchaînement des séquences tout en insistant sur la nature cyclique de l'Histoire et de l'existence humaine" 'facilitate the chain of sequences while insisting on the cyclical nature of History and human life' (33). While the novel provides no allusion to the issues of the census and the National Pact, the choice of 1932 to echo 1975 points to one of the key issues in the civil war. And yet at the same time, the accent on the "cyclical nature of history," as Miraglia phrased it, deemphasizes the historical processes or the reasons why history seems to be repeating itself.

Through a pair of siblings, Myriam and George, Chédid emphasizes the fratricidal aspect of the conflict, and therefore an imagined unity of Lebanon: "Les heurts traversés par le pays, par les régions avoisinantes, secouaient les deux adolescents, redoublant leur opposition" 'The clashes that occurred in the country, in neighboring regions, shook the two young people, intensifying their opposition to each other' (59, Schwartz 68). George joins an unnamed party, while his sister Myriam collaborates with Ammal to organize a peace walk. George's stance is intransigeant: "L'espoir de nous réunir tous n'est qu'une source de tensions. Regardez l'histoire! Des belles idées ne suffisent pas, rassembler des gens différents dans un même endroit crée la haine" 'The hope of uniting us all causes nothing but tension. Look at history! Fine ideas aren't enough, gathering different people in one place gives rise to hatred' (103, Schwartz 126). Nowhere in the novel is there an allusion to colonial history and how French influence and interference to privilege the Maronite community have contributed to shaping relationships between various groups. Elise Salem notes that when General Henri Gouraud proclaimed the creation of Greater Lebanon in 1920, his proclamation stressed the Phoenician, Greek, and Roman heritage of Lebanon and omitted any reference to its Arab and Islamic heritage (15). George's stance contrasts sharply with his sister's peace activism and the overall message of the book.

The emphasis on roots throughout the novel can be understood in terms of the Lebanese context and its struggles to define its national identity. Indeed, one of the epigraphs is taken from Khalil Gibran, the renowned American-Lebanese poet who became one of Lebanon's national icons when so few existed (Salem 33). As Michelle Hartman argues, the title of the novel can be read as meaning "the family without roots" by translating the word "house" into Arabic (*bayt*) and exploring its various denotations. She then interprets it as referring to how characters from one family explore their roots by spending time in their "native land" (62). As Hartman noted, Chédid problematizes the issue of pure identity through the plot, the main characters' background, and her use of epigraphs because "De-emphasizing roots, heritage and 'true origins' is also important in the context of war-torn Lebanon. A fixation on heritage and lineage can have negative connotations in a country with such a diverse population, particularly one in which people were divided by a war which emphasized sectarianism" (65-66). It might also be read as wishful thinking on Chédid's part that Lebanon should become a "country without roots," given the fact that sectarianism, and different views of Lebanese roots or history, were at the core of the conflict. Historian Salibi has titled his study of the various views of the Lebanese history *A House of Many Mansions*, after a Biblical verse (John 14:2), where house here stands for country.

Yet, despite the avoidance of naming and pointing fingers throughout the novel, the conflict seems to be framed exclusively in religious terms. In an incident at the beginning of the novel, two cab drivers (one a Muslim, the other a Christian) have an argument. The narrator comments: "Mêlé au moindre événement, à toutes les colères, à toutes les réconciliations, Dieu vient d'apparaître sur le devant de la scène. Son nom se prononce à tout bout de champ, soumis aux hommes, à leurs violences, à leurs amours" 'Involved in the most trivial incident, in every quarrel, in every reconciliation, God has just appeared center stage. His name is bandied about at the beck and call of men, their loves and hates' (14, Schwartz 11). Later on, Odette tells Kalya that "Ici, la religion prime tout, elle marque toute l'existence" 'Here, religion dominates everything. It affects our whole lives' (46, Schwartz 52), an indirect allusion to the National Pact and its confessional system, which are never referred to explicitly. The only elaboration that is offered in the course of the narrative are theological disputes that date back centuries and refer to the schism between Sunnis and Shiites in Islam, and within the Christian church regarding the nature of Christ (49), emphasizing the murderous consequences of these debates. Kalya's uncle, Mitry, who tells her about this history, links it to the present by saying "Jusqu'aujourd'hui, dans ce pays, il y a quatorze possibilités d'être croyant, monothéiste et fils d'Abraham!" 'Even today, in this country, there are fourteen ways of being a believer, a monotheist and a son of Abraham!' (49, Schwartz 56). This is a reference to fourteen (actually seventeen) denominations that are recognized by Lebanon's political system. However, it skews the reality, because the contemporary disputes between groups are not due to theological differences, but to the issue of distribution of power and fair representation. By insisting on theological differences and eluding the confessional political system of twentieth-century Lebanon, the novel promotes a clash of religion interpretation of the Lebanese civil war, since the internal socio-economic as well as the external factors (the Palestinian refugees) are only indirectly surfacing in the course of the narrative.

On the one hand, the novel's portrayal of a well-off Christian family with little contact with any other group could be seen as showing how out of touch its members are with what constitutes Lebanon as a whole. Contrary to the rest of the characters, Myriam and Ammal are aware of the socio-economic problems that plague some of the population of Lebanon, though this poverty is not associated with specific groups (76).

Religious Intertexts, Female Genital Cutting, and the Lebanese Civil War in Evelyne Accad's *L'excisée*

Female Genital Cutting (henceforth FGC, more widely known as FGM or Female Genital Mutilation)[4] has received significant international attention following the 1979 United Nations Conference on Traditional Practices Affecting the Health of Women and Children. When Accad recalls the impact that learning about FGC had on her while she was a doctoral student, she explains that she was "very shaken," "sick for several weeks," and that "the title of [her] first novel, *L'excisée*, was already determined" following this experience ("Writing" 59). Accad had left her native Lebanon to study in the United States, where she eventually became a university professor at the University of Illinois at Urbana-Champaign; she has published scholarly literary studies as well as novels and poems. When reflecting on what prompted her to write, she remembers that learning about the "cruel practice of sexual mutilations" was a turning point ("Writing" 59).

Accad's novel was conceived as an autobiographically inspired feminist stand against women's subjugation by oppressive practices and religions ("Writing" 59).[5] However, Accad herself has stated that "what one intended to say [is] not necessarily what the readers see" ("Writing" 47).[6] My reading does not contradict the feminist intention and interpretations that have dominated scholarship on that novel, but goes beyond; it also departs from it in that it is a critical analysis that examines closely how the religious intertexts favor one religion over the other, and the implications to be derived given the socio-political setting of the novel (whether it was intended by the author or not).

L'excisée is a hybrid text that mixes genres (novel, poetry), profane discourse and Scriptures, as well as religious traditions through citations and allusions to the Bible and the Qur'an. The narrative is interspersed with poetry and unmarked verbatim excerpts from the Christian and Muslim holy books, which are occasionally set off typographically, and which have yet to be analyzed by critics.[7] *L'excisée* tells the story of E., a Christian Lebanese young woman, unhappy with her life in Beirut in the aftermath of a bloody summer, and feeling oppressed by the patriarchal tradition brutally enforced by her father, a pastor. She meets P., a young Muslim Palestinian, and flees with him to a village in an unnamed country, in the hope of inventing a new future. Disillusion quickly sets in as her Muslim husband proves to be as engrained in patriarchal tradition as her Christian father. After she becomes pregnant, he neglects her, and it is implied that he might have taken another wife in the city. After witnessing the infibulation of young girls, she runs away, taking with her a child, Nour. Before committing suicide, E. entrusts the child to an Egyptian woman going to Switzerland. Nour (whose name means "light" in Arabic) is cast as the one who will return one day to her country and hopefully enlighten and liberate her sisters from FGC.

While Accad's novel can undoubtedly mobilize sentiment against the practice (as all narratives featuring FGC do), it does so in a very problematic manner. In one of her scholarly publications, Accad justifies her reliance on literature to understand the causes of the Lebanese civil war by stating that "[creative works] allow us to enter into the imaginary and unconscious world of the author. In expressing his or her own individual vision, an author also suggests links to the collective 'imaginary.' . . . literature . . . reflects and articulates the complexities of a situation" (*Sexuality* 5). While *L'excisée* gives us a glimpse of the author's imaginary about the power relations between Muslims and Christians in Lebanon through the very bleak future she portrays for both communities, I argue that using the very real practice of FGC as a trope for patriarchal oppression of women and combining it with political and religious issues that are contextually unrelated reinforces harmful religious stereotypes that can only impede progress rather than promote efforts to eradicate such practice.

L'excisée points the reader to an allegorical reading through the persistent avoidance of specifying a certain time (1958), a place (Egypt), and names (initials instead of names for the two main characters). The excised woman of the title is meant in a symbolic way, as is made clear by Accad in a recent article: "*L'excisée* shows a woman, E., Elle (She in French), Eve (woman everywhere, myself to a certain extent), woman excised symbolically by fanatical religion in war-torn Lebanon, socially by the tyranny of man" ("Writing" 59). The main character has not been physically excised, and the back cover of the book makes it clear that the title does not refer to the secondary character of the Egyptian woman, who has been excised, and whom E. meets twice by chance. The symbolism of the letter *p,* which represents patriarchy, is made obvious when her father and the Christian Father are indicted (20), and this before the appearance of the character of P. As for P., the religious connotation that his first name carries is the first thing that comes to both E.'s (19) and later her father's mind (48) upon hearing it, and for his name to unmistakably identify him as a Muslim Palestinian, it would have to be Arabic. However, the letter *p* does not exist in the Arabic alphabet.[8] Therefore the character of P., who becomes emblematic of both patriarchy and an (illusory) Palestine, cannot be read literally. The fact that a Muslim character becomes the symbol of patriarchy in this allegorical reading is not without implications, and the fact that the focus of the novel will turn to Islam needs to be unpacked.

While the novel deliberately avoids specifying the year in which the narrative takes place, it leaves markers that make it easy to identify. The novel starts at the end of what has been "un été de rage" 'a summer of rage' (9), and the beginning of the narrative proceeds to enumerate various events that took place during that summer: the U.S. Marines' Sixth Fleet has been called in, and there is a new regime in Iraq (9-13)[9]. These events point to 1958, when a six-month civil war erupted over the issue of pan-Arab unity under the leadership of Nasser, president of the United Arab Republic of Egypt (1958-1961); 1958 is seen as a precursor to the civil war that would rage in Lebanon from 1975 to 1990.[10] However, allusions to Israeli raids ("Tyr est violé par l'homme venu du Sud" 'Tyr is raped by the man who came from the south,' 36)[11] have been understood to refer to the 1982 Israeli invasion of Lebanon. Given that the novel was published in 1982, it more likely refers to some of the numerous raids conducted by the Israeli army in (Southern) Lebanon prior to 1982 (starting with the strike on Beirut International Airport in 1968). In any case, such an unclear allusion contributes to blurring the setting's specific historical moment.[12] This, like the refusal to name the country where E. and P. flee (to which I will return later), promotes the vision of Lebanon as a country stuck in religious strife. Although the beginning of the novel states that this is not a war of religion (12), but a war caused by social inequities that plagued Lebanon according to religious and ethnic lines, the refusal to ground the story in a specific year relegates specific historical processes and events to the background instead of foregrounding them. On the one hand, the failure of E. and P.'s marriage forecasts the civil war that fully broke out in 1975; on the other hand, the refusal to ground the story in a specific year implies that no peaceful coexistence is possible in Lebanon. Reflecting on her first novel in an article, Accad repeats some of the sentences that are printed on the book's back cover ("Where can this woman go? Is love between a Moslem and a Christian possible?" in "Writing" 59), which shows that the back cover statement (perhaps written by Accad herself) orients the reader in the direction intended by the author. Interestingly, in her study *Sexuality and War*, Accad criticizes the Israeli government for using Lebanon and thinking "it benefits from a war that, among other things, proves that peaceful cohabitation among different religions is an impossibility and a myth" (34). Yet her novel, through her depiction of the failed marriage of a Christian and a Muslim, offers the same conclusion because it orients the reader to an allegorical reading that, despite historical markers, refuses to be firmly grounded in time.

Thus, the novel can be read as an allegory of Lebanese society, where E. is representative of the Lebanese who thought that the Palestinian cause could revolutionize the Arab world (E. sees P. as "la Palestine de l'espoir" 'the Palestine of hope' (29). In *Sexuality and War,* Accad criticizes the novelist Etel Adnan and all Lebanese intellectuals who held similar convictions for their shortsightedness (73-5). In *L'excisée*, E. pays the price of her naïveté through her failed marriage. While the novel explicitly shows the patriarchal structure across the religious divide by identifying her Muslim husband P. with her father, the uneven power relationship between the couple (where Christian E. is subjugated by Muslim P.) is a problematic allegory of Lebanese society prior to the civil war. For one of the factors that triggered the war was the "disjuncture between representatives and the people they claimed to represent" (Cooke, *War's* 20), as the number of Muslims started to exceed the number of Christians. The proportional representation according to confessional criteria established in 1943 in the National Pact did not plan for an uneven population growth among the various religious groups (the Maronites were then the largest community, and political power was shared between Christians and Muslims on a six to five ratio in favor of Christians, who slightly outnumbered the Muslims, see Abul-Husn 77). Moreover, one can object to the reduction of Lebanon's numerous religious communities, which numbered seventeen in the 1932 census, into two seemingly homogenous Muslim and Christian groups.

The character of P. highlights the fact that one can be victim and oppressor at the same time. In the beginning of the novel, P. is emblematic of Palestine, and Palestine is associated with suffering women several times in the novel, be they excised women (33) or E. herself (47), for Palestine has been raped (55, no specific marker is given here). But P.'s status as a victim does not prevent him from becoming E.'s unexpected oppressor; and here again the allegorical reading supports the interpretation by some of the Palestinian problem as it affected Lebanon, where Palestinian refugees turned from victims into troublemakers.

Since the first influx of Palestinian refugees in 1948, international affairs have come to bear on Lebanon's domestic politics, as the (mostly Muslim) Palestinian refugees disrupted Lebanon's delicate balance between the various sectarian factions trying to get their share of power. This situation was exacerbated when the PLO established its headquarters in Beirut after Black September in 1970.

While P.'s intransigence regarding the religious diversity of the Arab world reflects a real threat, pitting an intolerant Muslim who refuses to consider Christianity as an Arab religion against a powerless Christian who embraces diversity (35, 140), it only reinforces the reductive dichotomy of the Lebanese civil war as a conflict between Christians and Muslims, which has pervaded the Western world's understanding of this history. In a passage where E. describes poverty in quarters that she discovers for the first time, these quarters happen to be in the Druze and Palestinian camps (57-58). While the novel does point out that the reasons for the war are more economic and class-based than religious (12), the allegory formed by the E. and P. couple relegates this fact to the background. Although the allegory of E. and P.'s couple illustrates Accad's thesis in *Sexuality and War* that "since the personal is the political, changes in relationships traditionally based on domination, oppression, and power games will inevitably rebound in other spheres of life" (167), it does not do justice to the reality of Lebanese society by depicting the Muslim as the primary oppressor. Christians not only controlled the political arena, they dominated all sectors of the Lebanese economy.[13] One could say that the text unconsciously reflects the fear of the Christian Lebanese, who, although in power, were feeling threatened by their new minority status in terms of numbers. Although I doubt that this was Accad's intention, *L'excisée* can nevertheless be seen as one example of what Shu-Mei Shih characterizes as

> deliberate national allegorical narratives with an eye to the market . . . When the signified is predetermined, allegories are easier to write or create and to understand and consume. A predetermined signified is produced by a consensus between the audience in the West and the Third World writer or director. It is a contractual relation of mutual benefit and favor that works first to confirm the stereotyped knowledge of the audience and second to bring financial rewards to the makers of those cultural products. (21)

Despite details in the novel that partially account for the complexity of the situation, *L'excisée* can be seen as an allegory tailored to fit the First World's stereotyped view of the Lebanese civil war. This pitting of an oppressive Muslim against a defenseless Christian reappears in the novel in a scene between women that revolves around FGC. While the novel explicitly indicts both the Christian and Muslim faiths for their oppression of women, I show how the religious intertext reinforces this pitting of Islam against Christianity. The inscription of verses from the Qur'an in Accad's text provides a stereotyped view of Islam while the Biblical citations implicitly reaffirm Christian values of sacrifice and redemption.

Although the title of the novel refers to excision or clitoridectomy, which consists of removing some or all of the clitoris and labia minora (and which, according to Elizabeth Boyle, is the most common form of FGC in Africa, 26), the procedure that is described in the novel is infibulation,[14] practiced mostly in the African Horn (Sudan, Somalia, part of Ethiopia), southern Egypt, and part of Mali.[15] Infibulation is the form of FGC that is most often brandished by activists and the media since it is the most extreme and the most prone to immediate medical complications and long-term after-effects. As often in the literature about FGC, the lack of hygiene and the rudimentary nature of the instruments are emphasized in *L'excisée* (121). In emphasizing the issues of physical pain and unsanitary conditions that lead to infections and complications as their main arguments for eradicating the practice, critics of FGC fall vulnerable to the fact that performing the procedure under anesthesia in a medical setting eliminates most of these problems. The particular emphasis on physical pain did not anticipate what is becoming an increasingly widespread phenomenon: the medicalization of FGC (see Fran Hosken 5-9, and Gerry Mackie 277 for a discussion of the implications of this issue). The medically founded opposition to FGC that characterized most efforts against the practice until the 1990s has come to be seen as a mistake by many (Boyle 140), especially those who are fighting against FGC performed on children.[16]

The novel is deliberately vague about the country where E. flees with P., all the while giving hints that allow it to be identified as Egypt (The Egyptian woman who boards the boat in Alexandria is fleeing the country E. and P. will go to [82-83]). Through contrived avoidance, the country is never named. By referring to the place with the terms "pays de sable" 'country of sand' (78), and "pays du désert" 'desert country' (62), the novel conjures stereotypes of an African continent stuck in time, antithetical to progress and modernity. Moreover, the overbearing omnipresence of flies in the village suggests decay and poverty. While FGC has been practiced in Egypt for over 2000 years—thus predating Islam—and is practiced by Africans of all faiths, including the Christian Copts in Egypt (Hosken 15, 55), *L'excisée* does very little to give the reader a sense of the diversity of the practice or of its practitioners, preferring instead to conflate the most extreme practice of FGC with Islamic teachings.

Accad's novel is critical of Christianity, but most of her criticism consists of quoting the Bible to highlight how Christians have strayed from its teachings. In a passage on page 45, which is not a word-for-word quotation, but rather a summary of Luke 6:27-29,[17] the narrator highlights the hypocrisy of people in E.'s church, who are incapable of compassion and forgiveness. The author also parodies Genesis 1:27 by stating "l'homme a rétréci Dieu et L'a fait à son image" 'man shrank God and created Him in his image' (91). Another Biblical allusion to David and Goliath (Samuel 17:4-51) highlights the racism E. encounters in Switzerland when she is sent to a Biblical camp. There, she overhears Europeans making a parallel between David and Goliath and Israel and Arabs, and viewing Israel as a "miracle de la résurrection" 'miracle of resurrection' (90).

Some scriptural allusions emphasize how religions have become so entangled with culture that both the Christian and Muslim codes of honor in Lebanon are very similar: "Oeil pour oeil, dent pour dent. Et quand il s'agit d'une femme: deux femmes pour un homme" 'an eye for an eye, a tooth for a tooth. And when it concerns a woman: two women for a man' (17), which allude respectively to Exodus (21:24) and Qur'anic legalistic prescriptions according to gender for testimony and inheritance.[18] Another allusion: "femme-faible, homme-fort/femme-terre, homme-charrue" 'woman-weak, man-strong/woman-earth, man-plough' (97) alludes to Peter 3:7, which posits women as weaker than men, and the Qur'anic verse 2:223 "Your wives are as a tilth unto you; so approach your tilth when or how ye will"[19] comparing women to a field and men to a plough, thereby linking women to passivity and to submission to men. The strongest condemnation of Christianity occurs when the New Testament is linked to excision on a metaphorical level, when the author writes: "Toutes les femmes acceptant le crucifix, l'épée qui les châtre" 'all women accepting the crucifix, the sword that castrates them' (72).

Accad's text is not as virulent in its criticism of Christianity as it is in its criticism of Islam. In one instance E. briefly associates both Christianity and Islam with excision: "sang coulant dans la plaine, croix à porter, croissant à brandir" 'blood flowing in the plain, cross to bear, crescent to brandish' (95), but the verbs' connotations are worth emphasizing: the image of the cross to be carried contrasts with the aggressive image of the crescent to be wielded, and pits a benign and suffering Christianity against an assertive and belligerent Islam. In another instance, Accad mixes up the two traditions and allows a biblical allusion to pass for a Qur'anic teaching. In a passage in which E. attempts to understand the custom of excision, a woman's gesture is described as follows: "elle lève les bras au ciel vers Allah en ajoutant:—toute notre vie, nous, femmes, n'est que souffrance. Dieu l'a prescrit" 'she raises her arms to the sky towards Allah while adding:—all our life, for us women, is only suffering. God prescribed it' (135). While Allah, the Arabic word for God, is used by Arab Christians as well as Muslims, in the novel it is only used by Muslim characters; in a French text it will immediately connote Islam. In attributing to Allah what is actually reminiscent of a quote from the Bible, in which women are punished with the pain of labor in childbirth,[20] Accad displaces a core Christian tenet onto Islam, which, despite the fact that it places itself in the continuity of the Judeo-Christian scriptures, does not adhere to the teaching that Eve was responsible for the Fall of man, nor that labor pains are a punishment inflicted on her and her kind.

The first Qur'anic verse quoted in the novel is the verse 24:31 in which women are enjoined to lower their gaze and cover their bosoms; because it ends with an injunction to go back to Allah, it will be associated with the Qur'an by any reader (*L'excisée* 14-15). That the author chose not to include the preceding verse, which enjoins men to "lower their gaze and be modest" (Qur'an 24:30), contributes to the stereotype that only women are subject to restrictions in Islam. That Qur'anic quote in the novel is preceded by a Biblical quote in which women are enjoined to be submissive to their husbands (Peter 3:1-7)[21] and which summons husbands to be kind to their wives. In the Biblical citation, women's inferiority compared to men is somewhat alleviated by the injunction of kindness to wives, whereas the fact that the author has truncated the part of the Qur'anic quote that dictated similar restrictions imposed on men as for women reinforces the stereotype that women fare better under Christian dogmas than under Islamic ones.

In the narrative taking place in the Muslim village, Accad conjures up all manner of Western stereotypes about Islam. As with infibulation in regards to FGC, the village women's dress is one of the most extreme to be found in the Muslim world: they wear a mask over their face in addition to a veil covering their head and body (105). To crown it all, all households are polygyneous (113). In the scene describing infibulation, she associates the Muslim veil with FGC:

Le couteau du sacrifice	The knife for sacrifice
La lame tranchante qui tue, qui sépare, qui arrache	The sharp blade that kills, that separates, that tears out
Les boutons du désir	The buds of desire
Les pétales de joie	The petals of joy
L'ouverture de l'extase	The opening of ecstasy
Fermé, cousu, scellé pour toujours	Closed, sewn, forever sealed
Comme un grand voile de fer	Like a large iron veil
Comme un masque de rouille	Like a mask of rust
Comme un rideau de plomb (121)	Like a lead curtain

The flower metaphor for the clitoris and labia contrasts with the metallic veil and mask that the infibulated genitalia have become; it is a battle in which nature has been destroyed by culture, and that culture is unmistakably identified as Islamic.

This intertwining of Islam with excision and oppressive practices is reinforced with quotations from the Qur'an. [22] While the quotes are not identified as verses from the Muslim holy book, they are among the most well-known verses about women (such as the verse of the veil, 143). Other Qur'anic verses are quoted and fulfill part of a narrative function; they are associated with E.'s misfortunes and make it seem as if Islam preordained for all women the downturn in events that E. experiences. Part of the verse on polygamy is quoted twice in the novel (96, 116); the second time the passage implies that E.'s husband has taken another wife after she became pregnant. The quote of the last part of verse 65:4 (about the waiting period for divorced women before they may be turned out of their husband's house) forecasts that E.'s fate will probably be divorce after she delivers her child (116).

Accad also selected parts of the first section of sura 56 (verses 4-6, 12-17, 22-24, 35-8), which deal with the rewards of paradise, and in particular the Houris, which have come to be understood in Islam as eternal virgins awaiting the righteous in Paradise. This truncated sura is inserted right after the description of the procession of women singing after the girls' excision (127). This insertion highlights one of the reasons given for infibulation, that is, guaranteeing the virginity of the future bride, but it gives the wrong impression that infibulation is sanctioned by the Qur'an (which it is not). The last quote from the Qur'an is inserted after the women have been described as reciting verses from it; the reader can infer that the verse quoted is what the women are reciting as they are about to throw in the river the genitalia of the girls who have just been excised (128-9). That verse is known as the pledge of allegiance given by women converting to Islam (60:12); inserting it in that section erroneously implies that the practice of infibulation is part of Muslim women's duties.

In another indented section that contains the Arabic word for God, the reader is misled to believe that infibulation is prescribed in the Qur'an by the presence of Arabic words:

Khatin, Tahara, Khatin	Khatin, Tahara, Khatin
Coupez, mais ne coupez pas trop	Cut, but do not cut too much
Coupez, coupez, coupez	Cut, cut, cut
mais	but
pas	not
trop	too much
Puis refermez et que Dieu soude bien	Then close and may God weld it
le tout	all well
Puis recoupez et resoudez et recoupez	Then recut and reweld and recut
Allah le veut (135)	Allah wants it

Khatin (circumcision) and *Tahara* (purification) are both Arabic words used to designate circumcision. This passage refers to infibulation, since it alludes to the fact that infibulated women need to undergo further cutting to have intercourse and to deliver children, after which they are commonly reinfibulated. There is no mention of excision in the Qur'an, and this paragraph is an allusion to a Hadith[23] regarding FGC, which reports the Prophet recommending that a midwife exert restraint. This Hadith is not found in the collections compiled by the scholars Bukhari and Muslim that are considered authentic. It is found in Abu Dawud's collection (41:5251) and is classified as weak because its chain of transmission is broken. It states: "Narrated Umm Atiyyah al-Ansariyyah: A woman used to perform circumcision in Medina. The Prophet (peace be upon him) said to her: Do not cut severely as that is better for a woman and more desirable for a husband."[24] Both supporters and opponents of FGC in Muslim countries have used this Hadith to defend their cause: with some arguing that only a moderate cutting of the skin covering the clitoris, analogous to male circumcision, is allowed; and others arguing that the Prophet's daughters were not circumcised and that the Hadith should be dismissed because of its classification. This Hadith has been used effectively in campaigns in Egypt, Mauritania,[25] and Sudan as a means to minimize the amount of tissue cut.

While this mixing of Qur'an, poetry, and Hadiths provides a distorted view of mainstream Islamic teachings, the Biblical intertext reaffirms the Christian theology of redemption. The most recurrent quote from the Bible comes from John 14:6: "Jésus a dit : Je suis le Chemin, la Vérité et la Vie. Nul ne vient au Père que par Moi" 'Jesus said to him, 'I am the way, and the truth, and the life. No one comes to the Father except through me.' This quote appears at least four times in the narrative (pages 16, 22, 72, 97). It stresses the importance of Christ as the divinely revealed reality of God, and suggests that Christ is the only way to Heaven. Other quotations, such as "Le sang de Christ vous lave de tout péché" 'the blood of Jesus Christ, his Son, cleanses us from all sin' (19), taken from John 1:7, reinforce the redemptive quality of Jesus' sacrifice.

In *L'excisée*, the parallels between E. and Jesus are numerous: Indeed, some quotations from the Bible, such as the one on page 43 (inserted in the narrative), taken from Revelation 5:1-5,[26] reinforce the association between E. and Christ, and provide a note of optimism in the text: E. being identified as the savior is confident that she will succeed, and she draws from the Bible the courage to go against her family's wishes. On the next page (44), the quote comes from Revelation 3:7-8 and 3:12,[27] which again implies at this point of the narrative that E. will triumph over her parents. Another allusion to Genesis 7 (to Noah and the flood) points to the little child Jesus/Nour as the savior of mankind (23). In fact, women in the text are all somehow associated with the sacrifice of Christ: E.'s mother (whose hand "accepte d'être clouée pour que les autres vivent et connaissent la Vérité" 'accepts to be nailed so that the others may live and know the Truth;' 49), as well as Mary, Jesus' mother (72). E. also becomes a female figure for Christ: first through the "crucifixion symbolique" when her father nails the shutters of her bedroom window shut (Marie 71), and when she sacrifices herself through her suicide-drowning at the end of the novel in order to save other women. The book opens with an unidentified citation from the Bible (Revelation 12:13-18),[28] about the Woman and the Dragon, followed by a short poem that the reader can retrospectively interpret as being about E.'s flight with Nour. This juxtaposition of scripture and poetry reinforces the association of E. with Mary and Nour with Christ. The sermon given by E.'s father in the tent also refers to the dragon and the child (21): the wait for the child savior (Jesus) parallels the anticipated return of Nour, who is expected to save her sisters from excision and other oppressive customs. Despite the condemnation of the fact that women are being sacrificed, the ending of the novel repeats and reinforces the Christian theology of redemption through sacrifice.

Paradoxically, this reappropriation of the Christ figure through the character of E, while interpreted as feminist by Marie (160), participates in the ethnocentrism that First World feminists have been criticized for regarding issues concerning Third World women. As Chandra Mohanty stated in her seminal article, the analytical strategies of assuming one's class and background as the norm applies to Third World women writing about their own cultures (52). At the beginning of the novel, E.'s orientalist attitude is obvious as she reflects while on her way to the village how she will "pénétrer ce monde des femmes derrière le voile, ce monde des êtres du silence, ce monde de l'attente, . . . ce monde qui l'appelle parce qu'elle a été choisie pour le comprendre" 'penetrate that world of the veil, that world of women behind the veil, that world of beings of silence, that world of waiting, . . . that world that calls her because she has been chosen to understand it' (103). E.'s attitude is similar to the one that First World feminists have been criticized for adopting: implying that the veil can only have one meaning, that veiled women cannot speak for themselves, and the quasi-messianic attitude of the character who ultimately fails (and one can argue there is no real attempt) to understand anything that goes on in the village in terms other than her own cultural values.[29] The same applies to the novel as a whole, which casts Qur'anic scriptures as the source of oppression for Muslim women while framing its narrative within Christian theology.

Women practicing FGC are seen by E. and the Egyptian character she meets on the boat as perpetuating the custom as an act of revenge, "heureuses de voir que . . . la souffrance ne s'est pas arrêtée à leur propre corps et que le cercle infernal se perpétue" 'happy to see that . . . the suffering did not stop with their body and the infernal circle perpetuates itself' (85). This portrayal of vengeful mothers is very problematic, for it shows a lack of understanding of the social contexts in which FGC is carried out. Researchers have emphasized that in the communities where FGC is the norm, parents would be considered irresponsible if they did not have their daughters conform to the custom. In *L'excisée*, a clear demonization of the midwife performing the infibulation takes place in the course of the narrative: the midwife comes to be designated as a witch. Like Alice Walker who connects her personal eye wound to FGC as a patriarchal wound in *Warrior Marks*,[30] Accad's character identifies with the excised girls, whose operation becomes the symbol and the height of all patriarchal oppression. E.'s psychological sufferings are mirrored and amplified in the infibulated girls' pain in a graphic scene towards the end of the novel. In a short exchange in which E. attempts to understand the reason for the custom, women are portrayed as passively accepting the tradition (134). There is no real dialogue taking place between E. and the Muslim women of the village, although this would have been an opportunity to insert some explanation for the custom in the narrative.

In addition, E. panics after the women ask her whether she has been excised or not, and she feels threatened when they make a gesture as if attempting to lift up her skirt to see for themselves: "Elle regarde les femmes avec effroi, mer en furie, houle prête à la submerger, à la noyer, à effacer la différence. . . . Comment se défendre contre ces femmes qui semblent assoiffées de sang et de sexes ensanglantés? . . . Pourquoi cette rage contre la différence?" 'She looks at the women with dread, infuriated sea, swell ready to submerge her, to drown her, to erase the difference. . . . How to defend oneself against these women who seem thirsty for blood and blood-soaked genitals? . . . Why this rage against difference?' (137). E.'s reaction appears rather disproportionate with the question and gesture of the women who never hint that they intend to excise her.[31] What is telling in this scene is how E. feels threatened by her distinction and how she constructs the women as hungry for erasure of that bodily difference, which parallels her religious difference with her husband. Just as P., as a Palestinian refugee, is both victim of injustice and E.'s worst oppressor, women, who are often associated with Palestine's sufferings throughout the novel, appear as oppressors of future women by perpetuating the tradition of FGC.

In *Sexuality and War*, Accad is aware that changing a society requires "a long process of in-depth political, economical, psychological, religious, sexual, familial, and social transformations established on an understanding of the different factors, causes and links between these various fields" (166). While *L'excisée* succeeds in making the reader empathize with the girls subjected to FGC, which is, as Ellen Gruenbaum states, a necessary first step to work on improving their living conditions (201), it falls short in providing the reader an understanding of the factors that perpetuate FGC.[32] The main character escapes from the village, taking along a little girl who has not yet been excised. After a chance encounter with the Egyptian woman who had first told her about the custom of infibulation, she entrusts Nour in her care to be taken to Switzerland. E. drowns in the sea, while Nour, who in a melodramatic tirade has gained sudden consciousness of the oppression women face in her village, is portrayed as determined to later return to her country to save her sisters (173).

E.'s failure is the failure of the outsider (in the sense that she does not come from that country) and in this the novel is in agreement with all who believe that change cannot be imposed from outside. History has shown that any imposition or threat from Western powers (such as the one to cut off foreign aid) are seen as imperial moves that threaten indigenous cultures and are not effective (Boyle 104). In Sudan and Kenya, attempts by colonial powers to eradicate FGC failed because it became a political issue (see Dareer 72 for Sudan, Gruenbaum 207 for Kenya). In a similar vein, international pressure in Egypt did succeed in making changes on paper (Boyle 2-5), but these changes seem to have had no impact on the ground: according to a 1996 survey, 97 percent of married women had been circumcised in Egypt (Boyle 2); according to a recent article, the prevalence rate stayed the same in Egypt between 1994 and 2003 (Mekay).

Moreover, the fact that Nour has to leave the village and get a Western education before she can hope to change her village's customs validates the ethnocentric view that the center of change and modernization is in the Western world, and that African countries are stuck with immutable traditions with no conceivable modifications coming from the inside, which is quite contrary to what is happening at the grassroots level. Even Hosken, one of the most vocal and controversial activists against FGC, has become conscious of the fact that action for change cannot come from outside but has to be led by African women who live in Africa (Hosken 9). This is also the recommendation of the Women's Caucus of the African Studies Association in a position paper issued in the early 1980s, with the additional warning that the issue should not be singled out from all others affecting women, especially economic ones (2).[33] The ending of Accad's novel, which forecasts Nour as the future savior of African women from FGC after she has been enlightened by the education she will receive in Switzerland,[34] runs counter to the recommendation mentioned above, and is symptomatic of the imperialism that Western feminists have been criticized for regarding issues concerning Third World women.[35] It demonstrates how tricky it can be to address practices outside of one's culture, since Accad herself is aware that Western feminism has been denounced for its colonial stench when it came to African women ("Author's" xii). And yet *L'excisée* can be said to reproduce such cultural imperialism by the way in which it portrays the women of the village, FGC, and Islam.

The fact that there are varied meanings (such as a rite of passage into adulthood, a code of chastity linked to Islam, cleanliness) assigned to the practice in different locations should influence the strategies used for elimination, since what will work in one area might not work in another (Boyle 31). Boyle has shown that Christian women, whose ideologies are more in line with international ideals (since the latter were formulated in Christian countries) were more likely to be responsive to efforts to eliminate FGC than Muslim women (120). Further, she found that Muslim women who live in cultures that support FGC will justify their opposition to it with medical arguments rather than human rights notions (138), since medicine is viewed as a neutral argument that does not call into question the cultural values of their society (146). As she points out, "although FGC did not originate with Islam, its continuation is tied up with Islamic beliefs in some areas" (30). The fact that one type of FGC is called *sunna* (which means the tradition of the Prophet) in some countries also reinforces the belief held by some that female circumcision is a religious Islamic duty.[36] Given that she chose a Muslim setting to describe infibulation in her novel, Accad's rejection of religion seems far removed from the reality on the ground. Asma Dareer emphasizes that Muslim religious leaders can play a crucial role in the fight against FGC, since they have a very strong influence on their communities (103). Gruenbaum also relates an interview with a Sudanese doctor who uses the Qur'an to show that any procedures that affect a woman's sexuality are against the teachings of Islam (189). This Sudanese doctor uses the Qur'anic verse 2:187,[37] which places sexual relations as a basic need like hunger and thirst, and that should be of mutual satisfaction to husband and wife, to advocate against FGC. If one is to use religious texts to combat infibulation in Muslim countries, educating people about what the religion actually says about the practice seems to be a more effective strategy.

Accad can be credited for being, to the best of my knowledge, the first Francophone writer from an area where FGC is not practiced, to take up the issue in a creative work when it first began to gain international attention.[38] *L'excisée* gave voice to the typical repulsed reaction of people for whom FGC is a foreign custom experience. Since then, however, much progress has been made in grasping the complexity of the issues surrounding this custom, but the absence of contextualization of FGC leads critics who read *L'excisée* to qualify the practice as child abuse (Hottell), or the affliction of a deformity (Marie 116).[39] Unfortunately, twenty years after the publication of *L'excisée*, Accad's reductive portrayal of Muslim customs and FGC does not seem to have been refined by the plethora of publications on the issue. In a recent article, she writes of her character E.: "how could she bend to his [her Muslim husband] customs, which crush women even more than those of her childhood?" ("Writing" 60). *L'excisée* is a telling example of how a Third World author can have as ethnocentric an attitude as the First World critic towards a part of the Third World other than her own.

Although Olayinka Koso-Thomas, an activist in Sierra Leone, ends her book, published in 1987, with the hope that by the year 2000 FGC will no longer be practiced in Africa (100), a recent report shows that figures for FGC remain stable.[40] Many researchers have noted the "discrepancies between the global discourse on female circumcision (with its images of maiming, murder, sexual dysfunction, mutilation, coercion, and oppression) and their own ethnographic experiences with indigenous discourses and with social and physical realities at their field settings and research sites" (Shweder 220). These discrepancies might be a factor in what seems to be an absence of improvement in overall numbers despite two decades of activism and attention. In a remarkable collection of articles on the diversity of FGC, Bettina Shell-Duncan and Ylva Hernlund emphasize the fact that "identifying the most effective and appropriate strategies for eliminating female genital cutting is among the most bitterly contested issues surrounding this practice" (24). Some activists argue for the complete eradication of the custom, whereas others find it more realistic to promote compromising measures, such as milder forms of FGC in Sudan, or banning the practice for children but legalizing it for adults (Boyle 18). In any case, combating FGC is a multifaceted issue that needs to be discussed in terms of specific contexts. As Françoise Lionnet points out, there is a "third way" to frame the debate other than between cultural relativism and human rights universalism: "to see [these practices] as part of a coherent, rational, and workable system—albeit one as flawed and unfair to women as our own can be" (165).

Conclusion

Events of the past few years have brought Lebanon back in the headlines: the assassination of Prime Minister Rafik Hariri in 2005 and the subsequent Cedar Revolution and withdrawal of Syrian troups, the 2006 July War with massive Israeli bombings that severely damaged Lebanon's infrastructure, and the crisis over the presidency in 2007-2008. These recent developments stem from the complexity of Lebanese domestic politics and their entanglement in the politics of the region, making it all the more urgent for critics to point out when writers such as Chédid and Accad have not been up to the task.

Notes

1. That census had been taken under the French Mandate, and "there was a general suspicion, even among many Christians, that it had been a rigged one, at least to some extent" (Salibi, *A House* 198).

2. For more details about such shifting alliance, see Salem 151, and 163-66.

3. For two other versions of the beginning of the war, see Salem (99-100) and Salibi (1976: 90-101).

4. Naming the practice (commonly referred to as mutilation or circumcision) has become a contested issue, and various terms, such as operation, surgery, and cutting are being used as alternatives. I will use the term Female Genital Cutting, which has been gaining popularity because of its neutral stance, instead of the more established Female Genital Mutilation, because the term "mutilation" connotes the intent to inflict harm. FGC ranges from a cut in the prepuce covering the clitoris to removal of the clitoris, all labia, and suturing of the vaginal opening. For explanations of the different types of cutting and terminologies, see Gruenbaum (2-4), and Boyle (25-26, including the fact that people do not always mean the same operation with the same terminology).

5. The book itself and the narrative are not presented as an autobiography.

6. Indeed, Accad knows first hand that a reader can see a lot more than the author intended, as evidenced by her exchange of letters with writer Halim Barakat, who disagreed with Accad's interpretation of his novel. All the endnotes to chapter eight of *Sexuality and War* are quotes from Barakat's letters refuting Accad's analysis (*Sexuality and War* 130-4).

7. In fact in some cases, it is clear that the religious intertext has not been identified and recognized for what it is. For instance, El-Khoury attributes an excerpt of the Qur'an to the novelist (142), while Karnoub and Issa, despite promising titles, do not even mention the Biblical references. Similarly, Cooke incorrectly assimilates all indented passages of the novel to poetry ("Dying" 16). Sullivan briefly mentions that the "narrative is disrupted by words from the Qur'an and the Bible demanding submission from wives and women" (73-4), but goes on to quote a poetry passage and never comes back to the religious intertext. Verthuy does recognize in a particular passage that one text is "Christian" and the other "Islamic" and that "both urge women to obey their husbands" (164), but does not go further.

8. Given that the novel was written in French and published in Paris, Accad's intended reader might not notice that.

9. Later on, there is a reference to the Algerian war of independence (34).

10. See Kamal Salibi's 1976 book for an account of 1958.

11. All translations from the novel are my own.

12. Accad told Elisabeth Marie during an interview that she had wanted to mix up both wars in order to describe the horrors that took place during both periods and to denounce all wars (Marie, note 22 p.15).

13. In 1975, the average income of Christians was 16 percent higher than that of Druzes and 58 percent higher than that of the Shiites. Literacy rates among Muslims ranged between one third and half that of the Christians (Abul-Husn 15)

14. In addition to excision, the labia majora are cut and the wound is sutured, leaving only a small opening for urine and menstrual flow.

15. The Western world has a history of FGC, albeit not well known. Clitoridectomy was used as a medical cure for masturbation and hysteria in Europe and in the U.S., from

the nineteenth to the mid-twentieth centuries (see Gruenbaum 9-12). A new trend has emerged: Female Genital Cosmetic Surgery or FGCS, which is being marketed as a positive advancement not just for medical but also for aesthetic reasons or beautification (see for instance http://www.labiaplastysurgeon.com). According to a *New York Times* article, "primarily, doctors say, aggressive marketing and fashion influences like flimsier swimsuits, the Brazilian bikini wax and more exposure to nudity in magazines, movies and on the Internet are driving attention to a physical zone still so private that some women do not dare, or care, to look at themselves closely" (Navarro).

16. However, others are advocating for some degree of medicalization, such as Fuambai Ahmadu, who as a willing adult underwent excision as part of the Kono initiation for women in Sierra Leone (308-310). See Zabus (*Between Rites* 214-221) for an analysis of Ahmadu's autobiographical vignette.

17. "But I say to you that listen, Love your enemies, do good to those who hate you, bless those who curse you; pray for those who abuse you. If anyone strikes you on the cheek, offer the other also; and from anyone who takes away your coat do not withhold even your shirt."

18. Qur'an 4:11: "to the male, a portion equal to that of two females"; 2:282: "if there are not two men, then a man and two women."

19. All verses from the Qur'an are taken from *The Holy Qur'an*.

20. Genesis 3:16: "To the woman he said, 'I will greatly increase your pangs in childbearing; in pain you shall bring forth children.'"

21. Peter 3:1 "Wives, in the same way, accept the authority of your husbands"; Peter 3:7 "Husbands, in the same way, show consideration for your wives in your life together, paying honor to the woman as the weaker sex."   All quotes from the Bible are taken from *The New Oxford Annotated Bible*.

22. Both opponents and supporters of FGC invoke Islamic teachings (for instance in Sudan, see Asma El Dareer 79).

23. Hadiths are narrations about the sayings and deeds of the Prophet Mohammed; they constitute the second source for Muslims after the Qur'an.

24.   This   translation   was   taken   from   the   following   web   site: http://www.usc.edu/dept/MSA/reference/searchhadith.html.

25. See Zainaba's lecture as an example.

26. Revelation 5:1 "I saw in the right hand of the One who sat on the throne a scroll with writing on both sides, and sealed with seven seals."

27. Revelation 3:7-8 "And to the angel of the church in Philadelphia write. These are the words of the holy one, the true one, who has the key of David, who opens and no one will shut, who shuts and no one opens: 'I know your works. Look, I have set before you an open door, which no one is able to shut. I know that you have but little power, and yet you have kept my word and have not denied my name.'" Revelation 3:12: "If you conquer, I will make you a pillar in the temple of my God; you will never go out of it. I will write on you the name of my God, and the name of the city of my God, the new Jerusalem that comes down from my God out of heaven, and my own new name."

28. Revelation 12:13-18: "So when the dragon saw that he had been thrown down to the earth, he pursued the woman who had given birth to the male child. But the woman was given the two wings of the great eagle, so that she could fly from the serpent into the wilderness, to her place where she is nourished for a time, and times, and half a time. Then from his mouth the serpent poured water like a river after the woman, to sweep her away with the flood. But the earth came to the help of the woman; it opened its mouth

and swallowed the river that the dragon had poured from his mouth. Then the dragon was angry with the woman, and went off to make war on the rest of her children, those who keep the commandments of God and hold the testimony of Jesus."

29. For an analysis of parallels between E. and Christ, see Marie.

30. For a remarkable analysis, see Inderpal Grewal and Caren Kaplan's article.

31. Some critics read the scene where E. sees the women as threatening to excise her to the extreme by stating that E. "escapes physical excision by leaving the community" (Hottell). I concur with Marie who thinks that the women were kidding her (52).

32. In her first scholarly book, Accad incorrectly states that a girl is more likely to be circumcised if she is from the lower classes, and that this is the reason why it is rarely mentioned in fiction from North Africa and the Arab world (*Veil of Shame* 20-21). As Shweder states, ethnicity and cultural group affiliation are the best predictor of circumcision (220), while education and economic status have no influence on it (230). Moreover, the reason it is absent from North African fiction is that FGC is nonexistent there.

33. The success of the Tostan program in Senegal is attributed to the fact that FGC is only part of one of several basic education modules and that people are never told what they should do, instead they are given facts and trusted to make the right decisions for themselves (see Mackie 256-261).

34. The choice of Switzerland is ironic given that it has been one of the slowest European countries to affirm women's rights (right to vote in 1971 and legalization of abortion in 2002).

35. See Chandra Talpade Mohanty's article.

36. The *sunna* type in Sudan is supposed to be the mildest form of FGC and analogous to male circumcision because it consists in removing the tip of the prepuce of the clitoris, although one of the intermediate types of FGC is also called *sunna* by many (Dareer 2-4).

37. "Permitted to you, on the night of the fasts, is the approach to your wives. They are your garments and ye are their garments."

38. Other writers for whom FGC is a foreign custom have incorporated the practice in their novels. Ben Jelloun's *La nuit sacrée* [*The Sacred Night*] features a scene where a group of women, portrayed as fanatical Muslims, infibulate their sister as an act of revenge (159-60). The first person narrator, who is the victim of the operation, "pratiquée couramment en Afrique noire, dans certaines régions d'Egypte et du Soudan" 'commonly practiced in black Africa, in some areas of Egypt and Sudan,' undisputedly calls it a "torture," "mutilation," a "barbarian idea," a "massacre," and the Sudanese guardian, who is blamed for giving the idea to the sisters, is "une sorcière, experte dans les méthodes de torture" 'a witch, expert in methods of torture' (163). While the excision that is performed on the narrator no doubt deserves the epithets that the narrator uses, for it is in that novel an imported cultural practice put to use with the intent to harm an individual, the casual mention that it is performed in black Africa orientalizes the practice and does nothing to inform the reader. While the narrative is careful to mention that such a practice in unknown in the Maghreb and forbidden by Islam (163), Ben Jelloun did not escape criticism of sensationalism. A novel by Canadian writer Marie Auger (pseudonym) is titled *L'excision* [The Excision]. The title refers to a self-inflicted excision by a woman whose body can feel neither pain nor pleasure. The narrator briefly mentions the fact that some women excise their daughters, and refuses to try to understand why, because, in a categorical judgment, "Il est plus facile d'accepter l'incompréhensible que de compren-

dre l'inacceptable" 'it is easier to accept the incomprehensible than to understand the unacceptable' (105).

39. "La femme excisée est affligée d'une sorte de difformité. Cette dernière a cependant l'avantage d'être non apparente et lui évite d'être davantage exclue de la société qu'elle ne l'est déjà" 'The excised woman is afflicted with a kind of deformity. The latter however has the advantage of not being apparent and prevents her from being further excluded from society than she already is' (Marie 116). On the contrary, one of the reasons given for performing FGC is aesthetic (Koso-Thomas 7), and in many communities, the uncircumcised woman is the one who would be ostracized.

40. "The prevalence of FGC in Egypt, for example, stayed roughly the same—about 97 percent—between 1994 and 2003, while it rose in Cote d'Ivoire from 43 percent to 45 percent, slipped back from 95 percent to 89 percent in Eritrea and to 34 percent from 38 percent in Kenya, in the same time period" (Mekay).

Chapter 4

The Algerian Civil War: Rachid Boudjedra's *Le FIS de la haine*, Rachid Mimouni's *De la barbarie en général et de l'intégrisme en particulier*, and *Une enfance algérienne*

The French colonization of Algeria stands out among the other North African countries by the length of time (132 years) and the bloody war that was fought to gain independence. Algeria came back in the news in the late 1980s and 1990s with the rise of an Islamist political party and a devastating civil war. During that period, France was slowly coming out of a period of amnesia, as historians Benjamin Stora and Mohammed Harbi put it, about its painful colonial past and the atrocities it committed in Algeria before and especially during the 1954-1962 war for independence. This is the context in which the books analyzed in this chapter were published.

As the sole party since it won the war in 1962, the FLN had maintained a strong hold on Algerian politics thanks to oil revenues. The drop of the price of oil in 1986 brought this fragile equilibrium to a halt. Adding to this, a high birth rate, lagging infrastructure, and high unemployment rate took their toll and triggered riots in October 1988, that were severely repressed by the government. As Philip Naylor phrased it, "On the surface, the riots stemmed from economic pressures, but they were deeply rooted in political, social, and cultural frustration" (165). These events led to the adoption of a new constitution in early 1989 opening the political arena. One of the newly established political parties was the FIS (Front Islamique du Salut), founded in March 1989, a party that went on to win the first two free elections held in Algeria since Independence: for the local governments in June 1990, and for the National Assembly in December 1991.

1991 was a watershed year for Algerian politics, because the FIS took center stage as the only viable opposition party to the FLN. Tensions grew between the government and the FIS leaders following the imposition of a redistricting before the legislative elections to minimize the FIS's projected gain at the polls.

A siege was declared, the FIS leaders (Benhadj and Madani) arrested, and the elections postponed for six months. Some Islamists refused to engage in the elections which they saw as a dupery and took to the maquis, committing violent acts (over which the FIS had no control). After the FIS emerged victorious from the first round of elections in December 1991, the army's coup d'état in January 1992 (making the president resign, cancelling the elections' second round, dissolving the FIS and arresting its militants) marked the beginning of the civil war that would last until 1999 and in which Algerian civilians became targets. The civil war spilled over to France when the GIA hijacked an Air France plane in 1994 and orchestrated terrorist attacks in Paris in 1995.[1] These events offered dramatic proof of the neocolonial relationship extant between the two countries; they brought to the fore the fact that France and Algeria's paths had remained intertwined. Despite decolonization,[2] economic dependencies, such as the presence of French *coopérants* in Algeria, of Algerian emigrant workers in France, and agreements regulating the exploitation of Algeria's hydrocarbons, existed.[3] Naylor notes that "Though France was politically ambivalent [about the annulment of the elections], it consistently provided Algeria with indispensable economic support" (196), notably through rescheduling of Algeria's debt. According to him, "by exercising its influence in multilateral organizations and circles, France disguised its extraordinary economic support to Algeria," a support that was crucial in saving Algeria from financial disaster (207).

This chapter analyzes representations of the rise of the FIS to political prominence and the civil war in nonfiction works. The first section examines two essays that were triggered by the FIS's electoral victory and that were published the year of the annulment of the elections: Rachid Mimouni's *De la barbarie en général et de l'intégrisme en particulier*, and Rachid Boudjedra's *Le FIS de la haine*. My purpose here is not to weigh in on the question of whether intellectuals were right or not in supporting the annulment of the elections.[4] My analysis demonstrates that both essays reduce the diversity of Islamist movements to the fundamentalism of the FIS. In addition, I contend that word choices (Mimouni's title and Boudjedra's inflammatory rhetoric) do more to feed the flames of fear than to further our understanding of the events under scrutiny.

A surge of novels and autobiographical accounts set during the civil war were published during the 1990s in Paris by Algerians, but instead of analyzing some of these works in the second section (it would take a book to do them justice), I focus on a collection of short autobiographical narratives where the civil war trespasses on the colonial past. Also published in the 1990s, *Une enfance algérienne* is set during colonial Algeria, a time period well before the civil war even started, and yet the civil war intrudes in the collection. I give particular consideration to the fact that the devastating effects of colonialism are mostly erased or strikingly downplayed, while the violence that surfaces in places is mainly associated with the Algerian nationalist movement during the war for independence and with the rise of Islamic fundamentalism that constitutes the backdrop to the publication of the text, commissioned in the 1990s. I draw out the implications of the civil war's intrusion into narratives taking place well before the 1990s, and of this shift of perpetrators of violence given the context of publication of the volume.

The FIS's Electoral Victory in Essays

Rachid Boudjedra's *Le FIS de la haine*

In *Le FIS de la haine* (2002), Boudjedra identifies several causes for the birth of the Islamist party. In the process, he does not spare any one, as he successively lays the blame on several actors: the West and the Algerian government, the Algerian people and intellectuals are all held accountable. The West is castigated for its double standards (17), its shameless capitalism and neocolonialism not only in the economic, political, but also in the cultural sphere with the concept of *Francophonie* (20-31, 89-95), and its scorn of the Arabic language and Islamic culture inherited from colonial times that has contributed to the rise of religious fundamentalism (32-34). Regarding the West's project to improve the economic situation, Boudjedra points out that "on a l'impression que les pays riches sont prêts à s'accommoder de la peste intégriste si leurs intérêts économiques les plus égoïstes sont garantis par les islamistes" 'it seems that rich countries are ready to tolerate the fundamentalist plague provided that their most selfish economic interests are guaranteed by Islamists' (133). One can object that there is nothing new here in terms of Western foreign policy in the Middle East overall, for the same has been true with the FLN's authoritarian rule. As Frédéric Volpi noted, the West has been more concerned with its short-term economic requirements than with Algeria's long-term needs to develop a democracy (129). Boudjedra blames the Algerian people for the unrestrained birth rate and the ensuing problems caused by such high demographics.[5] Intellectuals are also blamed (56-58). Another factor listed as a cause for the rise of the FIS is the FLN's corruption and its Arabisation policy, which led the government to bring in teachers from abroad, especially from Egypt, some of whom turned out to be members of the Muslim Brotherhood who spread fundamentalism.

Scholars have pointed to the same factors as contributing to the Algerian crisis, so it is not so much the content of Boudjedra's essay, but its rhetoric that is objectionable. *Le FIS de la haine* has been labeled as a pamphlet (Memmi, "La folie" 32), a category that is fitting given its virulent tone. While Boudjedra's writing is caustic throughout, I argue that his explicit demonization of the FIS and oversimplification of certain issues to the benefit of the FLN and detriment of the FIS skews Boudjedra's argument. This disproportion, both in quantity and quality, in the criticism of the FIS leaves little space to emphasize the damages caused by the FLN since independence.

Boudjedra is able to paint a nuanced portrait of the West and the FLN, underlining both their achievements and their shortcomings, but he fails to do the same for the FIS. The writer can differentiate between on the one hand, the West that oppresses other nations and its multinationals governed by greed, and on the other hand the West of intellectuals and artists (104-105), but he cannot make the same distinction when it comes to the Algerian Islamist movement. Gilles Kepel has noted that from the very beginning in the early 1980s, the Islamist movement in Algeria has had two trends: an extremist one that advocates armed struggle and a reformist one that works through political channels (*Jihad* 170). Although Boudjedra does recognize that there are different "islams" (120), his depiction of the Islamist movement in Algeria is monolithic, with the FIS presented as the sole Islamist party, and with no distinction between different groups. After its formation, the FIS did not include all major representatives of the Islamist movement (Kepel, *Jihad* 173); there were other Islamic parties on the Algerian scene (such as Mahfoudh Nahnah's Hamas, and Abdallah Jaballah's Nahda), who participated in the elections. Indeed, Michael Willis notes that several senior Islamists (such as Ahmed Sahnoun and Mohammed Saïd) refused to join the party, and that from its inception the FIS represented only part of Algeria's Islamist movement (117), but Boudjedra fails to mention any of this.

Boudjedra faults the FIS leadership for its inconsistencies, which he sees as double talk (with Abassi's public statements differing sharply from Belhadj's hardline rhetoric), but these discrepancies also reflected real divisions between the two leaders of the FIS (Willis 146-48). In addition, there is a difference between the Islamic militants involved in the political process and the Emirs of armed groups, the latter usually composed of marginal people outside the religious sphere until they joined the jihad (Martinez, *The Algerian* 96). But by lumping them all together under the Islamic fundamentalist label, the atrocities committed by the latter indelibly taint the former. Boudjedra has fallen into the trap of overemphasizing the violent and discriminatory aspect of the Islamic movement in Algeria, thus failing to explain how it came to have such support, whether one situates it in an international context of Islamic fundamentalism, or as a consequence of the evolution of the postcolonial state and society.

Boudjedra portrays FLN leaders in a somewhat more nuanced fashion. Ben Bella was a "despote . . . grisé par le pouvoir" 'despot, intoxicated by power,' "inculte, démagogue" 'uneducated, demagogue' (38). While Boudjedra describes how Ben Bella had people arrested and executed, he does not describe him as thirsty for blood (as he does the FIS, more on that later). In his most virulent attack, Boudjedra refers to ministers under Boumediene as "obsédés sexuels" 'sexual maniacs' (42). The FLN's role in bringing about the birth of the FIS is broached briefly (11), but that brief sentence is overshadowed by two pages that praise the party for creating a modern independent state (13-14). Although Boudjedra admits that the FLN was "autoritaire, méprisant, dictatorial, corrompu, perverti, à un point inimaginable" 'authoritarian, comtemptuous, dictatorial, corrupt, perverted, to some unimaginable degree' (14), he exonerates it by intimating that these are characteristics of all political powers. Later on, he finds excuses for the FLN's corruption by recalling the harsh treatment its members endured during colonial times and the war for Independence (53), but shows no such leniency for the FIS leaders.

On the issue of corruption and poor economic planning, Boudjedra first states that both the state and the FIS are responsible (81); later on he criticizes the West as well as the FIS by naming it twice, but forgets the FLN (102). This is an example of Boudjedra's double standard: the FIS, which controlled the local governments for a year and a half, gets more blame than the FLN, which controlled all levels of government for close to thirty years, as if commensurability existed between the decades of FLN state rule and the brief period when the FIS held local offices. Louis Martinez has pointed out that the FIS could not carry out its policies after its victory in the local elections in June 1990 for lack of financial support from the government, something its victory at the legislative level could have changed (*The Algerian* 90-1, see also Willis 159-60).[6]

But more than his selective presentation of facts, it is the vocabulary that Boudjedra uses to disparage the FIS's leaders and its members that is striking: Ali Belhadj is "ignare" 'ignorant,' a "petit avorton" 'small squirt' whose weekly sermons leave its audience "avide de sang" 'eager for blood' (11), "ils [leaders of the FIS] sont devenus aujourd'hui parce que cancres, parce que incompétents, les bourreaux de l'Algérie contemporaine, les fous de Dieu qui éructent des insanités" 'because they are dunces, incompetent, they became the executioners of contemporary Algeria, the madmen of God who eruct insanities' (65), "les monstres qui dirigent le FIS. . . . Horde d'incultes" 'the monsters that lead the FIS. . . A horde of uneducated people' (40);[7] "requins voraces qui aiment la couleur du sang et son odeur" (140), 'voracious sharks that like the color and smell of blood' (15) "maquereaux qui balafrent et vitriolent les femmes" 'pimps who gash and throw vitriol at women,' "des débiles attardés" 'backward feebles,' "rats enragés et pestiférés" 'rabid and plague-stricken rats' (16). Boudjedra reserves his vitriolic rhetoric for the FIS, the words he uses animalize the FIS leaders and its members, who are reduced to monsters thirsty for blood. Animalizing one's target is a common colonialist and genocidal rhetorical ploy, used among others by the French in Algeria to refer to the FLN. Given that the pejorative term "raton" 'small rat' is still used to designate North Africans, for an Algerian to call other Algerians rats is to be purposefully provocative. Moreover, Boudjedra's accusations are not well informed: Madani held a Ph.D. in education and had published three books (Willis 147-8); Benhadj possessed great oratory talents (Kepel, *Jihad* 174).

The party and Islamism are variously called "un fascisme rampant et gluant" 'a crawling and gluey facism' (10); "la peste verte" 'the green plague' (111, 135); "monstre verdâtre" 'greenish monster' (114); "le pus vert" 'green pus' (137); "un parti ordurier et nauséabond" 'a filthy and foul party' (16); "Parti de la mort, il a la passion du sang, du bain de sang, de la tuerie. La majorité écrasante de ses responsables sont des cas psychiatriques. La pathologie du FIS est très profonde" 'the party of death, it has a passion for blood, blood bath, slaughter. The overwhelming majority of its leaders are psychiatric cases. The pathology of the FIS is very deep' (108). The following hyperbole, stating that the intent of the FIS regarding women is to "imprison them in concentration camps" ("la femme il la parquerait dans des camps de concentration" (93), crowns it all. One can see clearly here the measure of exaggeration in Boudjedra's text, for if indeed the FIS did not promote gender equality, its sexist pronouncements[8] were a far cry from incitement to genocide.

Boudjedra also engages in personal attacks on historians Harbi and Stora (122-23), and rails against Lahouari Addi's statement that the election of the FIS was a "régression féconde" 'fertile regression' (110-11). Regarding the latter, Boudjedra deprecates the scholar ("un petit sociologue" 'a petty sociologist') to better denigrate the argument, with which he does not really engage.[9] Boudjedra blames some journalists, whom he faults for believing that "ils sont objectifs et que toute autre analyse que la leur est passionnelle et subjective" 'they are objective and that all analysis other than their own is emotional and subjective' (115). However, the vocabulary and hyperbole detailed above are ground enough to turn that same critique against Boudjedra himself. Similarly, the attacks leveled against some journalists for simplifying a complex situation (118) can also be applied to his book.

Le FIS de la haine was reedited with a new afterword by the author in 1994, two years after the original edition. The back cover, signed by Boudjedra, sets the tone: only the FIS is blamed for electoral fraud and terror. He asserts that his book was written "sans tabous, sans barrières et sans préjugés" 'without any taboos, barriers, or prejudice' (backcover). In this new edition, Boudjedra keeps on blaming the FIS, and ignores the military exactions (including torture) committed by the regime, such as the measures taken starting in April 1993 to reconquer the Islamist communes of Greater Algiers (Martinez, *The Algerian* 22). There is no mention in Boudjedra of the crackdown perpetrated by the government on the FIS in June 1991 and in January 1992 (Volpi 51, 58), of the dissolution of the party and the repression against its members—more than ten thousand prisoners in detention camps (Burgat 304). The new afterword keeps blaming the FIS for all the gruesome news coming out of Algeria, and does not make any mention of the GIA at all, an armed group that split with the FIS and that was responsible for some of the atrocities that Boudjedra attributes to the FIS (Volpi 68).[10] In addition, Boudjedra accuses the FIS of propaganda,[11] but there is not a single word on the FLN's censorship of the media (Volpi 59).

According to Boudjedra, "le FIS n'est qu'un élément de l'internationale intégriste islamique qui fait tant de mal à l'Islam" 'the FIS is only one component of the Islamic fundamentalist Internationale that wrongs Islam so much' (119). The term "Islamic fundamentalism" is used as a blanket term to denote a wide spectrum of movements.[12] Boudjedra does not make the distinction that Volpi deems crucial in a Muslim context between Islamic fundamentalism as "the set of political and ethical precepts which may (or may not) help people to organize their social world better, and Islamic fundamentalism as a name attributed to the activities of a group of political actors . . . claiming to represent Islamic orthodoxy" (Volpi 10). Boudjedra's statement "Le FIS n'a qu'un credo: le pouvoir, de n'importe quelle façon" 'the FIS has only one creed: power, by all means' ("Postface" 127), could very well be said of the FLN. Boudjedra cannot come to terms with the fact that the Islamic movement does have a certain appeal, as attested by its capacity for mobilization (Burgat 2), not just to the poor urban youth but also to the pious middle class (Kepel 174),[13] with the fact that Muslims may find an ethics and an understanding of modernity governed by Qur'anic principles (Majid, *Unveiling* 21), and with the fact that democracy and Islam may not be incompatible (Layachi 59).

Rachid Mimouni's *De la barbarie en général et de l'intégrisme en particulier*

Mimouni's *De la barbarie en général et de l'intégrisme en particulier* adopts a perspective similar to Boudjedra's position. The first part, entitled "Qu'est-ce que le FIS?" 'what is the FIS?' purports to demonstrate how retrograde the FIS is by focusing on its alleged archaism (fixation of fundamentalists on the past), and its hatred of women, culture, and intellectuals. Mimouni does stress the difference between Islam and Islamic fundamentalism (particularly in his discussion of women), but does not differentiate different tendencies within the Islamic movement (153, 166, 170). The second part underlines that the power in place shares some responsibility in the rise of Islamic fundamentalism in Algeria (poor handling of the economy, using the fundamentalists to counter the Berber movement in 1980). The intellectuals are also blamed for their lack of courage and their absence at key moments.[14] The third part focuses on the factors that promoted fundamentalism (moral crisis, demographic explosion, dual tracks in education). The fourth part talks about obstacles to democracy in Algeria (no tradition of democracy in Algeria, tribalism and illiteracy).

Mimouni's essay perpetuates some of the same stereotypes as Boudjedra's, starting with its title that clearly qualifies Islamic fundamentalism as a barbaric movement, made explicit in the course of the essay: "ce retour de la barbarie" 'this return of barbarity' (87). In addition, the treatment of the shortcomings of the FLN and the FIS lacks balance. For instance, only the FIS is presented as benefiting from *trabendo* (black market, 64), although *trabendo* predates the 1988 riots (Kepel 167). Even when there might be something positive to be said about the FIS, it is phrased in such a way as to turn it into a negative. For instance, Mimouni acknowledges the FIS's charity work, but in a manner that ends up turning it into a coldly calculated tactic to win more support (66). Several parallelisms between Algerian and French history are made: an interesting comparison is made between Boudiaf's return in 1992 and De Gaulle's in 1958 to solve the Algerian crisis (86), but a rather dubious one between the FIS and the OAS reduces a legally constituted political party that won elections to an underground terrorist organization (166).

Despite these shortcomings, Mimouni's essay endeavors to achieve a rational examination of the situation. The last two pages seem to forecast the civil war that was to unfold (166-67). To his credit, Mimouni also acknowledges that the Islamic tendency is there to stay and must be taken into account,[15] and that the dissolution of the FIS is not a long-term solution (165). Robert Mortimer has pointed out that "What was needed, well before the fateful elections of December 1991, was a dialogue between secularists and Islamists about pluralism and civil liberties" (19), and added that the urgency for dialogue has been rendered all the more critical by the civil war. Azzedine Layachi envisions the need for a democratic front including Islamists and secularists in order for change to occur; he states that "the Islamists and the secularists must both change the way they perceive and relate to each other" (63). Layachi acknowledges that this will be a challenge, but not an impossible task (63). Boudjedra's essay, with its virulent rhetoric, does not demonstrate that kind of willingness from its author, while Mimouni is definitely a step closer. However, the portrayal of Islamism as a barbaric movement does not foster the conditions necessary for dialogue or analysis.

Criticism of the FIS was undoubtedly warranted. Party policies were characterized by vagueness and lack of innovation in terms of economic policy and political institutions. A majority of its pronouncements focused upon social, educational, and cultural issues, mostly advocating Arabization of education and segregation of the sexes (Willis 138-47), and its leadership was fragmented due to a clear cleavage between the two leaders about crucial issues (Willis 145-46, Naylor 220). However, Boudjedra and Mimouni's essays fail to point out that political violence began with the arbitrary arrests and torture of pro-Islamic demonstrators by the government, a fact that historians and political scientists writing about the Algerian crisis underline (see for instance Volpi vii). The fact that the so-called "Islamist" violence is a response to state violence is too often occulted (Burgat 115).

Moreover, Burgat noted that the "interruption of the electoral process and flare up of repression open[ed] a breach in the arguments of the FIS' legalists to the advantage of their most radical challengers" (318). Mimouni does anticipate that state repression will radicalize the Islamist movement and promote the most extremist leaders (166). As for Boudjedra, he does not reflect in the new edition of his work on the fact that the level of violence was caused by the state's measures, and that the state was responsible for a significant proportion of the exactions committed, whether directly or indirectly by infiltrating Islamic movements (Volpi 90). Burgat notes that this government infiltration of the GIA was designed "to keep the necessary repulsion in international public opinion and thus block any rational analysis of the crisis" (328). Thus, the regime in Algeria succeeded in limiting the visibility of its opposition to the excesses of the most radical elements with the cooperation (conscious or not) of the international media (Burgat 316). With their titles, Boudjedra and Mimouni's essays have contributed to that current. In a similar vein, Willis noted the eagerness of the Algerian (and French) government to report items when the FIS implemented measures to conform Algeria's social life to their idea of an Islamic society, some true, but others turned out to be fabricated, distorted, or measures taken by previously FLN-controlled authorities (158-59).

Boudjedra (96) and Mimouni (84) both accuse the FIS of burning a baby in Ouargla in 1989. Boudjedra recalls this incident again at the closing of the book (140-41), and compares it to the burning of the Reichstag in 1933 (which marked the end of the democratic republic of Weimar). He invokes lessons from Nazism (137), and from Iran (139). Similarly, Mimouni makes a parallelism between Nazism and the Weimar Republic and Algeria to counter those who defend that the electoral process should have been respected (152), as well as a parallelism with Iran (154). According to journalist Rabha Attaf (who opens her article by quoting Boudjedra's mention of it in his essay), this incident was nothing but a "sordide affaire de moeurs" 'sordid sexual immorality case' (202), yet it was exploited and told over and over again as a proof that the FIS hated women. According to her, "l'utilisation mensongère de cette affaire a un objectif bien précis: disqualifier le FIS et justifier, a posteriori, un anti-islamisme primaire alimentant une répression sanglante sous couvert de lutte pour le droit des femmes" 'the deceitful use of this case has a very specific goal: to disqualify the FIS and a posteriori justify a simplistic anti-Islamism that feeds a bloody repression under the guise of a struggle for women's rights' (202). The references to Iran bring foreign history and events to bear on the Algerian context, putting more emphasis on transnational Islamism, and not placing the rise of the FIS within the context of Algeria's unfinished history of (de)colonization.

As Willis points out, "the high-profile backing the French media gave to the [secular opposition parties and the FLN] . . . seemed to confirm the FIS' propaganda against the other parties that they were the vehicles of Western and anti-Islamic values" (153). With its numerous invectives and incendiary tone, *Le FIS de la haine* can be seen as partaking (unwittingly) in this counter-productive campaign, and most definitely does not help look at the crisis rationally. After 1995 and the election of Zeroual as president, the labeling of the violence as terrorist and Islamic allowed the regime to create a confusion between marginal elements of its opposition (which its brutal repression helped to radicalize), and the entire opposition; this enables it to justify to the West the postponement of democratization indefinitely (Burgat 332).

Burgat has stressed that "one needs to see beyond its extreme expressions to the essence of the Islamist dialectic that it is possible to understand why it has such a remarkable capacity for mobilization" (4). Refusing to recognize the appeal that Islamist parties can have in Algeria (and other parts of the Muslim world) will not enhance our understanding of the dynamics of the region. The fact that in several countries Islamist parties have emerged as the main opposition to authoritarian, Western-backed governments must be confronted and understood.

Volpi noted that the problem for Western democracies was that "the process of democratisation was accompanied by a process of 'Islamicisation,'" and that "Western democracies had to make a difficult compromise between their short-term economic and domestic political objectives and the long-term developmental needs of liberal democracy in a Muslim polity" (129). Moreover, Western democracies are complicit in the ruling elite's system of governance of "buy[ing] social peace with political repression and economic redistribution" (131), a system whose stability depends on the price of hydrocarbons. No Francophone writer has noted the contradiction noted by Martinez: "by refusing to make the FIS a partner in power in 1991 despite its success in the elections, . . . and then giving a privileged role to the AIS, the Presidency showed that the way to power is not through the ballot box but through armed resistance" (*The Algerian* 19).

Réda Bensmaïa rightfully noted the striking "contrast between the sociopolitical insignificance of intellectuals as a 'group' and the violence carried out against them" during the civil war in Algeria (86). If during the Algerian crisis Algerian intellectuals played the role of "Phantom Mediators" (as Bensmaïa phrased it in the title of his article), works published in France contributed to a demonization of Islam that had some repercussions in that context, most notably with the "affaire du foulard" 'headscarf affair,' which I discuss in the next chapter.[16] In any case, Boudjedra's pamphlet would not have fulfilled the function of intellectuals, which Bensmaïa qualifies as "mediators between the cultures, languages, and morals of the country and to translate the variety of statements coming from the different communities for the . . . nation, so that these could be understood in the different political, ethnic, cultural, and religious idioms" (90). Although Boudjedra has specified that *Le FIS de la haine* had been specifically written for the French public (qtd. in Gafaïti, 72), it does not further the French public's understanding of the situation that led to the rise of the Islamic party. Mortimer identified one of the reasons why a third democratic and secular alternative did not materialize as an alternative to the FLN and the FIS, as "the isolation of the elite from the grass roots" (25). The essays discussed here are emblematic of that isolation. While the authors denounce the corruption and abuse of the FLN during its thirty years in power, neither Boudjedra nor Mimouni published essays focusing on the FLN, similar to these essays on the FIS. That, in itself, speaks volumes about the authors and the French market conditions.

Remembering Colonial Algeria in the 1990s: *Une enfance algérienne*

Une enfance algérienne first appeared in Paris in 1997, and was translated into English as *An Algerian Childhood* in 2001. Edited by Leïla Sebbar, a Franco-Algerian author, this collection is the second in what can be labeled a trilogy of collections of autobiographical short stories.[17] In the first, *Une enfance d'ailleurs*, co-edited with Nancy Huston, the common denominator of the writers (some of whom come from Poland and Russia) is French as a language for written expression. The third volume, *Une enfance outremer*, features writers from former French colonies. As its title indicates, the second volume focuses on one country; it is the only text in the trilogy to do so. Asked about the genesis of this project, Sebbar explained that she has followed the same approach for all the collections: after selecting a topic of interest to her, linked to the themes of her works (colonization, exile, war, etc.), she then asked writers for an unpublished autobiographical piece on the theme of the book (personal correspondence with the author).

Une enfance algérienne features sixteen pieces by Francophone writers from diverse backgrounds (Arabs, Jews, French settlers, as well as people of mixed descent), who have in common the fact that they spent their childhood in Algeria. The authors' backgrounds emphasize the diversity of the population of colonial Algeria and the experiences of various constituents. The authors' birthdates range from the 1920s to the 1950s, and thus the stories cover the period from post World War I to the Algerian war. In addition to their Algerian childhood, these writers also have in common the fact that they all have been living in France for decades, with the exception of one contributor who goes back and forth (according to the short biographical notices that precede each story). Indeed, these writers were chosen because they had to leave Algeria for one reason or another (Donadey, "Foreword" xiv). This fact in part explains the nostalgic tone that characterizes several of the stories.

Overall, the narratives seem to stress the cordial relations that existed between the different groups that peopled colonial Algeria. Here are some examples: Arab and Jewish women exchange food (Bencheikh 28), Arab and European kids play together (Alloula 20, Pélégri 193), the diverse ethnic groups enjoy the same doughnuts, their various languages are like soothing lullabies (Dadoun 88, 96), and the diverse religions form a polyphony (Daniel 111). There is an emphasis on the common lot of all, with epidemics (Dib 119) and natural disasters that do not differentiate between the backgrounds of their victims (Pélégri 201). The nostalgia present in several of the stories is expressed through frequent interjections (Bencheikh), and the transfiguration of a weekly routine into an odyssey where prosaic chores are compared to artistic endeavors (Dadoun). William Cohen has noted that "The pieds-noirs have a vision of history they wish to see adopted by the metropole. The most important 'truth' the pieds-noirs wanted to establish was that they lived in harmony with the other ethnic groups in Algeria" (132).[18] However, the pieds-noirs are not the only ones who "embellish" inter-ethnic relations, as Tengour's story for instance emphasizes the fact that his grandfather remained friends with French settlers during the war, while his son was in prison for his nationalist involvement. As Anne Donadey points out in her introduction to the English translation, this volume creates "a utopia, an imaginary homeland whose foundation rests on reconciliation and respect for differences. This volume brings into being an open Algerian community that is unfortunately impossible to put together today except within the pages of a book" (xvii).[19]

However, cracks surface in this "utopian" Algeria where different groups supposedly coexisted peacefully. Some passages mention or talk about the misconceptions and prejudices of one group towards another: against Arabs (Annie Cohen 79), Muslims (Daniel 109), and Jews (Tengour 223). In Jean Pélégri's contribution, the earthquake leads Areski, an Arab, to realize the common humanity he shares with his employer, a settler, whom he now sees as his brother, but that acknowledgment is not reciprocal. While Areski insists that they are united in the face of natural disaster, his employer's answer is to stress what differentiates them: in the circumstances, the arbitrariness of grammatical gender. Although the French and Arabic languages do have grammatical gender, they assign opposite gender to the moon and the sun (202). The settlers' indifference to the indigenous population transpires in some stories. Daniel recalls that he and his teacher had no desire to learn Arabic (104). Millecam points out that as a child, he had no awareness of the colonial situation, of the fact that this territory used to belong to the ancestors of the children who are now the most destitute and whom he cannot even name, but only designates as "les autres" 'the others' (180). The use of the vague non-descriptive words "les autres" to refer to the indigenous children betrays an awareness, even if vague, of the colonial divide accompanied by a refusal to acknowledge who these "others" were. Cixous' story strongly contradicts that myth of harmony (more on that particular piece later).

While the juxtaposition of short stories emphasizes the plurality of perspectives, this collection overall glosses over the brutalities of colonialism in two ways: by humor, or by emphasizing subsequent violence. In "Mes enfances exotiques" 'my exotic childhood,' Alloula mentions the colonial situation in passing, when he locates the story in his "village colonial de l'Oranie" 'colonial village of Oran' (11, de Jager 5), and talks about "la population européenne" 'the European population (19, de Jager 12). The metaphor that compares the French school to a guillotine using the words "billots" 'chopping block,' "bourreau" 'tormentor,' and "calvaire" 'suffering' (10, de Jager 4-5) could be read as an indictment of the role played by the French school system in the colonies to further the imperial project, but it could also be applied to a non-colonial context, where children have to submit to a strictly enforced discipline. The story starts with the mention of a "loustic non scolarisé" 'uneducated kid' [not enrolled in school] (9, de Jager 3) and the obscenities he would yell to the children attending school through the classroom window. The French school is described as "ce lieu qui lui était inaccessible mais qu'il ne nous enviait pas" 'that place that was inaccessible to him, but which he did not envy us' (10, de Jager 4). In 1954, 90 percent of the colonized Algerian population was illiterate (Carlier 361, Naylor 8), and only one out of ten Muslim children was enrolled in elementary school. The word "inaccessible" is a euphemism, considering the fact that colonial policies did not make school accessible to all children, and that among numerous inequities, European children had priority over indigenous children (Stora, *Les trois exils* 66). In addition, that discrimination is tempered by the fact that the child was not eager to go to school. The focus of the story remains on the awakening to sexuality and the tone humoristic throughout, particularly in the skillful description loaded with poetic metaphors that accentuate the grotesque coupling of two adulterous villagers.

Another story in the same vein is Mohamed Kacimi-El-Hassani's "A la claire indépendance" 'By Independence Clear,' set at the beginning of the first school year after independence. The narrator and his friends cannot fathom why they are still being sent to the French school. Convinced that they are the only village in Algeria still under French colonization, they decide to skip school to assess the situation in the next village. The story highlights that colonialism has given way to a neocolonialism that is even harsher, subtly symbolized by the teacher's ruler, changed from wood to steel. The chorus of the French children's song "A la claire fontaine" 'by the fountain clear,' whose lyrics serve as a connecting thread throughout, close the story: "Il y a longtemps que je t'aime/ Jamais je ne t'oublierai" 'I've loved you for a long time And I shall never forget you' (de Jager 147). These lyrics emphasize the long lasting relationship fostered by colonialism and forecast that, as Naylor pointed out, "the referendum [for independence] marked a reformulation rather than a repudiation of the relationship between the metropolitan power and the ex-colony" (1), where the colonizer was replaced by the *coopérant*. Despite the strong vocabulary used to describe the school routine, where corporeal punishment seems to be an integral part of the curriculum and the teacher is compared to an executioner, the tone of the story is very light and humoristic thanks to the naïve point of view of the child.

Likewise Mohammed Dib's story, where his encounters with foreigners are all positive: the Greek doctor who saved his leg, his French teacher, and the French language which was to become his language of literary writing. The ironic allusion to the Eurocentric curriculum of the school he will attend is made in the context of the Greek doctor and therefore removed from the otherwise positive portrayal of his French school experience: "Celui-ci ne descendait pas de ces Gaulois dont je saurai plus tard, à l'école, qu'ils étaient mes ancêtres" 'He was not a descendant of the Gauls who, as I later learned at school, were my ancestors' (118, de Jager 106).

The second means by which the narratives downplay the impact of colonization is by emphasizing violence in the post 1962 era. Even the few stories that mention the brutality of colonialism fit into the pattern of lessening the blame through mentioning violence committed after Independence, thereby relativizing the colonial brutality to subsequent events. Kacimi-El-Hassani alludes to post-independence internal violence when he mentions that Ben Bella, the first Algerian president, killed Colonel Chaâbani, after the latter led an insurrection against him. The war of Independence was multifaceted: a war of Independence waged by Algerians against France, a Franco-French civil war about the fate of French Algeria, and an Algero-Algerian civil war over the leadership of the Independence movement (Stora, "1999-2003" 507). In *Une enfance algérienne* however, only the Franco-Algerian (with emphasis on the Algerian) and the Algero-Algerian dimensions appear.

Farès points out the discrimination and violence perpetuated by different parties at different times: from the banning of indigenous children from school in 1940 and their continued discrimination even after they are readmitted to school once WWII was over, to the civil war that targeted Francophone secular intellectuals. There are explicit parallels drawn between the internal strife following the capitulation of France and the Vichy government, and the events of the 1990s. In a very dense passage, Farès alludes to some of the pivotal moments in Algerian history:

> A chaque crise, répondent les fantasia et les grandes manœuvres militaires, en septembre, au sud du village de Berrouaghia: fin du nazisme, en Europe; refus de la subtile émancipation politique, en Algérie; l'est du pays déjà flambe; le sud se met en ligne sur la longue piste des chevaux! Deux fois les chars: la première en 1947 à l'inauguration—mauvais augure—des grandes manœuvres de la guerre.
> La seconde en 1962, lors des charniers de Boumediene. (136)
> With each crisis, cavalcades and huge military maneuvers respond, in September to the south of the village of Berrouaghia: the end of Nazism in Europe; refusal of fragile political emancipation in Algeria; the East of the country is already in flames; the South lines up on the long road of horses! Tanks twice: the first time in 1947 at the inauguration—a bad omen!—of the great war maneuvers.
> The second in 1962 at the time of Boumedienne's mass graves. (de Jager 123-24)

The defeat of Hitler in 1945 is juxtaposed with an indirect allusion to the 1945 riots (most commonly known as the Sétif riots) that shook the country when nationalist demands were brutally suppressed. While Farès' style is reputed for being difficult and obtuse, in this passage the allusions to internal postcolonial Algerian violence carried out by Boumedienne are more clearly identified than those committed by the colonial authority. 1947, for instance, is the year of the law giving more representation to Muslim Algerians. The Berrouaghia prison is mentioned twice in the story (136, 141). This prison was founded by the French where they incarcerated revolutionaries; it has kept this function post-independence and has housed leaders of the Berber Spring[20] and FIS members. In November 1994, Islamist prisoners died there in suspect circumstances (that could not be investigated because of censorship by the authorities, which claimed that prisoners were trying to escape or caused a mutiny).

Jean-Pierre Millecam revisits his childhood as the Eden before the original sin, from the point of view of the child, but as a grown-up narrator he knows that "la faute avait été commise quelque cent ans plus tôt" 'the sin had been committed some hundred years before' (181, de Jager 167). Colonialism compared to the original sin forecasts the demise of French Algeria, and the flooding of a town announces the fascism that will sweep his town. The conscription of indigenous soldiers sent to Europe as a "chair à canon" 'cannon fodder' (188, de Jager 173) is denounced. WWII, the Algerian war, and the civil war as a continuation of it are compared to apocalypses (188). The religious reference of the title, and the quotation from the Bible ("dans la cuve de la colère divine" 'in the vat of divine wrath' 182, de Jager 168) taken from Revelation 14:19, downplay human agency in historical processes.

Sebbar's story, dedicated to her parents who were both teachers, touches on her ambivalence about the role of teachers in the colonial project. The two violent incidents that are recalled in the story are chosen because they target teach-ers, and are committed by Algerians who are trying to put an end to the colonial domination. Sebbar intertwines a memory she has of hearing her parents talk about teachers being killed, with her research in library archives trying to find more information about these incidents. Describing a newly arrived couple of teachers who were killed on the first day of the war of independence, Sebbar asks: "Ils ne savent pas que c'est la Colonie et sa langue qu'ils viennent servir, sur ces Hauts Plateaux étrangers, hostiles et beaux?" 'Don't they know they've come to serve the colony and its language, there on the foreign High Plateaus, hostile and beautiful?' (212, de Jager 195). By describing them as having "la candeur curieuse des enfants de la République" 'the curious candor of children of the French Republic' (212, de Jager 196), she tilts the balance to their inno-cence and naivety regarding the role they play, as teachers, in furthering the do-mination of the settlers' culture. The focus on teachers, together with the men-tion of burnt libraries (208), puts the emphasis on repositories of knowledge that are targeted during the war. The other incident that Sebbar discovers in archives took place in 1901, when rebellious villagers threatened a teacher. In the context of the publication of the book, the physical violence French teachers are victims of in this story will likely evoke the targeting of indigenous (Francophone) intel-lectuals during the civil war.

Two stories offer a striking counterpoint about the depiction of the relations between Muslims and Jews in Algeria. Albert Bensoussan's "L'enfant perdu" 'The Lost Child' and Hélène Cixous' "Pieds nus" 'Bare Feet' happen to follow one another by chance, since the narratives appear according to the alphabetical order of their author. Although both narratives have in common the narration of an encounter between a Muslim and a Jewish child, they could not be more dis-similar: positive and nostalgic for Bensoussan, who fondly recalls how he met and lost his friend Fatiha, and negative for Cixous, who was implicitly reminded of her privileged status, despite the abrogation by the Vichy government of the Crémieux decree granting citizenship to all Jews, during an encounter with a shoe shine boy. Both stories take place in 1941, a year that is specified in Cix-ous' piece, and that can be implied from Bensoussan's story. I contrast both sto-ries, and analyze the implication of Cixous' casting of the Arab shoe shiner boy, who belonged to the most disenfranchised group during colonial Algeria, into an aggressor and symbolic murderer of the little Jewish girl that she was, when he put red shoe polish on her white sandals. A detailed analysis of "Pieds nus" shows that the contemporary conditions of its writing distort what was the actual reality on the ground for Algerian Jews and their relationship with Muslims, thereby fueling stereotypes of Arab-Muslim hatred for Jews.

"L'enfant perdu" tells the story of the friendship between the narrator, a six-year old Jewish boy, and a Muslim girl, Fatiha, and its abrupt ending. After Al-bert gets lost while shopping in the market with his mother, he is found by an Arab man, who takes him home, where his daughter Fatiha takes care of him until his family is contacted. Thereafter, his mother drops him off at Fatiha's house every Thursday for about three years while she goes shopping. Bensoussan fondly recalls the games played with Fatiha. Suddenly, he was no longer taken to Fatiha's house, without really knowing why. It is only years later that he understood that as she had reached puberty, Fatiha could no longer play with a boy.

The title of the story is polysemic. It refers to Bensoussan as the lost child in the market, and evokes the distance between the narrator and his childhood, many years behind him.[21] The emotion felt by the loss of his friend is poignantly expressed by the narrator in an apostrophe: "Fatiha, mon amie, qu'étais-tu devenue?" 'what became of you, Fatiha, my friend?' (52, de Jager 46). Bensoussan's nostalgic tone can be read in two different ways. On the one hand, it can be seen as nostalgia for life prior to what Stora has called the first of three exiles experienced by Algerian Jews. Stora has detailed how the 1870 Crémieux decree, which gave the French citizenship to indigenous Jews, triggered the gradual assimilation of the Jewish community with the European community in Algeria,[22] and therefore its separation from the Muslim population. This entailed a gradual loss of Arabic (Les trois exils 13). In the story, Albert's mother speaks Arabic, but he does not, and it is in French that he communicates with Fatiha. The process of Frenchification and assimilation of Algerian Jews to French culture is evident in some of the linguistic choices between the two generations of the mother and the child: the narrator's mother uses the Arabic term "Roumis" to designate Christians, as Arabs do, but the son uses the word "communion"— pointing out "comme on disait, pour bien dire" 'as they said to put it nicely' (52, de Jager 45)—to talk about what must have been his bar-mitzvah. What separates the two friends is not their different religious background nor the disconnect that took place between the two groups as a consequence of the Crémieux decree, but gender relations as defined by Muslim Arab culture. Calling Fatiha's family his "famille arabe" 'Arab family' (51), Bensoussan's text seems to endeavor to recapture the time when there were still bonds between the two communities.

Bensoussan's story can also be seen as partaking in the nostalgia that is symptomatic of the "desire to create and hold on to a memory, to recapture the world that was lost, existing prior to the fall of 'Algérie française,' French Algeria" (William Cohen 129). William Cohen states that, with a few exceptions, "What is striking about the many novels and memoirs on French Algeria is the absence in them of any account of strife between Europeans and Muslims. It is as if memories of such incidents had been repressed" (William Cohen 132).[23] Bensoussan's piece fits perfectly in that category. Stora specifies that after the 1962 exile,[24] it was not until the 1990s that Algerian Jews began making a distinction between themselves and the pied-noir community (Stora, Les trois exils 9, see also "L'impossible" 289). Once Algerian Jews abandoned a pied-noir identity, they were no longer interested in furthering the myth of a French Algeria where the three monotheist communities lived in perfect harmony (William Cohen 136). One can see that change reflected in Cixous' "Pieds nus," albeit in a problematic way.

Cixous' story starts with a description of her native city of Oran. References to two different worlds are sprinkled throughout the narrative; it is not always clear for the child what exactly those two worlds are (60, 62), but the divide created by colonization is clear. Colonial Oran is described in negative terms as a sick body, where hatred predominates: "Le corps d'Oran . . . était un corps politique, tuméfié, articulations enflammées, un monstre peuple, les bouches haletantes les langues chargées de glaviots prêtes à se les cracher au visage, les genoux boursouflés, les gorges grosses d'arrière-pensées, à soi-même étranger, étrangers, furieux" 'Oran's body . . . was a political body, swollen, limbs inflamed, a monster people, mouths gasping tongues laden with gobs of saliva ready to be spit in each other's faces, puffy knees, throats thick with afterthoughts, strangers to themselves, foreign, furious' (62, de Jager 55-56).

Cixous fondly recalls the Sundays her family spent on the mountain (which stands as a sharp contrast with the city) as a happy time:

> On renouait plaisamment avec les morts. C'était des maures qui dormaient familièrement tout au long du flanc de la montagne, à peine recouverts d'un pan herbu et sur la tête une jolie mosaïque aux couleurs vives. On marchait entre eux sur eux on s'asseyait avec eux, c'était bon, cet accompagnement hospitalier, jamais plus tard je ne retrouverai cette congénialité paisible, ce partage de la terre, cet acquiescement. (58)
>
> One reconnected pleasantly with the dead. It was the Moors who slept informally all along the side of the mountain, barely covered with a grassy patch and a pretty, brightly colored mosaic on their head. We would walk between them, on them, we'd sit down with them, and it was good, this hospitable company; never again did I find that peaceful congeniality later on, that sharing of the earth, that acquiescence. (de Jager 51-52)

Nicholas Harrison notes that the choice of the word "maures" 'Moors' and its assonance with "morts" 'deads' translates "a child's confusion at much of what she hears," and that it "may carry positive connotations," since it evokes the Golden Andalusian age, when Muslims, Jews, and Christians lived in peace and contributed to a vibrant culture (24). In keeping with Cixous' description of the city as unharmonious, I propose a radically different interpretation of this paragraph: the play on the homonymy between "morts" and "maures" emphasizes the fact that the only time she and her family enjoy peaceful relations with the Arabs is when the latter are dead, and, to continue on the allusion to the Andalusian era, that the time of peaceful coexistence is long gone.

After the abrogation of the Crémieux decree by the Vichy government stripped Algerian Jews of their French citizenship, the little girl that she was felt relieved of her guilt, as she considered that she no longer belonged to the oppressive side (63). Her father, who was forbidden to practice as a doctor, was forced to become a chiropodist. A clever play on the homonyms "corps" 'body' and "cor" 'corn' highlights the absurdity of the *numerus clausus*[25] that was imposed on professional Jews: "Pour survivre mon père se fit pédicure. Je ne sais pas pourquoi Vichy qui lui ôtait le soin des corps lui avait cependant abandonné les cors aux pieds" 'In order to survive, my father became a pedicure. I don't know why Vichy, which had taken the care of bodies away from him, still left him the care of corns' (62-63, de Jager 56).

Cixous likens her new status of outcast to the sensation of being barefoot when she walks on the mountain between the Muslim graves: "Que nous fussions parias cela obscurément me soulageait, comme d'être vrais, comme d'être pieds nus sur le chemin des Planteurs parmi les tombes" 'That we were pariahs consoled me in an obscure way, like true beings [like being true], like barefoot beings [like being barefoot] on the path of the Planters among the tombs' (62, de Jager 56). The motif of walking barefoot in the mountain suggests an organic link with the land. On the mountain, she feels a kinship with the "maures/morts" through her bare feet ("En grimpant j'ôtais mes sandales et je mettais mes pieds dans les mains des morts, et je caressais l'empreinte de leurs pieds avec les paumes de mes pieds" 'Clambering up I would take off my sandals and put my feet in the hands of the dead, and I'd caress the imprint of their feet with the soles of my own' (59, de Jager 53). The indigenous of the city (those who are alive) are portrayed as anchored in the ground ("encore inséparés de la terre et des pavés" 'not yet separated from the earth and the pavement' 61, de Jager 55) to denote their belonging to Algerian soil. According to Stora, the abrogation of the Crémieux Decree marks the second exile of Algerian Jews, this time not from the Muslim natives, but from the French Republic to which they had assimilated (*Les trois exils* 13). Cixous' take on the abrogation of the Crémieux Decree is unique, as she first presents it as a (short-lived) hope for reversing that first exile. No other Algerian Jewish writer, to the best of my knowledge, had anything positive to say about being stripped of their French citizenship.

After someone donates to her a brand new pair of sandals, she is reminded that she still enjoys class privileges when an Arab shoeshine boy smears her white sandals with red shoe polish. Their encounter is presented as a rehearsal for the play that will be staged on the scene of independent Algeria (64). The scene is compared to a trial: "J'avouai. J'étais coupable. Devant son tribunal à lui, l'acquittement dont je jouissais à mes yeux depuis Vichy n'avait aucune valeur. J'habitais rue Philippe au deuxième étage et j'avais des sandales données à l'état neuf" 'I confessed. I was guilty. Before his tribunal, the acquittal I had enjoyed since Vichy was of no value whatsoever. I lived in the rue Philippe on the second floor, and I had been given sandals that were almost entirely new' (65, de Jager 58). Ronnie Scharfman has argued that "by foregrounding the suffering implied by their exclusion, as Jews, between 1940 and 1943, from an already problematic French identity, both writers [Cixous and Derrida] effect an identification with contemporary Algeria from which they were excluded, paradoxically and painfully, when they lived there as children and were perceived by the Arabs and Berbers as part of the French colonial regime" ("Cixous" 89). Indeed, in the Manichean colonial order, there is no conceptual place for the status of Algerian Jews as both insiders and outsiders. But Scharfman does not comment on the fact that the little girl is aware that she has been on the oppressive side of the colonial divide, and that this knowledge gives her a guilty conscience that is at the core of the story. The focus on the sandals emphasizes class over ethnicity; it is because the sandals seem to indicate a privileged status that the shoe shiner associates her with the colonizer. However, some statements suggest that the Arab boy identifies her as being Jewish, such as the sentence quoted above in which she states that her new status since Vichy did not make a difference to him, and later on when she states: "Nous savions tout" 'we knew everything' (65, de Jager 58).

While esthetically Cixous' story is undoubtedly a masterpiece, the roles she attributes to the children are problematic in light of historical evidence. The red polish on her sandals is compared to blood (66), this act is for her a symbolic murder with a double edge: anti-colonial and gendered. On the one hand, the violence she is subjected to forecasts the Jews' exile from Algeria after the war of independence. During the narration of this encounter, she sees herself and the shoe shine boy as suddenly becoming adults. This helps to blur the time between 1941, when the scene is set, and when the independence war will be fought. By being cast as a rehearsal for what will unfold during the war for independence, the scene does anticipate some of the attacks that were committed by the FLN against Jews during the war for Independence to push them to side with the Algerians' cause, but it posits the Arab child as the sole embodiment of anti-Semitic violence (even if only symbolic) since the text is mute about violence committed at the time by Europeans (including the future OAS).[26]

Waves of European anti-Semitism, in the 1890s and 1930s, did not spare Algeria (Stora, Les trois exils 58-59). The Crémieux Decree was vehemently opposed by some pieds-noirs, who considered it as putting natives on the same footing with Europeans. Although anti-Semitism among the European population of Algeria was strong, it is occulted in Cixous' story. Indeed, the discriminatory measures of the Vichy government were overzealously applied in Algeria, where the oppression of Jews during WWII was in some aspects worse than in France, and this despite the fact that there was no German occupation in Algeria (Stora, Les trois exils 87). To top it all, the abrogation of the Crémieux decree was belatedly reversed in 1943, almost a year after the Allied controlled North Africa (Stora, "L'impossible" 294). Given that Stora credits the Muslim population for not committing any hostile act against the Jews during the WWII period ("L'impossible" 295, 303), Cixous' story goes against the historical record. By casting the Arab boy murdering the Jewish girl, Cixous lends credence to one of the anti-Semites' arguments for repealing the Crémieux decree: that it was causing resentment against France in the Muslim population (Stora, Les trois exils 79), although Stora points out that Muslim leaders did not fall into the trap that tried to antagonize both communities (Les trois exils 79, 97). I surmise that the culpability that Cixous feels for having been on the privileged side is assuaged by her casting the boy as a would-be murderer that forecasts the exile of the Jewish and French communities from Algeria, as well as other developments of Algerian history, particularly gender discrimination in post-independence Algeria (with the 1984 Family Code, and attacks targeting women during the civil war).

In addition to the colonial dimension, this scene could also be interpreted as defloration, since there is a glimpse of desire in the boy's eyes, and a symbolic loss of innocence for the child. The gender issue is more obvious in "Mon algériance," at the beginning of which Cixous recalls one image present in "Pieds nus," albeit with a slightly different formulation: she knew that the Arabs were the "true" indigenous people of Algeria, and her unease would vanish when she walked bare feet on their graves (71).[27] She recalls how she unsuccessfully tried to befriend the three Muslim girls that attended her high school class during 1951-1953,[28] and therefore explains her surprise when Algeria came back to her decades later through her friendship with Algerian women exiled in France to escape the atrocities of the civil war (74). Several paragraphs later, she implicitly refers to the violence committed against women in postcolonial Algeria, and labels Algeria "ennemie des femmes" 'enemy of women' (74, Prenowitz 172).

In "My Algériance," Cixous decries and elaborates on the violence of colonialism (and particularly the Arabs' dispossession) as well as the French population's anti-Semitism,[29] but this is passed over in "Pieds nus." In the context in which "Pieds nus" appeared, and with the historical shifts within the story, the shoe shine boy embodies the oppressive Algerian man, be it the FLN militants who will chase the pieds-noirs out of independent Algeria, or the extremists (religious and nationalist) who will chase women out of public space. The *hic et nunc* of the narration of the anecdote projects an anachronistic rendering that skews the historical reality. In addition, the fact that Cixous' ethnicity is foregrounded in the narrative will color its reading, as any story involving a Jew and an Arab read from an end of the twentieth-century's standpoint is inevitably colored by the legacy of the Arab-Israeli conflict.

Unlike the war of independence, none of the writers' childhoods unfolded during the civil war, and yet the 1990s events lurk in some stories. One can object to the mention of the 1990s' civil war because these events are anachronistic to the stories about the authors' childhoods, which for all of them ended well before the last decade of the twentieth century. However, autobiographical writing implies a narrator grounded in the present of narration, with a distance that allows some perspective on the events of one's life. As Philippe Lejeune has pointed out, the "I" of an autobiographical narrative is multiple: the one of the child at the time of the event, and the one of the narrator at the time the story is told. Therefore, given the time during which these stories were commissioned, it seems understandable, at the very least, that the tragedy of the 1990s surfaces here and there.

Jamel Eddine Bencheikh's "Tlemcen la haute" is a series of vignettes told in a stream of consciousness from the author's recollection of the summers he used to spend in his parents' native town, that also pays tribute to Arab and Tlemcenian poets and artists. The only mention of violence relates to the civil war. The last page is presented as reality that turned into a nightmare the author wishes to wake up from. The blurring between reality and nightmare emphasizes the horrendousness of the situation, and that Tlemcen is unrecognizable because of it. The descriptions of women veiled in black (instead of the traditional white North African veil) and men sporting Afghani clothing and beards, signal an imported fundamentalism that has been gaining ground. The murders of singers and writers (Alloula, Cheb Hasni, and Djaout) are put in line with Ibn Khamis', a thirteenth-century poet from Tlemcen exiled in Granada where he was assassinated, because of disagreements with the powers in place.

Nabile Farès' story talks about various wars, and his last page picks up the issue of continuity between the war of independence with its internal strife between various factions and the 1990s' civil war. The narrator says that it is either another war, or that the first one in fact never ended, that "il est *encore* question de démocratie" 'it is *still* a question of democracy' (141, de Jager 127). Some historians see the origin of the 1990s' war as going back to unresolved issues from the war of Independence (Harbi, "L'Algérie" 43) or before. Stora lists the similarities between the two wars, but is quick to add the differences and underlines that the latter weighs more than the former, and that "ce qui rapproche surtout cette 'seconde' guerre d'Algérie de la 'première', c'est la *persistence des préjugés et des stéréotypes* qui ont fabriqué une mémoire de la guerre d'Algérie en France" 'what brings this second war closer to the first Algerian war is the persistence of prejudice and stereotypes that made a memory of the Algerian war in France' (*La guerre* 65). Omar Carlier insists that the extreme violence that took place during these years is not due to a historical determinism ruling Algeria, but to specific historical processes (379). Similarly, Stora repeatedly warns that a comparison between the war of independence and the civil war reinforces the stereotype of Algeria as a country plagued by a never-ending violence (*La guerre* 10, 52, 56).

In a humorous postscript, Farès imagines what his mother, who used to wash the nationalist militants' clothes, would do with the current insurgents (which would be to boil the men rather than their clothes). He is silent about the series of events that brought about the war. All direct and indirect references to the civil war in the collection blame the Islamists for the violence that has swept the country, although historians have singled out events during which violence emanated from the state, not the Islamists, as catalysts. For instance, although Stora stresses that it is hard to pinpoint the beginning of the civil war, he identifies several moments as possible starting points: the October 1988 riots, the cancellation of the second round of the January 1992 elections,[30] and the murder of president Boudiaf in June 1992 (*La guerre* 15-17). Martinez refutes the economic and religious factors as satisfactory explanations for the level of violence during the civil war and singles out "the failure of democratic transition" ("Why the Violence" 16-17). He assessed that the violence was a "product of the cancellation of the December 1991 legislative elections and the policy of repression conducted from 1992 to 1994" ("Why the Violence" 22), these being committed by the military-controlled state.

The consequences of some of the colonial policies that sustained the dominance of the European minority over the Algerian majority (such as massive land expropriations, the "Code de l'Indigénat," occultation of the indigenous culture,

the status of Arabic as a foreign language) surface here and there, but the policies are not subjected to criticism, nor are their effects on the Algerian population presented as direct consequences of institutionalized discrimination and
violence. The poverty of the Algerians, which characterized the overwhelming
majority (Carlier 361), is not saliant at all. Habib Tengour seems to be the person whose direct family suffered the most from the colonial yoke. His indigence
becomes obvious when he mentions having to skip school when his grandfather
could not afford a pair of cheap shoes. We learn that his father, a nationalist, was
imprisoned and tortured by the French, but that is mentioned in passing in the
space of one sentence. The emphasis of the story is on fostering relationships
with others, and on knowing people as the best means to dissipate erroneous
stereotypes, such as his grandfather's friendship with settlers despite political
problems, and his own friendship with a Jewish family that dispels prejudices
conveyed in popular culture.

One could object that people's lives were not solely determined by the colonial situation, and that in a short piece writers cannot possibly render all aspects of their childhood. Moreover, since they were children at the time, they
might not have been fully aware of the gravity of some situations. Some of the
Arab authors belonged to the upper class (such as Fatima Gallaire as indicated
by the number of servants), and their class privilege mitigated their status of
colonial subject. The writers of this collection represent the various groups that
peopled colonial Algeria, yet some escape easy cataloguing, since some, such as
Sebbar, are the product of mixed marriages. Alain Vircondelet talks about the
atrocities of the war of independence (231) and victims on both sides. The child
of a Frenchman and an Algerian woman, he takes the side of Algerians (234).
To their credit, some of the criticism of colonialism comes from Europeans,
even if belatedly. This compilation of short stories by different authors could
very well have been called "Enfances algériennes" 'Algerian Childhoods' with
the plural emphasizing the diversity. The choice of a singular title for the collection signals a desire to emphasize what binds these people together.

While the collection seems to be representative of the diversity of the
people who lived in Algeria between the 1920s and the 1960s, it is actually de-
ceptive in that it is limited to writers who express themselves in French. Given
the high rate of illiteracy when the country became independent (at least 80 percent), these writers, schooled in French, can only be the voice of a small minority. As such, *Une enfance algérienne* is emblematic of the limitations of the field
of Francophone Literature.

This book was published right before the beginning of the end of amnesia,
with 1999 as the key date according to Stora since this is when the French government formally acknowledged that the Algerian "events" indeed constituted a
war, as well as the publications of articles and books by victims of torture and
torturers ("1999-2003" 502). Sebbar's collection is still situated at a time when
the Algerian war is still not fully dealt with by collective memory. Nevertheless,
I contend that the context in which this collection was published makes it an
important issue. Farid Laroussi points out that many books by Algerian women

about the desperate conditions of women in Algeria were published in the 1990s, in which "The sociopolitical situation in Algeria rightly comes under attack but only as a way to reassert France's own representation as a land of Enlightenment" (88). My analysis of *Une enfance algérienne* shows that this process seems to be at play here as well, where past French exactions are minimized to better emphasize Algerian violence (past and present), thereby fueling stereotypes of Arab-Muslim violence, and hatred for Jews in the case of Cixous' story. Stora notes that a plethora of images showing the atrocities committed by Islamist groups in the media, coupled with the absence of images showing the suffering caused by the government's exactions puts all the focus and the blame on the Islamists while dispensing with a critical reflection on the origins of the conflict (*La guerre* 82). As demonstrated by this collection of short stories and the essays analyzed in the previous section, I argue that Francophone writers have contributed to this phenomenon through their writings. The context in which this collection was published as well as the implications of the civil war's intrusion in narratives taking place before the 1990s adds to the simplistic rendering of the civil war, blamed solely on Islamists, all conveniently lumped into a homogeneous, dangerous, and threatening mass to be eradicated at all cost, all the while being mute on the role played by other elements, as well as history itself.

Recent cinematic production, such as Nadir Moknèche's *Viva Laldjérie*, has questioned the simplistic view of Islamic fundamentalism as being the sole responsible agent of violence during the Algerian civil war. As Sylvie Durmelat points out, the only murder in the film is committed by a high ranking member of the State's security forces, thus suggesting that "les terroristes ne sont pas ceux que l'on croit" 'the terrorists are not who we think' ("L'Algérie" 110). It is significant that since 1992, no leader has repelled the Family code (Stora, *La guerre* 64). Therefore, the Islamists are not the ones (or at least not the only ones) to oppress women, though they are (conveniently) blamed for Algeria's woes and the status of women there in particular.

Notes

1. This summary of events is based on Kepel's chapter "Algérie: les années FIS" in *Jihad* (166-82). For more detailed studies, see Martinez, Volpi, and Willis.

2. This relationship has been rendered by Etienne Balibar as the following numerical equation: that France and Algeria are neither one nor two nations, but that "l'Algérie et la France, prises ensemble, ne font pas deux, mais quelque chose comme *un et demi*, comme si chacune d'entre elles, dans leur addition, contribuait toujours déjà pour une part de l'autre" 'Algeria and France, put together, do not make two, but something in the order of *one and a half*, as if each one, when added together, always already contributed to part of the other' (76).

3. See Naylor for a detailed study of complex hydrocarbons contracts between France and Algeria after independence that shows a "privileged French economic posi-

tion in Algeria's development plans" (145), and Aït-Embarek (120-30) about the economic support and pressure of France and the European union for the junta during the civil war.

4. Many saw this as a lesser evil despite the contradiction of having to resort to authoritarian measures to "save" democracy (that Algeria was a democracy is highly contestable, given the status of the FLN as sole political party until 1989). Layachi notes that "people's growing apathy toward the political process" as evident in the 2002 elections does not foster democracy and seems to indicate little progress (61). There were "eradicators" and "conciliators" on both sides of the Mediterranean (Naylor 210).

5. "Dans le subconscient collectif et populaire, il y avait quelque chose de rageur et de pervers dans cette façon de faire surchauffer les statistiques de la natalité galopante" 'in the collective and popular subconscious, there was something furious and perverse in this way of overheating the statistics of runaway natality' (59).

6. Willis stresses that "even the most competent of local authorities (let alone totally inexperienced ones like those of the FIS) could [not] be expected to make an impact in the shorter term" (160).

7. While Boudjedra castigates the FIS leaders for their ignorance, he himself demonstrates some lacunae, such as stating that the Qur'an is composed of 60 suras instead of 114 (12).

8. In their study of the pronouncements of *El Mounquid*, official journal of the FIS, on women, Imache and Nour found that the party asserts women's rights to schooling, inheritance, vote, jihad, and work—although the latter comes with restrictions (45-46).

9. The FIS claimed a filiation with the FLN's ideology, while criticizing the party for deviating from it (Kepel, *Jihad* 177). In a footnote, Kepel recalls Lahouari Addi's statement that "le FLN est le père du FIS," playing on the homonymy between FIS and "fils" ('son') in French, interpreting it in two ways: that the FIS situates itself in the FLN's ideology, but also that they share the same view of a totalitarian, monolithic society (Kepel, *Jihad* note 26 p.391).

10. It will later be revealed that some of these atrocities were committed by government forces but attributed to Islamic groups to better discredit them (Burgat 278 and note 19 p.319), and others were due to the government's infiltration and manipulation of the GIA (Burgat 327, Volpi 90).

11. "Il n'arrête pas de manier l'intox" 'he keeps on using propaganda' (Boudjedra 1994: 116).

12. "Since its transformation into a political force in the 1980s, the Islamist movement has constituted a wide and heterogeneous phenomenon with three main fronts: a cultural front aiming at the 're-Islamisation' of society; a non-violent political front acting inside or outside of the system for gradual, peaceful and comprehensive change; and a violent political front aiming at bringing down the regime by force and at instituting a rigid Islamic order" (Layachi 53). See Layachi (54-56) for more details on the various Algerian Islamist organizations; the FIS is listed under the non-violent Islamist organizations.

13. "In its essence, populist Islam speaks to the millions of men and women in the MENA who feel marginalized, alienated and abused by their rulers. . . . Whether through religious instruction, education and tutoring, social services, welfare functions, emergency assistance or associational activity, Islamism has come to fulfill basic needs in society that the state has been increasingly ignoring or economically unable to sustain" (Entelis 207).

14. Willis has stressed the absence of a third unified alternative to the FIS and the FLN because numerous secular political parties ended up fragmenting this opposition (152-53).

15. This is also acknowledged by Layachi (59).

16. Boudjedra sees Algerian women wearing the veil and fighting against fundamentalism as a contradiction, because modernity is to be taken whole or not at all (85), thereby perpetuating stereotypes about covered Muslim women that I will discuss at length in chapter five. Similarly, Mimouni has a very simplistic view of the hijab (49).

17. Other autobiographical collections edited by Sebbar include *C'était leur France* and *Mon père*. I exclude them from the "trilogy" based on the titles, which do not follow the same format of "une enfance . . . " and do not put the emphasis on childhood.

18. Cohen also notes that the pieds-noirs, with very few exceptions, did not speak Arabic.

19. The last part of this sentence may allude to the fact that Christian clerics became targets and were murdered in Algeria starting in 1994 (Naylor 206).

20. The Berber Spring, a protest movement to claim recognition for the Berber language and culture, took place in 1980. It started when Mouloud Mammeri was prevented from giving a talk on ancient Berber poetry, and was severely repressed by the FLN.

21. In the English translation, it could also refer to Fatiha as the childhood friend he no longer sees by the end of the story (to refer to Fatiha in French there would need to be a silent "e" at the end of the adjective).

22. Stora interprets this event as a colonization of Algerian Judaism by French Judaism (292).

23. For an interesting account of how the pieds-noirs' memory and efforts to cultivate and bring their selective memory of French Algeria to the national level, through memorials, see William Cohen's article.

24. This complete assimilation made the Jews particularly attached to France, and made it impossible for most of them to support an Algeria divorced from France (Stora, "L'impossible" 303).

25. That law limited the number of Jews to small percentages in various fields (Stora, "L'impossible" 295). See Stora (*Les trois exils* 82-84) for more details.

26. This double violence is most "tragically symbolized by the well-publicized killings of William Lévy . . . by the OAS, and of his son by the FLN" (Naylor 44). Naylor adds that the FLN declared in 1961 "For the first time in History the Jews have been claimed—and by a government composed of followers of another religion—as the sons of one and the same country" (qtd. in Naylor, 44).

27. "Un autre sentiment dans l'ombre: la certitude jamais entamable que 'les Arabes' étaient les vrais rejetons de ce sol poussiéreux et parfumé. Mais quand je marchais pieds nus avec mon frère sur les chemins chauds d'Oran, je sentais la plante de mon corps caressée par les paumes accueillantes des anciens morts du pays, et le tourment de mon âme s'apaisait" (71) 'Another feeling in the shadows: the unshakeable certainty that 'the Arabs' were the true offspring of this dusty and perfumed soil. But when I walked barefoot with my brother on the hot trails of Oran, I felt the sole of my body caressed by the welcoming palms of the country's ancient dead, and the torment of my soul was assuaged' (126).

This and a reference to the abrogation of the Crémieux decree in 1940 are the only elements common between "Pieds nus" and the French version of "Mon algériance." However, as Harrison pointed out, the English translation of "Mon algériance" includes additions to the French original, including the section from "Pieds nus" that features the encounter with the shoe shine boy (note 10 p.30).

28. "Je sus immédiatement qu'elles étaient l'Algérie qui se préparait. Je leur tendais la main, je voulais faire alliance avec elles contre les Françaises. En vain. Pour elles j'étais la France" (74) "I knew immediately that they were the Algeria that was in store. I held out my hand to them, I wanted to ally myself with them against the French. In vain. For them I was France" (170).

29. "Two hates shared the hearts differently between themselves. One of them, which I will never forgive, the colonialists' hate, was made of the scorn from which thieves and usurpers, like all despots, forge deceitful arms. In response there was the other one, which I forgive, even until today, the hate with eyes burning with tears of the humiliated and deprived, the hate of the 'Arabs' for all that was collected in the 'F' [French] group" (162, this paragraph does not appear in the French original). But even in that text, when it comes to her personal experience in colonial Algeria, there is an over-emphasis on the fact that she wanted to be accepted and loved by the Arabs but was only met with hatred.

30. President Bouteflika admitted later on in July 1999 that the government was responsible for the origin of the civil war with the cancellation of these elections, which was a violent act (Stora, *La guerre* 19).

Chapter 5

Islam and the French Republic: The Affair of the Muslim Headscarf in works by Tahar Ben Jelloun, Abdelwahab Meddeb, Amin Maalouf, Albert Memmi, Leïla Sebbar, and Yamina Benguigui

In the second half of the twentieth century, metropolitan France has become home to a substantial, albeit invisible until the 1980s, Muslim minority, composed mostly of immigrant Maghrebian workers and their descendants confined to the outskirts of French society. The number of Muslims in France is notoriously elusive, and estimates range between three and a half and seven million, with five million as the most accepted estimate, for a total population of about sixty-one million. Although the inauguration of Paris' Great Mosque in 1920[1] would seem to give official recognition, at least symbolically, to the presence of Islam on French soil, its conception is entangled with French colonial history and its policy towards its Muslim subjects. The project was first conceived to strengthen France's power over its Muslim colonies, and then as a monument to honor Muslim soldiers who lost their lives for France during World War I (Kepel, *Les banlieues* 64-76). In fact, the Paris Great Mosque was not built to serve Muslims living in the capital, which numbered very few at the time (Kepel, *Les banlieues* 65).

In recent decades, the Muslim French have been struggling to gain acceptance by French society. The notorious "affaire du foulard," 'affair of the [Muslim] scarf,'[2] sparked in 1989 when three teenage girls were expelled from their public middle school for refusing to remove their headscarves, received much coverage from the media.[3] Similar incidents reoccurred over the years and culminated into the 2004 law that bans certain religious signs in public schools.[4] Similar affairs have broken out in other Western countries such as England, the United States, etc., but France stands out by the level of divisiveness, the length of time of the controversy, and the resort to legislation to solve it. Although the debate on the issue of the scarf was framed exclusively around the issue of secularism, with concerns over the equality of the sexes adding fuel to the fire, several scholars, including Christine Delphy, Saïd Bouamama, Gérard Noiriel, Pierre Bourdieu, Françoise Gaspard, and Farhad Khosrokhavar, have pointed out that what was really at stake was the issue of immigration, and, more specifically, the realization that a population that was considered foreign and composed of temporary immigrants had actually settled down and was there to stay.[5]

In addition to this heated domestic debate about the issue of the veil in public schools, Islam has been associated with distressing national and international headlines in the 1990s. France was the site of terrorist attacks in 1994 and 1995, carried out by the Algerian extremist GIA (Groupe Islamiste Armé "armed islamist group"). The debate over the headscarf affair in France was tainted by international news at a time when the rise of Islamic fundamentalism was regularly making headlines, more specifically during the time in question with the Algerian civil war that ravaged Algeria during the 1990s and the Taliban's government in Afghanistan, both with disastrous consequences, particularly for women.

Images have played an important role during the affair of the scarf. French magazine covers had the tendency to depict Islam as a women-oppressing fundamentalist religion (Gaspard and Khosrokhavar 31), by presenting pictures of veiled women (sometimes burqa style afghani) that most often than not had nothing to do with the scarf worn by the girls concerned. For example, on December 8, 1994, *Le nouvel observateur* featured a young woman whose head and face were covered, with the cloth molding the face to suggest gagging and suffocation, on the cover of a special issue on women and Islam.

These images contributed to blurring the difference between the French and foreign contexts, and made the veil a symbol of fanaticism, since pictures of veiled women often accompany articles that deal with fundamentalism in news magazines. Significantly, this so-called debate on secularism was triggered by the presence of a Muslim sign in what is supposed to be the gateway to integration, namely the public school. The French public school became the symbolic place where the various crises plaguing French society converged, including the crisis of the nation-state, for which the public education system is the spearhead (Gaspard and Khosrokhavar 40-41). John Bowen's comprehensive study has demonstrated that explaining the 2004 law on the prohibition of religious signs in public schools, which ended the affair,

> would require unpacking a great deal about France, including France's very particular history of religion and the state, the great hopes placed in the public schools, ideas about citizens and integration (and the challenge posed by Muslims and Islam to those ideas), the continued weight of the colonial past, the role of television in shaping public opinion, and the tendency to think that passing a law will resolve a social problem. (2)

As he (and others) noted, the issue of the veil in public schools became the symbol of what were seen as both internal and external threats to France, and its prohibition as an expedient to solve social problems of Islamism, sexism, and violence in the suburbs.

In *Intellectuals and Politics in Post-War France*, David Drake explains that French intellectuals were split over the affair of the scarf (176-82). His book does not include any Arab intellectual, although some of them (the most famous being Ben Jelloun) have been living and publishing in France for a long time, and did publish opinion pieces on the issue. Because of their status as privileged interpreters on anything linked to Arab-Muslim issues, their writings can influence and shape the terms of the debate. Indeed, Ben Jelloun and Sebbar published on the issue in newspapers, and Meddeb testified in front of a government-appointed commission.

This chapter examines how Arab writers who were living in France have presented the affair of the scarf in non-fiction writings. The writers treated are representative of the diversity of the Francophone Arab world with their various backgrounds (Muslim for Benguigui, Ben Jelloun, and Meddeb, Christian for Maalouf, Jewish for Memmi, secular for Sebbar; and Moroccan for Ben Jelloun, Franco-Algerian for Sebbar and Benguigui, Tunisian for Memmi and Meddeb, Lebanese for Maalouf). The headscarf affair split French public opinion, but not along lines determined by ethnic, gender, cultural, or religious backgrounds. It would be absurd to assume that just because these writers are Arabs (or of Muslim origin for some), they would side with the veiled girls.[6] However, it is fair to expect that because they have ties with countries with majority Muslim population, they might provide a better understanding of the problems faced by Muslims in France. In addition, since they have cogently addressed the devastating effects of colonialism and its role in shaping current events in parts of the Arab world in their writings (often by successfully presenting the point of view or plight of the colonized), one would hope that they could bring a fresh perspective that would enrich the debate. But as this chapter demonstrates, the opposite is the case. Despite such awareness of the legacies of the colonial era, they (with the exception of Benguigui) have failed in two notable ways: they did not help people understand the issue from the point of view of the girls concerned (which would have required depoliticizing the issue), and they did not prod French society to see its blind spots regarding secularism, which has framed the debate. The purpose of this chapter is not to redress the silencing of women.[7] Rather, the aim is to demonstrate that prominent Francophone authors limit their readers' understanding of the Muslim world, by refusing to come to terms with the challenge that women who choose to don Islamic garb poses to Western feminism and secular thought.

9/11 and the French Islamic Veil Affair in Essays: Tahar Ben Jelloun's *L'Islam expliqué aux enfants* and Abdelwahab Meddeb's *La maladie de l'islam*[8]

Ben Jelloun and Meddeb's essays are part of an effort to counter reductive representations of Islam that have been going on for decades, as Said demonstrated in *Covering Islam*. 9/11 has further exacerbated the association made in the Western media between Islam and terrorism. As a defining moment marking the turn of the century, 9/11 has not only impelled writers from the Francophone Arab world to respond creatively with fiction,[9] but also in essays. Ben Jelloun and Meddeb, of Moroccan and Tunisian origins, respectively, who have both been living in France for decades, published books in Paris in 2002 that use 9/11 as a point of departure for reflection on the Muslim faith. These essays are aimed at different readerships: Ben Jelloun's *L'Islam expliqué aux enfants* 'Islam explained to children'[10] is a slim, ninety-page book that targets ten- to fifteen-year-olds, while Meddeb's *La maladie de l'islam* 'The malady of Islam' is highly erudite. Both texts, however, share the similar intent and didactic function of countering reductive representations of Islam fostered by Islamic fundamentalists and the media, as well as explaining and historically tracing the link between terrorism and the Muslim faith.

It is worth noting that, in these essays, Ben Jelloun and Meddeb's first attempts to explain Islam to their fellow French citizens take 9/11, an attack on a foreign country,[11] as a point of departure when Islam, in fact, had been making domestic headlines well before 2001. How do these essays present the affair of the Muslim scarf that ignited such divisive debates and measures? Moreover, what are the implications of discussing Islam in general, and the affair of the scarf in France in the light of 9/11? How do these writers handle their pedagogical project given the French context of their publications? I will take up these questions focusing on the essays published in 2002 and Meddeb's *Face à l'islam* 'Facing Islam' (2004).

Ben Jelloun's *L'Islam expliqué aux enfants*

Ben Jelloun's essay is part of a series for youth published by the prestigious Parisian press Seuil, to which he already contributed *Le racisme expliqué à ma fille* "racism explained to my daughter" in 1998. The structure of *L'Islam expliqué aux enfants* is in accordance with the model of the series, following the format of questions and answers between a child and the author. This text differs from all other titles in the series in that instead of foregrounding a biological link with one child, it addresses all children. This suggests that contrary to the other books in the series, all addressed to "my daughter/son, my grand-children, or my children," Islam has to be made explicitly relevant to all children since it is not immediately perceived to be so in the way topics such as racism, the French Resistance, or Auschwitz are.[12]

The first chapter, entitled "Le 11 septembre expliqué aux enfants" '11 September explained to children' makes it clear that Ben Jelloun's daughter's reaction to the coverage of these attacks motivated the writing of the book. Ben Jelloun blames the media's amalgam between terrorists, Arabs, and Muslims for the confusion and denial experienced by his daughter, who refuses to be associated with her Arab and Muslim heritage (7). He then proceeds to tell the story of Islam as a fairy tale, beginning with the story of Mohammed, the five pillars, the Golden Age, and the contributions of Arabs to various fields of knowledge, all of which are interspersed with allusions or brief discussions of contemporary issues in international and domestic politics.

Keeping in mind that the target audience is identified by the author as children between the ages of ten and fifteen, it seems inevitable that such a book cannot engage in highly complex discussions of the various issues mentioned. But this limitation notwithstanding, Ben Jelloun also seems overly concerned to explain Islam, as well as colonization, and the affair of the scarf, in ways that will not alienate his intended readership. On several occasions, for instance, his assertions contradict mainstream Muslim views. It is the case with his interpretation of the word 'alaq as really meaning "sperm" (19).[13] In the same vein, his assessment that the Qur'an does not prescribe women's veiling (68-69) is in accordance with what a few scholars reinterpreting Islamic traditions have concluded,[14] but it is not widely accepted. Moreover, some of the recommendations issued by Ben Jelloun's father, and which he uses to discharge himself of the daily prayer requirements, are reminiscent of the Bible's Ten Commandments (12). They are therefore more intelligible to a readership coming mostly from a Judeo-Christian tradition, but they gloss over the fact that the daily prayers are one of the five pillars of Islam, and therefore cannot be avoided lightly, except in specific circumstances, none of which apply to Ben Jelloun.

Ben Jelloun's conciliatory efforts with its assumed French readership even leads to distortions in his account of the colonization of North Africa, which states that people revolted only decades after being colonized, and is inaccurate:

Ce qui a permis l'occupation de ces pays arabes et musulmans, c'est le déclin qu'ils connaissaient. C'est comme un corps malade qui ne peut pas se défendre et se voit envahi par d'autres maladies.
—Est-ce que les gens se sont révoltés?
—Oui, après quelques décennies, ils se sont réveillés. (71)
What made the occupation of these Arab and Muslim countries possible was their decline. It's like a sick body that cannot defend itself and is invaded by other diseases.
—Did people revolt?
—Yes, after a few decades, they woke up.

Ben Jelloun portrays the Arabs as very passive towards colonization, thus writing off resistance movements such as those led by Abdelkader in Algeria and

Abdelkrim in Morocco.[15] In *Le racisme expliqué à ma fille*, Ben Jelloun was noticeably more virulent about colonialism in general, and the French colonization in particular (48-49), thus the downplay of the effect of colonization in *L'Islam expliqué aux enfants* is all the more striking. A statement such as "les croisades sont un lointain souvenir, la colonisation aussi" 'the Crusades are a distant memory, so is colonization' (65), is certainly not the case in the French context at the turn of the twenty-first century, with France finally coming to "the end of amnesia," as the title of a book edited by historians Stora and Harbi puts it, about its colonial past and the war Algerians fought for independence.

Similarly, by shifting the blame to an unidentified entity—with the use of the indefinite subject pronoun "on" 'one'—to explain the rise of fundamentalism in Muslim countries, Ben Jelloun makes short shrift of the colonial legacy in this historical development:

> S'il y a parmi les musulmans des jeunes devenus violents et fanatiques, c'est que leur éducation a été mal faite, on les a laissés entre les mains de gens ignorants et sans scrupules. On n'a pas su ou voulu leur faire aimer le développement, la culture et la vie. On a laissé se développer la pauvreté et l'analphabétisme. On a eu peur de la liberté et on n'a rien fait contre la corruption et les injustices (*L'Islam* 65).
>
> If there are among Muslims young people who have become violent and fanatical, it is because their education was poorly done, they were left in the hands of uneducated and unscrupulous people. One was unable or unwilling to make them like development, culture, and life. One has let poverty and illiteracy develop. One was afraid of freedom and has not done anything against corruption and injustices.

This excessive generalization may be unavoidable because of the limited scope and intended reader, but it underestimates the role that Western nations, including France, have played in various parts of the Muslim world to fuel extremism. The use of the indefinite pronoun masks the fact that no nation exists in a vacuum and that former colonial power structures have been superseded by other, less obvious but no less damaging institutions and neocolonial politics.

By far, the most conciliatory pages of *L'Islam expliqué aux enfants* deal with the affair of the scarf. When Ben Jelloun insists that Muslims in France must respect the 1905 law on the separation of church and state, he brings up the affair of the veil.[16] He subscribes to the often repeated argument that religion should remain in the private realm (12). Many have said during the course of the debate (and indeed this is what was done in some schools) that girls had to take off their headscarves as soon as they entered school. As Rosello pointed out, in the framework of the Muslim faith and customs, this does not make sense (140), since a Muslim girl is only required to cover in the presence of unrelated men, which is not likely to be necessary in her home, unlike in public. In contrast to his 1984 book about French racism, in which he acted as an effective spokesperson responsible for explaining cultural issues to the French public, Ben Jelloun fails to point out the absurdity of the mandate from the point of view of an observant Muslim. Devout Muslim women would not concede to only veiling in the private realm.

In addition, his explanation of the consequences of the affair shows that like most accounts in the media, the veiled girls are never credited with any sense of agency in their decision to cover, despite solid evidence to the contrary: "certaines filles ont renoncé à porter le foulard. D'autres ont été retirées de l'école par leurs parents. Ils ont eu tort de les priver d'enseignement" 'some gave up wearing the scarf. Others were taken out of school by their parents. They were wrong to deprive them of an education' (67-68). Books such as Gaspard and Khoskhovar's, Dounia Bouzar and Saïda Kada's, and Alma and Lila Lévy's,[17] clearly dispelled the stereotype that the majority of French girls who wear the veil are coerced into doing so.[18] Although he later criticizes the custom of taking girls out of school once they have reached puberty in some Muslim communities (88) and sees the school as the place to start establishing gender equality in Islam, he never considers the consequences of denying an education to girls who refuse to take off their headscarves.[19]

Subsequently, Ben Jelloun states that "les musulmans de France ont la chance de vivre dans un pays démocratique qui leur garantit le droit de pratiquer librement leur religion" 'Muslims of France are lucky to live in a democratic country that guaranties them the right to practice their religion freely' (76). Needless to say that from the covered girls' point of view, their expulsion from school because they are dressed as they believe their religion mandates is hardly guaranteeing their right to practice.[20] Ben Jelloun's statement implies that the French Republic's principle is fully implemented, which is far from true. There is no mention here (nor elsewhere in the text) of the difficulties Muslims are encountering when trying to establish adequate infrastructure to accommodate their faith. For instance, obtaining building permits for mosques is notoriously difficult. Similarly, the French government refuses to use the Concordat,[21] still in place in Alsace-Moselle, to train imams,[22] which many recognize as essential to the development of a "French Islam." Failure to exploit well-established structures to the benefit of the French Muslim community is symptomatic of the denial to consider Islam as what it is: the second religion in France.

Meddeb's *La maladie de l'islam*

Meddeb's *La maladie de l'islam* is also inspired by the 9/11 attacks, which the author condemns in the very first sentence of the book. The book's title echoes Voltaire's writings, such as his *Traité sur la tolérance*, as acknowledged by Meddeb, but also his entry on "fanaticism" (which he sees as having sullied all religions) in *Dictionnaire philosophique*.[23] In contrast to Voltaire, Meddeb's title implies that Islam as a whole is subject to a disease intrinsic to it, as if fundamentalism was Islam's prerogative and other religions were immune to it. Indeed, Meddeb asserts: "Si le fanatisme fut la maladie du catholicisme, si le nazisme fut la maladie de l'Allemagne, il est sûr que l'intégrisme est la maladie de l'islam" 'if fanaticism was Catholicism's disease, if Nazism was Germany's disease, it is certain that fundamentalism is Islam's disease' (12).

Meddeb's book endeavors to trace the history and intellectual genealogy of Islamic fundamentalism. Although Meddeb acknowledges that there are internal and external reasons for Islamic fundamentalism, he justifies his focus on internal factors by stating:

> Il est du rôle de l'écrivain de pointer la dérive des siens et d'aider à leur ouvrir les yeux sur ce qui les aveugle. Je tiens, comme on dit, à commencer par balayer devant ma porte. Ce texte, écrit en français, sera lu par de nombreux lecteurs connaissant le français et concernés d'une manière ou d'une autre par le drame de leur origine islamique. Je m'adresse à tout lecteur, mais j'ai une pensée particulière pour les lecteurs qui, comme moi, se sont symboliquement constitués dans la croyance d'islam. (10)
> The writer's role is to point out his people's drift and to help open their eyes on what blinds them. I insist, as we say, in starting by sweeping in front of my door. This text, written in French, will be read by numerous readers who know French and who are concerned one way or another by the tragedy of their Islamic origin. I address any reader, but I have a special thought for readers who, like me, formed themselves symbolically in Islam's belief.

Meddeb's personal experience of being a Muslim in France might have been tragic, but extending his subjective experience to the whole Muslim population in France without addressing the socio-political context tags Islam negatively without proper justification. When Meddeb talks about "sweeping in front of his door," he positions himself as part of the Muslim world, since his book expressly focuses on problems within Islam. Although the quote above shows Meddeb's awareness of his French readership, it does not demonstrate that he has fully thought out the implication of the fact that his "door" is in fact not in the Muslim world, but has been located in Paris for decades.

Like Ben Jelloun, Meddeb gives a distorted view of what mainstream Islam believes to be the proper dress code for women in his subsequent book *Face à l'islam*. In a sentence whose syntax obscures its meaning, Meddeb proposes to only consider the verses of the Qur'an and gives an interpretation that does not render the headscarf compulsory, while admitting that this is not mainstream: "Le voile peut n'être pas assimilable à un signe religieux si l'on prend la décision de ne pas suivre l'unanimité des docteurs et de lire uniquement en eux-même les versets coraniques invoqués pour légitimer sa prescription" 'the scarf may not be assimilable to a religious sign if one takes the decision not to follow the unanimity of scholars and to read only the Koranic verses invoked to legitimize its prescription in themselves' (*Face* 198). Meddeb also fails to mention that the decision not to take into account the Tradition by the Prophet would be unacceptable to most Muslims, since these narratives play a crucial role in Qur'anic exegesis.

Although Meddeb is very careful in his argument about not essentializing Islam (*La maladie* 64), he fails to apply his own caution to the issue of the veil. He admits being shocked at witnessing veiling in Paris (*La maladie* 49) because the reveiling of women for him is a sure sign of going backwards. This statement also presupposes that the veil had disappeared from all Muslim countries, which it had not. He takes pity on veiled women in Egypt, as if the veil could only have the meaning of oppression, thus ignoring that the phenomenon of (re)veiling can have different meanings depending on the context in which it occurs, and can even be a revolutionary gesture.[24]

Meddeb deplores the standardization of the veil throughout the world, as opposed to the time when each Muslim culture had a distinct way of veiling, as if this standardization, if standardization there is (this is highly debatable), could not be a sign of new exigencies. This contradicts what others have noticed, such as Leïla Ahmed, who sees the variety of new styles in Cairo as "adoption of a 'modern' version of the conventions of dress they . . . were accustomed to" (222). In the French context, this is also contradicted by the picture on the cover of the Lévy sisters' book, which shows two young women in turtlenecks wearing headscarves tied at the nape of the neck. This innovative use of a turtleneck sweater, a "Western" garment, which allows for tying the scarf behind rather than in front to cover the neck, debunks the standardization deplored by Meddeb. In addition, the tricolor headscarves mimicking the French flag worn by some of the women demonstrating against the law banning religious signs were very much grounded in the French socio-political context and cannot be seen as partaking in standardization.

Overlooking the contradictory nature of his position and the subjectivity of his statements, Meddeb asserts that the veil is a cultural sign only if it is seductive. When it ceases to be attractive, it becomes ideological and a sign of women's subservience to men. This reasoning is particularly evident when he evokes the image of the silk *haïk* worn by traditional Tunisian women. While he finds the garb, "froufroutant à chaque pas" 'rustling with each step' (*Face* 198), sexually provocative, one of the young women in Mernissi's autobiography explains that this traditional and impractical dress was "probably designed to make a woman's trip through the streets so torturous that she would quickly tire from the effort, rush back home, and never dream of going out again" (*Dreams* 118).[25] It is quite ironic that Meddeb, who poses as a champion of women's rights, looks nostalgically at the *haïk*, a garment that discourages women from being outside, while he denigrates the headcover that enables them to move freely in public space. It is also disputable whether women in general fared better under the Golden Age of Islam that Meddeb looks upon so fondly because of its openness to sensuality. And he is downright orientalist when he laments:

Quelle chape de pudeur a couvert les pays qui virent Flaubert s'abîmer dans la jouissance! Pour en retrouver la scène, que faire sinon rappeler les heures ardentes que l'écrivain normand avait passées avec l'almée Kuchuk-Hanem sur les bords du Nil. (*La maladie* 136)
What cope of modesty has covered the countries that saw Flaubert sunk in pleasure! To remember its scene, what can we do, other than recall the passionate hours spent by the Normand writer with the almah Kuchuk-Hanem on the Nile's banks.

This allusion to the most famous pages of Flaubert's *Voyage en Orient* glorifies Flaubert's encounter with a prostitute in Cairo without drawing any attention to the ethnic, class, and gender issues in a passage that portrays Arab women as stupid, eager sensual objects of male desire, of whom Kuchuk Hanem, as Said pointed out in *Orientalism*, is the prototype (207).

Although he only indirectly alludes to the affair of the headscarf in *Maladie*, Meddeb unequivocally affirms his support for the way the law against religious signs in public schools has been justified. He praises the French model of integration as a better system than the American model of multiculturalism, as if the periodical violence in French suburbs, certainly the riots of fall 2005, did not attest to major flaws: "je reste surpris par ceux qui, en invoquant leur islam, demandent à la République de changer" 'I am still surprised by those who, invoking their Islam, ask the Republic to change' (*La maladie* 221), and adds that this is a "prétention déraisonnable" 'unreasonable claim.' He follows this with a quote from the Torah to counter this "unreasonable claim," without giving pause to the oddity of invoking Jewish scripture to argue for secularism as a response to concerns expressed by Muslims. In his subsequent book *Face à l'islam*, he is more explicit about the headscarf affair. He interprets the veil as a sign of sexual discrimination against women (159). His delight about the legislation of the law, which he somehow helped to bring about as a consultant for the Debré commission (197), is clearly evident.

Like Ben Jelloun, Meddeb advocates education of his fellow Muslims as a remedy against fundamentalism and women's oppression, but does not consider the fact that the decision to exclude veiled Muslim girls from schools is actually depriving the ones who, according to him, need education the most. To combat fundamentalism, Meddeb also advocates the following: "au lieu de distinguer le bon islam du mauvais, il vaut mieux que l'islam retrouve le débat et la discussion, qu'il redécouvre la pluralité des opinions, qu'il aménage une place au désaccord et à la différence, qu'il accepte que le voisin ait la liberté de penser autrement" 'instead of distinguishing between a good and a bad Islam, it is better that Islam find again debate and discussion, that it rediscover the plurality of opinions, that it carve out a place for disagreement and difference, that it accept that the neighbor be free to think differently' (*La maladie* 13). However, when it comes to the issue of the veil, he fails to apply his own recommendation.

Unlike Ben Jelloun's and Meddeb's essays, Benguigui, Maalouf, Sebbar and Memmi do not focus on Islam per se in the works discussed here, and were not triggered by 9/11. But their respective topics do lead them to talk more or less about France's colonial legacy and Muslims, and briefly about the issue of the headscarf in public schools.

The Affair of the Headscarf in Amin Maalouf's *Identités meutrières* and Albert Memmi's *Portrait du décolonisé arabo-musulman et de quelques autres*

Amin Maalouf's *Identités meutrières*

In *Identités meutrières*, an essay published in 1996, Amin Maalouf sets out to explore the question of multiple belongings, and the disastrous consequences that can ensue when we are pressed to deny some of our affiliations. Drawing on his personal situation as a Christian Arab, a "paradoxical" fact (23) that puts him at the border and allows him to affiliate with Christians and Muslims alike, Maalouf gives examples of situations when one's identity can change because of political events. He strongly advocates that one should be encouraged to see one's identity as multiple, and warns of the dangers that come with pushing people to single out one element and repress the others (183). Maalouf advocates learning languages as a remedy to two forces that crush plurality: essentialist identity politics and globalization. In the process of this argument, Maalouf reminds us that religious fundamentalism has not been the first choice of Arabs and Muslims, but a last resort when everything else failed (96). Maalouf contrasts languages with religion, in the way that one can speak several languages, but only belong to one religion. This leads Maalouf to write: "Il faudrait faire en sorte que personne ne se sente exclu de la civilisation commune qui est en train de naître, que chacun puisse y retrouver sa langue identitaire, et certains symboles de sa culture propre" (187-88) 'We must act in such a way as to bring about a situation in which no one feels excluded from the common civilisation that is coming into existence; and in which everyone may be able to find the language of his own identity and some symbols of his own culture' (Bray 163). This is a very general statement and Maalouf abstains from giving examples of what to retain and what to keep, yet that is the thorny issue. However, the Muslim headscarf is not one of the symbols he seems to deem appropriate to display, as I will explain shortly.

Maalouf does mention the affair of the scarf, but does not elaborate on it. After a development on the situation of migrants, and the fact that the host society is "ni une page blanche, ni une page achevée, c'est une page en train de s'écrire" 'neither a tabula rasa, nor a fait accompli, but a page in the process of being written' (50, Bray 40), Maalouf asks a crucial question that deserves to be quoted at length:

> il s'agit, à vrai dire, d'un contrat moral dont les éléments gagneraient à être précisés dans chaque cas de figure: qu'est-ce qui, dans la culture du pays d'accueil, fait partie du bagage minimal auquel toute personne est censée adhérer, et qu'est-ce qui peut être légitimement contesté, ou refusé? La même interrogation étant valable concernant la culture d'origine des immigrés: quelles composantes de cette culture méritent d'être transmises au pays d'adoption

comme une dot précieuse, et lesquelles—quelles habitudes? quelles prati-
ques?—devraient être laissées "au vestiaire"? (51-52).
What we are really talking about—a moral contract, the elements of which
need to be defined in each case to which it is applied: what, in the culture of a
host country, is the minimum equipment that everyone is supposed to possess,
and what may legitimately be challenged or rejected? The same question may
be asked about the immigrants' own original culture: which parts of it deserve
to be transmitted like a valuable dowry to the country of adoption, and which—
which habits? which practices?—ought to be left at the door [cloakroom]?
(Bray 41)

The use of the word "vestiaire" 'cloakroom' is important (and is missing in the
English translation), since it is a place where one leaves clothing; it indirectly
alludes to the affair of the headscarf that will be mentioned later. By using a
term associated with clothing, Maalouf's statement can be read as implicitly
suggesting that the veil, an article of clothing that has been the source of great
polemics, should be left in the cloakroom. Four paragraphs later, Maalouf resorts to a paralipsis to mention the affair: "Aurais-je à l'esprit, en disant cela, des
controverses comme celle qui s'est engagée, dans divers pays, autour du 'voile
islamique'? Ce n'est pas l'essentiel de mon propos" 'Am I thinking of contro-
versies like that which has arisen in various countries over the 'Islamic veil'?
These are not my main concern' (53, Bray 42). The paralipsis, a rhetorical figure
of speech that allows one to bring up a topic while denying it should be discussed, allows Maalouf to mention the affair while distancing himself from it.
However, he continues using vocabulary that is associated with the debate over
the issue of the scarf in France: "Lorsqu'on sent sa langue méprisée, sa religion
bafouée, sa culture dévalorisée, on réagit en affichant avec ostentation les signes
de sa différence" 'When one feels that his language is despised, his religion ridi-
culed and his culture disparaged, he is likely to react by flaunting the signs of his
difference' (53, Bray 43). The word "ostentation" recalls the language used in
the directive issued in 1994 by the French Minister of Education that aimed to
exclude headscarves from public schools and led to the expulsion of more than a
hundred girls.[26] When Maalouf returns to the issue of the scarf explicitly a couple of paragraphs later, he qualifies it as "un comportement passéiste et rétro-
grade" 'a reactionary, backward-looking behavior' (54, Bray 43). His interpretation of the resurgence of religion here as something that valorizes the past to the
detriment of the present and progress does not take into account women's explanations and understanding of this gesture. Bowen has noted that many young
women draw a clear distinction between the Islam that they practice and the one
of their parents, which shows that it is not simply a return to the past (71). To his
credit, Maalouf adds that the real question that needs to be asked is to understand why sometimes modernity is not perceived as a progress (54), but he never
questions that the only possible path to modernity is the French and Western
model. Although he is acutely aware of the discrimination that immigrants and
their children have been victims of, Maalouf refuses to consider that the decision
to wear the scarf can be "the result of a personal commitment rather than an in-

tention to signal something to others" from the point of view of the girls (Bowen 81).

Albert Memmi's *Portrait du décolonisé arabo-musulman et de quelques autres*

In an essay that aims to examine the situation of the formerly colonized, in the same vein as his landmark *Portrait du colonisé*, Memmi talks about the issue of the scarf in a very brief section entitled "Le voile ou le métissage" 'Head Scarves and *Métissage*' (105, Bononno 86). In two pages, he constructs an imaginary dialogue with veiled girls that begins as follows:

> Passons sur leurs arguments, médiocres ou rusés; au nom de la liberté, par exemple: "On est libre en France, non? Eh bien, je suis libre de porter le voile!"; être libre de ne pas l'être, est-ce encore de la liberté? Ces petites sottes ne voient pas qu'elles agissent contre elles-mêmes, en refusant des lois qui les libèrent au profit de dogmes qui les asservissent. Elles exigent, au nom d'une laïcité mal interprétée, de ne pas être laïques. (106)
> Their arguments, some weak, some clever, often had to do with freedom. For example, "We're free in France, aren't we? So, I'm free to wear a headscarf, right?" It is a foolish argument. For they [these stupid girls] fail to see that they are acting against their own interests in rejecting the laws that freed them in favor of the dogmas that enslaved them. In the name of a poorly understood secularism, they demand not to be secular. (Bononno 86-87)

Although the question and answer format can been seen as indirectly giving voice to some of the girls' motivation for wearing a scarf, Memmi chooses and frames arguments so as to immediately discredit them in a manner reminiscent of the asymmetry of roles played by guests on various programs on French TV in 2003-2004 (Bowen 240-41). Bowen noticed in a specific program that included the Lévy sisters that "they [the Lévy sisters] were only allowed to speak as examples of the problem, the real understanding of which was provided by the 'experts'" (240). Memmi's use of the adjective "sotte" 'stupid' for the girls (lost in the translation) is harsh and condescending, and although Memmi's tone is very sarcastic throughout the book, this is the only instance that I have noticed when he disparages the intelligence of people (in this instance young women) to better attack their arguments. His dismissal of arguments advanced by young women is symptomatic of the general silencing of the women concerned during the affair. For example, Bowen notes that the Stasi Commission[27] did not hear from any girl who had been expelled (117), and only from one "token" veiled woman (118). He also notes that the media coverage of the affair perpetuated the stereotype that only uncovered women were seen as having earned the agency to speak for themselves, whereas covered girls were perceived as only parroting words dictated to them by men (245). Indeed, what Mohanty's ground-breaking article "Under Western Eyes" denounced well over a decade ago, can be seen operating in full swing here. First World feminists working on Third World issues posited themselves as the norm and in the process refused the idioms of agency that are relevant for Third World women. As for the issue of the interpretation of secularism, there is no acknowledgement here of the fact that the French have interpreted it in different ways, including the ruling of the *Conseil d'Etat* during the first affair, which stated that students' wearing of religious signs was not in itself incompatible with secularism.[28] Indeed, Drake underlines that both the intellectuals who opposed the headscarf in schools and those who opposed exclusion of the veiled girls did so in the name of secularism, a term that they understood in different ways (178). There is no hint of the complexity of the French debate about the issue of secularism during the second half of the twentieth century, most notably with the issue of public subsidies of private religious schools.[29]

After dismissing the argument based on the issue of freedom, Memmi dismisses other arguments (of the veil as a protection, and as a religious obligation) in a similarly expedient manner, invoking, after secularism, the equality of the sexes, jeopardized by the meaning of the veil:

> "Le voile protège les femmes du regard des hommes"; pourquoi ne pas protéger également les hommes du regard des femmes? N'est-ce pas un traitement particulier pour la sexualité féminine? Pour les protéger du désir des hommes, faut-il qu'elles ne soient pas désirables, comme les dévotes juives qui se font raser la tête? Et surtout: respecter celles qui souhaitent être ainsi protégées ne donne pas le droit de vitrioler celles qui ne le souhaitent pas. (106)
> "The headscarf protects women from men's stares," they say. Why not also protect men from the stares of women? Aren't we showing favoritism to the female sex? To protect them from men's desires, is it necessary that they be undesirable, like those Orthodox Jewish women who shave their head? What's more, respecting those who wish to be protected in this way does not give you the right to criticize [throw vitriol at] those who do not wish to be so protected. (Bononno 87)

When Memmi gets indignant in the first two rhetorical questions that the head covering is a "special treatment" and therefore violates the equality of the sexes, there is no question that the French model is taken as the desired norm, despite the fact that the advertisement industry has long been basing many campaigns on the very premise of a different treatment of the female body. Memmi's question "faut-il qu'elles ne soient pas désirables" betrays an assumption in the prerogative of the male spectator to look at attractive women that has been fostered in Western art, and most notably the traditional European nude painting, as demonstrated by John Berger's *Ways of Seeing*. In fact, I would argue that one of the reasons why the veil has crystallized public attention is because it goes against the Western pictorial tradition from the Renaissance to contemporary advertising that depicts women as sexual objects for the gaze of a male spectator. This includes the Orientalist tradition of languid odalisques that has been analyzed at length, and contemporary French society's tendency to undress women, from contemporary fashion styles to the topless and thong trends on the beach.[30] The opponents of the scarf in public schools who use the gender discrimination argument are not able to see it simply as a dress code nor look critically at French society's norms. Western societies have long had different dress codes for men and women, yet it would not come to anybody's mind to propose banning skirts from public schools on the ground that they promote inequality between the sexes because only girls wear them (not to mention the historical and religious reasons behind that fact).

There is a striking slip in the last sentence of the quote above between one issue and another: the use of the verb "vitrioler" (again, lost in the English translation), which can be used literally and figuratively, will not just mean "to criticize" for a French reader. It will evoke real-life cases of women who were disfigured by men who threw vitriol in their faces. These incidents happened in Muslim countries such as Algeria and Bangladesh during the 1990s and were reported in the media during Taslima Nasreen's visit to France, in particular, in the case of Bangladesh. Here, foreign contexts are brought to bear on the domestic one. The argument of forbidding the veil to better protect women who do not want to wear it was a powerful one (Bowen 208). Arab-Muslim culture was blamed for much of the violence that affected women in the poor suburbs, and as a sign of that culture, the veil was judged guilty in contributing to perpetuate this violence. The *tournantes* (gang rapes) that made sensational headlines during 2001-2003 helped give more momentum for the law (Bowen 214-17). According to a study cited by Bowen, the only new feature about gang rapes, which date back to the 1960s and were committed by non-immigrants, is the (false, though convenient) claim that they are due to Arab-Muslim culture (214).

Memmi counters the girls' argument that wearing a headscarf is a divine obligation by asserting that it is only suggested by the Qur'an (106), and that it boils down to men controlling women's sexuality. Here again, Memmi refuses to recognize that there are various interpretations of the Qur'an, and that those that have challenged the compulsory head cover do not represent the beliefs of the Muslim majority. The last sentence he attributes to the girls alludes to the fact that the veil is a reaction to the non-acceptance of French society:

> En fait, par delà les arguties, on a vu apparaître un aspect revendicatif, sinon provocant: le voile est devenu le drapeau d'une cause: "Vous n'aimez pas les musulmans, leur vue vous irrite? Eh bien, je le proclame, je suis musulmane, je vous en impose la vue! Celle d'un membre du groupe honni par vous." (107)
> But underlying the arguments we find an element of protest, if not downright provocation: the headscarf has become the flag of a cause. "You don't like Muslims, the sight of them irritates you? Well, I'm proclaiming my Muslimhood; I'm forcing you to see it. To see a member of a group you have made to feel ashamed." (Bononno 87-88)

Although the discrimination faced by Muslims in France is acknowledged, the girls are faulted for resorting to the veil, a "ghetto portatif" 'portable ghetto' (107, Bononno 88). Their choice is constructed as a provocation, which runs counter to all the accounts that have been published telling about the various paths and motivations behind French women's decisions to cover (see Gaspard and Khosrokhavar, Bowen, Bouamama). This is a clear example of what Noiriel, quoted earlier, has pointed out: how the victims are transformed into aggressors by changing a social issue into a religious problem. Although a key argument in the affair was to see the veil as a symbol of patriarchal oppression, the girls, who are then constructed as double victims of patriarchal oppression and social discrimination, as acknowledged by the above quote, are paradoxically turned into deliberate aggressors of French secularism.

Missing Images of Veiled Girls: Leïla Sebbar's *Journal de mes Algéries en France* and *Mes Algéries en France*, and Yamina Benguigui's *Mémoires d'immigrés: L'héritage maghrébin*[31]

A few writers have nonetheless displayed a more complex attitude towards the young women concerned and showed more discrimination in their representation of the scarf affair than those just examined. The works I focus on have in common that they either feature texts and images, such as *Journal de mes Algéries en France* and *Mes Algéries en France*, Sebbar's illustrated (auto)biographical narratives, or blur the boundaries between the two, such as the film and book by Benguigui, which bear the same title, *Mémoires d'immigrés: L'héritage maghrébin,* and whose contents overlap without being completely identical. Sebbar and Benguigui are both Franco-Algerian. Sebbar was born in Algeria of an Algerian father and a French mother; she moved to France at the age of 18. Benguigui was born in France of Algerian parents. Despite different situations and a generation separating them, they are both at the threshold between two communities, and the works examined unearth the links that have been woven by history between the Maghreb (and specifically Algeria) and France in order to fill a void through texts and images.

While Benguigui and Sebbar's works share the goal of giving its proper place to the Algerian and Maghrebian communities in France in the French collective memory, they also have in common a "visual omission": they do not include any pictures or any shots of veiled girls in France.[32] The affair of the scarf is mentioned to various degrees in the texts, but the scarf worn by middle and high school girls in contemporary France does not appear, as if one could talk about it but not show it.[33]

Sebbar's *Journal de mes Algéries en France* and *Mes Algéries en France*

At the very beginning of the affair, Sebbar sarcastically mentions in an article published in *Le Monde* the case of "laïcité aiguë" 'acute secularism' that is plaguing the teaching profession, and the irrational panic caused by the scarves that are seen as a war sign of the advance of a fanatical Islam. Already, Sebbar maintained what others have since elaborated on: that secularism is not threatened by the religious signs worn by students, that the veil expresses modesty ("un foulard qui cache leurs cheveux comme on cache ses cuisses et ses seins" 'a scarf that hides their hair just as one hides one's thighs and breasts')[34] and that the real victims in this case are the young girls who are excluded from the very institution supposed to promote equal opportunity.

Mes Algéries en France and Journal de mes Algéries en France are books that mix (auto)biographical narratives, portraits, and diary; both are illustrated with images ranging from textbook pages[35] to Orientalists paintings and personnal photographs. The narratives feature the experiences of diverse groups, including those of pieds-noirs in Algeria, children of immigrants in contemporary France, etc. In her foreword to Journal, Sebbar explains her project by saying: "Prise par un besoin fébrile de mêler l'Algérie à la France . . . je tente par les mots, la voix, l'image, obstinément, d'abolir ce qui sépare" 'Caught by a feverish need to mix Algeria with France, I try with words, voice, image, to abolish what separates.' Since the affair was such a divisive topic, one could expect to see Sebbar give it some attention in these texts. In Mes Algéries, the headscarf issue is briefly mentioned via a third party. In a section entitled "le foulard. . . . Je ne suis pas jacobine," Michelle Perrot (who also happens to have written a preface to Sebbar's book), is reported to have said in 1999 that she was against the expulsion of veiled girls from school, and therefore had not signed Badinter's text.[36] However, a footnote informs the reader that Perrot did sign a petition to support the law prohibiting religious signs in December 2003 (Sebbar, Mes Algéries 167), thus underlining her change of mind. This footnote is the only (indirect) comment by Sebbar on the issue in that book, and demonstrates a hardening of opinion.[37] Bowen also noted that more politicians gradually came to support the law (105).

In Journal de mes Algéries en France, Sebbar dedicates a few lines to the affair. While Mes Algéries was organized thematically, Journal is a diary written between March 2004 and January 2005; therefore, the news is mentioned occasionally. Her diary starts the very month that the law was passed, but only two paragraphs evoke the issue later on. First, she recalls French Muslim organizations' stand and mobilization to obtain the release of French journalists kidnapped in Iraq, but does not mention that the kidnappers had demanded the abrogation of the law as a ransom for the hostages (61-62). She then follows up with the following sentence: "Par ailleurs, les jeunes filles au hijeb ont accepté d'être semblables à leurs condisciples sans hijeb (sauf en Alsace), conscientes peut-être qu'elles seront les bénéficiaires de l'école laïque française" 'besides, the young women wearing a headscarf have agreed to be like their fellow students without headscarves (except in Alsace), conscious maybe that they will be the beneficiaries of the French secular school' (62). Given that this entry is dated September 3rd, it most probably alludes to the beginning of the first school year under the 2004 law that prohibits religious signs in schools. Although Sebbar is quick to point out the ineptitude of French politicians regarding equal opportunity for all (*Journal* 131), she no longer has anything to say about the cases of girls excluded.[38] While the parenthesis "sauf en Alsace" indirectly alludes to the fact that the 1905 law of separation between Church and State, which defines the principle of secularism in France, does not apply to some parts of the Hexagon, it only does so in the context of the headscarf affair. Sebbar has nothing to say about the fact that the Concordat statute that governs the area of Alsace and Moselle constitutes a breach of secularism, since according to the Concordat the president is involved in the appointment of religious clerics remunerated by the state, which also funds religious instruction in public schools (Haarscher 32, Baubérot 119-20).[39] Indeed, this has been one of the most salient omissions by those invoking the fate of secularism during the debate: the failure to acknowledge the double standard hidden in the argument, since in fact the law of separation of Church and State is not being applied in all parts of France, not to mention the fact that the Concordat statutes benefit only Judeo-Christian religions.

One can surmise that Sebbar's change of mind on the issue, expressed indirectly in her photographical essays, and confirmed to me directly during an interview conducted in June 2006 in Paris, probably unconsciously influenced her choice of pictures.[40] The only pictures of veiled women included in her books were taken in Algeria, and all the young women of Algerian origins living in France are bareheaded. In works endeavoring to document the diversity of the Algerian-French connection, it would have been pertinent to include in *Mes Algéries en France* a picture of the girls wearing tricolor headscarves and singing the French national anthem during several demonstrations that took place at the beginning of 2004 (see Ternisien). The blue, white, and red headscarves were meant as a symbol of these young women's identity, claiming their attachment to both Islam and France. If, as Roland Barthes puts it, "toute photographie est un certificat de présence" 'every photograph is a certificate of presence' (135), the absence of images of veiled French girls in Sebbar's books contributes to their rejection by French society.

Yamina Benguigui's *Mémoires d'immigrés: L'héritage maghrébin*

Benguigui's successful documentary film, *Mémoires d'immigrés*, broadcast on Canal + in May 1997, was followed by the publication of the book in July of the same year (Durmelat, "Transmission" 172). While there are some differences between the testimonies in the film and the book, the narratives match up and describe similar experiences. The headscarf affair is not mentioned at all in the film, and the only shots of veiled women were either filmed in Algeria, or are of immigrant women in black-and-white archival footage.

In contrast to the film, the first paragraph of Benguigui's book puts the headscarf affair in the foreground, and sees it as a key event in France's awareness of the definitive presence of a Muslim population in the Hexagon: "Un foulard islamique apparu sur la tête de trois adolescentes d'un collège de Creil, en septembre 1989, a vite semé l'inquiétude. D'où viennent ces musulmanes?

Comment sont-elles parvenues à se faufiler au cœur des établissements scolaires?" 'A Muslim scarf on the head of three teenage girls in a middle school in Creil, in September 1989, quickly spread anxiety. Where were these Muslim girls coming from? How did they manage to sneak in the heart of schools?'(7). Similar questions are asked a couple of pages later.[41] The questions that Benguigui attributes to public opinion and the choice of verbs give the impression that the presence of Islam is considered illegal on French soil.

Furthermore, one chapter of the book is dedicated to Naïma, a young woman who challenges the stereotypes, since she decided to wear the veil under no pressure from her family. To the contrary, her father was worried by it and feared he would be expelled from the country (186). Her mother and sister are dressed European style. Benguigui is startled when she first sees Naïma, her reaction is emblematic of the ambivalence and uneasiness that the scarf triggers in France, even for those who opposed the exclusion of veiled girls from school (178). While one can object to Benguigui's interpretation of Naïma's choice in Christian idiom (see Durmelat "Transmission," Bourget "A l'écrit"), Benguigui stands out in that she does give voice to a veiled girl in her book without demonizing or dismissing her choice of dress, taking a step to bridge the gap of misunderstanding by letting the silenced party speak for herself. One can only regret that she did not include Naïma in the film, since, if "photographic images are pieces of evidence in an ongoing biography or history" (Sontag 166), the non-inclusion of veiled girls in the contemporary French landscape contributes to relegating these girls to the margins.

Conclusion

Ben Jelloun, Maalouf, Meddeb, and Memmi seem to belong to the "hard-line secularists" (Drake 181) who were the most vocal during the fifteen-year affair. In their works that focus on Islam, neither Meddeb nor Ben Jelloun alludes to the various sides of the debate regarding the issue of the veil. By only presenting the opinions of a minority regarding certain religious rulings and by silencing the French girls' motivations for veiling, they contribute to deepening the gap of misunderstanding rather than bridging it. Since both writers lament the absence of debate in the Muslim world (indeed Meddeb's main argument is that fundamentalism is caused by the lack of debate and its intolerance of diverse opinions), the least we could have expected of them would be to render the plurality of voices in the debate surrounding the veil. For two writers who pose as champions for the emancipation of Arab women, it is unfortunate that they contribute to what Bouamama has noted as one of the characteristics of the debate: the absence of the voice of the women concerned.

By waiting for the terrorist attacks of 9/11 to try to explain Islam to the French, Ben Jelloun and Meddeb are exacerbating the main problem that Muslim French, many of whom are descendants of immigrants, face in France: they are not recognized as full-fledged and trustworthy citizens solely because of their choice to practice the religion of their ancestors. This choice is seen as incompatible with French values and subject to foreign allegiance. Thus, international news is made to bear on domestic issues even though they are not directly related to them. Not only do these essays fail to present a balanced account of the issue of the veil in France, they contribute to the confusion between Islam and terrorism by the mere fact of mentioning the affair in essays motivated by 9/11.

Ben Jelloun, Maalouf, Meddeb, and Memmi fail on two counts: they do not present a balanced account of the issues surrounding the headscarf affair in France, nor do they draw attention to the use and abuse of the concept of secularism in an affair that, as Gérard Noiriel pointed out, was more a "sous-produit des polémiques sur l'immigration lancées par les conservateurs au début des années 1980" 'by-product of polemics about immigration launched by conservatives at the beginning of the 1980s' (181).[42] According to Noiriel, the 2004 law on religious signs was a victory for the most conservative government intellectuals, who managed to reverse the relationship between victims and aggressors by transforming a social question into a religious one. The phrase "identité nationale" 'national identity' was dropped because it brought to memory extreme right-wing slogans, "nation" was replaced by "République" and "identité" by "laïcité" 'secularism.' Thus when one used to say "Les étrangers ne s'assimilent pas et menacent notre nation, parce qu'ils sont de connivence avec l'ennemi" 'foreigners do not assimilate and threaten our nation, because they are in connivance with the enemy,' one now says "les Maghrébins ne s'intègrent pas et menacent la laïcité républicaine car ils sont de mèche avec les islamistes" 'Maghrebians do not integrate and threaten republican secularism because they are hand in glove with Islamists' (Noiriel 182).

Why did these writers not underline the "extraordinary symbolic weight given to a scarf worn on the head by a small number of schoolgirls" (Bowen 7)? Why did they not give some recognition to the girls' effort to reconcile their Muslim and French identity as they saw fit? These are writers who have risen up to the challenge of showing the shortcomings of French society in the past, particularly regarding racism. The climate of course has changed. In a chapter of *Jihad* entitled "Europe, terre d'islam: le voile et la *fatwa*," Kepel puts the Islamic scarf affair in the international context of the rise of Islamism. Unlike Bowen, who, among other factors, demonstrates that the scarf affair brought to light the contradictions that already existed regarding secularism in France, Kepel takes it for granted that there is a well-established consensus about the definition of secularism, something that is debunked by two contrary developments: the 1989 ruling of the Conseil d'Etat that stated that the headscarf was not in itself a breach to secularism, and the 2004 law that forbids it. Kepel rightly underscores the role played by the international rise of Islamism, and particularly Khomeini's *fatwa* against Salman Rushdie, and its role in the change that considered Western countries that are home to Muslim citizens as part of *dar el islam*. His analysis puts the international political situation to the foreground, and the headscarf as one manifestation of political Islam, and only that. This is mostly what was disseminated in the media. The guilt by association factor (to which I will return in the next chapter), which prompts writers to take a strong stance to distance themselves clearly from any fundamentalist association, comes into play. However, this analysis reduces Islam to its political dimension and does not take the girls' point of view into account at all. Gaspard and Khosrokhavar noted that no link had been established between the veiled girls and Islamist groups in France (54). As for link to foreign groups, they note that the FIS had issued a call asking these girls to remove their scarves, that went ignored during the second affair in 1994 (29), thereby putting into question the notion that the girls were merely puppets in the hands of (foreign) fundamentalists. This shows a gap between political analysis and sociological fieldwork, a gap that one also finds between the writers discussed in this chapter and personal accounts of veiled women.

A telling statistic during the affair was that 91 percent of French teachers had never seen a veiled girl at their school (Bowen 121), and yet the teaching profession overwhelmingly supported the law. Of the writers discussed in this chapter, Benguigui might be the only one who actually met in person a girl who decided to wear a headscarf (Sebbar told me during an interview in 2006 that she did not meet veiled girls and did not want to because she already knew their discourse). Benguigui put aside the politics, both internal and external, and listened with an open mind and a sympathetic ear.

While Sebbar went from supporting the girls to supporting the law that excludes them, Benguigui does not take a position, but her work moves from exclusion to inclusion, albeit in a different way. The works of both, however, meet in excluding pictures of covered girls. This brings me, in closing, to comment on a picture that accompanied a 2006 article in L'Express on the rise of Islam in Europe (see Conan). As John Bowen noted, the weekly magazine L'Express' coverage of the scarf affair was strongly anti-veil from the very beginning (107). The picture features a girl wearing a tricolor headscarf and holding a French flag on her face, as a face veil.[43] The article warns about the danger of the rise of Islam in Europe, in general. The picture was probably chosen as an illustration of the rise of Islam in France because of the two icons it contained, and which summed up the gist of the article: a veiled girl representing Islam, and the tricolor flag for the French republic. I would suggest another reading of that picture, which I can only surmise was taken during a demonstration against the law on the prohibition of religious signs in public schools. I would read the girl's gesture as showing that it is the French flag, the icon of the French Republic, which is silencing and occulting Muslim women from public space and debate.

In his book, Bowen notes that he is gratified when, after people listen to him speaking on the 2004 law, they still do not know where he stands (7). Like Bowen in his study, my aim is not to take a position, although my view has probably become obvious to my reader. If anything, the 2005 riots seemed to confirm to me that the time, resources, and energy spent on the single issue of the scarf during the past fifteen years could have been more fruitful had they been directed towards concrete and pressing, and not symbolic, issues. There were no veiled girls burning cars all over the country that fall. One consequence of the affair is that it will have, ironically, triggered the establishment of private Islamic schools that will eventually receive government subsidies, like their Jewish and Catholic counterparts.

Notes

1. Incidentally, this mosque was partially funded by the French government, despite a 1905 law (much-brandished during the headscarf affair) that prohibits governmental funding of religious entities.

2. In France, the incident was referred to as "l'affaire du foulard" 'the affair of the scarf,' with the words "foulard," "voile," and hijab used interchangeably to denote a cloth covering the hair and neck. The Muslim veil comes in many shapes and colors throughout the Muslim world, with specific forms and vocabulary associated with some countries (for instance the Iranian chador, the Afghan burqa). I use the terms scarf and veil interchangeably, as was done in France, to refer to a head cover only, and not something that hides the face and/or the whole body.

3. Disproportionate attention was given to the affair. Alec Hargreaves notes that in 1994, the number of girls concerned constituted less than 1 percent of the number of Muslim girls in public schools. Bouamama points out that there was no increase in these numbers in 2003, the year when the move to legislate gained momentum (70).

4. For excellent analysis of the controversy, see Gaspard and Khosrokhavar (of which a short excerpt translated into English appears in *Beyond French Feminisms*) as well as Bouamama, the collection of essays edited by Nordmann, and Bowen.

5. In his provocative study, Bouamama places the law in the context of social regression for the working class. According to him, the headscarf affair was a timely way to divide the 2003 social movements that unified the teaching profession.

6. Indeed, one should not assume that a specific religious background entails better representation (see Bowen about the only Muslim member on the Stasi commission).

7. For the motivations behind some girls' choice to wear the scarf, see excerpts of interviews in the books by Bouzar and Kada, Gaspard and Khosrokhavar, Giraud, Sintomer, and the Lévy sisters.

8. This section has appeared as "9/11 and the Affair of the Muslim Headscarf in Essays by Tahar Ben Jelloun and Abdelwahab Meddeb." *French Cultural Studies* 19.1 (February 2008): 71-84. It has been revised.

9. A particular subset of novels that endeavors to imagine the mindset and indoctrination of a 9/11 hijacker is the subject of chapter 5.

10. These works have been translated into English (see bibliography). However, unless indicated otherwise, most translations in this chapter are mine.

11. The famous editorial published in *Le Monde* on 9/13/2001, "Nous sommes tous Américains" 'we are all Americans' had so much resonance probably in part because France still had vivid memories of terrorist attacks on its soil.

12. See Aubrac and Wieviorka.

13. Ben Jelloun explains that "Certains ont traduit ce mot par 'caillot de sang.' En vérité, il s'agit du liquide visqueux formé par les spermatozoïdes; on l'appelle 'sperme.' C'est grâce aux spermatozoïdes que les êtres humains se reproduisent" 'some have trans-

lated this word by 'blood clot.' Actually, it's the viscous liquid formed by spermatozoa; it's called 'sperm.' Human beings multiply thanks to spermatozoa' (19). Jacques Berque's translation (among others) favor the term "adhérence" 'adhesion' which renders another meaning of the word *'alaq* (which also translates as "a sticky thing") and would refer in this context to the embryo). References to semen occur in other parts of the Qur'an using a different word. Not to mention that such a statement, which completely occults the woman's biological reproductive role, is quite patriarchal for a man who otherwise poses as a champion of women's rights.

14. See Mernissi's *Le harem politique* as one example, although her approach is radically different from Ben Jelloun's. Mernissi knows that in order to be taken seriously and to have an impact, she cannot disregard summarily the body of *hadiths* as Ben Jelloun does, which would be totally unacceptable for mainstream Islam.

15. Abdelkader fought the French invasion of Algeria from 1832 till 1847, when he was forced to surrender. Abdelkrim was imprisoned in 1917 for his opposition to Spanish rule in Morocco. He escaped in 1919 and led the Moroccan resistance against Spanish and French colonial expansion from 1921 until 1926, when he was defeated.

16. Ben Jelloun made it clear in a newspaper article that he fully supported the 2004 ban on religious signs in public schools (see "Contamination").

17. These last two were published after Ben Jelloun and Meddeb's texts. For the Lévy sisters, see Giraud.

18. The Lévy sisters point out that the media gave inaccurate accounts of their story in slant articles and news reports that portrayed them as intransigent fundamentalists when they were expelled from their high school in 2003 (see pages 37 and 42).

19. There was a split among French feminists about the issue: none supported the veil, but several recognized that taking a hard stance and expelling the girls would definitely not be in the latter's best interests, and would not help promote equality between the sexes.

20. The French government's position on the issue changed over the years, but follows a pattern of hardening public opinion. In 1989, the *Conseil d'Etat* ruled that the veil worn by students was not incompatible with secularism. In 1994, the minister of education issued a circular, making a distinction between signs that are discrete versus ostentatious. In fact, cases were generally handled at the discretion of the schools' principals.

21. The Concordat is an agreement reached between Napoleon and the Pope in 1801, according to which Catholicism is no longer the religion of the State, although the State nominates and remunerates the clergy. This agreement covers Protestantism and Judaism as well. The Concordat ended in 1905 with the law of separation of Church and State, except in the areas of Alsace-Moselle which were at the time annexed by Germany. The Concordat was left untouched in Alsace-Moselle even after they were reincorporated into French territory following WWII. This has seldom been mentioned as a danger in debates about secularism.

22. Some intellectuals, such as Mohammed Arkoun, have been advocating the creation of a degree in Islamic theology to be offered at the University of Strasbourg (which already offers degrees in Catholic and Protestant theology, the only French public university accredited to do so).

23. "Lorsqu'une fois le fanatisme a gangrené un cerveau, la maladie est presque incurable" 'once fanaticism has gangrened a brain, the disease is almost incurable' (254)

24. See for instance El-Solh and Mabro, and Ahmed.

25. Memmi recalls how he used to joke that his Jewish grandmother, who would not leave the house without her *haïk*, looked like a ghost (105-06).

26. For more on that, see Bowen 89-91.

27. This was the commission appointed by the president to issue recommendations in 2003, one of which was to pass a law banning religious signs in public schools. For a critique of the Stasi commission, see Bowen (for instance, the members ignored the sociological studies that had been carried out about the girls, and did not interview a single girl that had been expelled from school because of her headscarf (70, 117).

28. http://www.conseil-etat.fr/ce/rappor/index_ra_cg03_01.shtml.

29. For more on that issue see Baubérot and Haarscher.

30. The compromise solutions adopted in certain cases, which modified the ways the scarf is worn (by showing the hairline, or the earlobes and neck, or wearing a bandana), demonstrate an attempt to align the head cover with practices accepted by mainstream French society (and showing more skin).

31. This section has appeared as part of "A l'écrit sans images: le foulard islamique dans des oeuvres de Leïla Sebbar et Yamina Benguigui." *Expressions maghrébines* 6.1 (Summer 2007): 19-35. It has been revised and augmented.

32. It is important to stress that the immigrant women's scarves never bothered anyone. According to Dounia Bouzar, "jusqu'à ces dernières années, les femmes en foulard qui faisaient le ménage dans les administrations ne posaient aucun problème ni à la société, ni à la laïcité: un islam infériorisé . . . est acceptable, c'est lorsqu'il revendique d'intervenir dans l'espace public en situation d'égalité qu'il apparaît intolérable" 'till the last few years, women in headscarves cleaning the government's buildings never posed a problem either to society or to secularism: an inferiorized Islam . . . is acceptable, it is when it claims to intervene in public space on equal footing that it appears unbearable' ("Françaises" 61).

33. For a detailed analysis of the presence and absence of Muslim icons in the images of these works, see my article "A l'écrit sans images: le foulard islamique dans des œuvres de Leïla Sebbar et Yamina Benguigui."

34. It is important to remember that as a sign of modesty the headscarf goes against the current, at a time when images of naked women's bodies are commonplace. Georgette Hamonou, a teacher who opposed the exclusion of two girls from her middle school, states: "Je souris lorsque j'entends Mme Badinter s'insurger contre le foulard qu'elle distingue à peine de la burka afghane, et qui ne dit mot de la façon dont on galvaude le corps féminin, cent fois plus qu'il y a trente ans, au bon temps du féminisme!" 'I smile when I hear Mrs. Badinter rising up against the headscarf which she barely distinguishes from the Afghan burka, and who does not say a word about the way the female body is debased, and this a hundred times more than was the case thirty years ago, at the good old time of feminism!' (Bouamama 141)

35. The copy of a page of a textbook entitled *Histoire de France et d'Algérie* shows the history of both countries presented side by side: a lesson on one side on Charlemagne for French history, on the kingdom of Tiaret for Algerian history (Sebbar, *Mes Algéries* 41). This questions the commonplace idea of the Eurocentrism of the curriculum in colonial schools evoked by the phrase "nos ancêtres les Gaulois" 'our ancestors the Gauls,' so often cited ironically by writers and scholars in Francophone studies.

36. The text she refers to here is the letter signed by intellectuals and published in *Le Nouvel Observateur* on November 2, 1989, protesting the stand against exclusion taken by the Minister of Education in front of the National Assembly. For a close analysis of that letter, see Gaspard and Khosrokhavar (22-24).

37. Emmanuel Terray applies Bibo's concept of political hysteria to the debate of the headscarf in France. Political hysteria consists in substituting to a real problem "un

problème fictif, imaginaire, construit de telle sorte qu'il puisse être traité avec les seules ressources du discours et par le seul maniement des symboles" 'a fictitious, imaginary problem, framed in such a way that it can be dealt with the sole resources of discourse and symbols' (103). According to him, the fact that many people changed their minds during the course of the affair, mostly in favor of the law, shows that this case of political hysteria was "highly contagious," and not a sign of an open debate (117).

38. See Laronche and the following articles in *Le Monde*: "Dix fois moins de foulards" (published in the September 4, 2004 issue) and "Premières exclusions scolaires après la loi sur le voile" (October 21, 2004).

39. Haarscher (32) and Baubérot (120) both point this out by means of rhetorical questions.

40. Sebbar explained to me during the interview that the Islamisation of the suburbs had triggered her change of mind on the issue. Her reversal is far from unique. She justified that the absence of veiled girls was due to the fact that her books were about people she had met personally, and that she would not try to meet with veiled girls because she already knew their discourse. However, the two books I discuss here include reproductions that do not fit the criteria just mentioned (for instance, the picture of an anonymous man—maybe a Chibani—in *Journal* page 90). The assumption that Sebbar already knows these girls' discourse is symptomatic of what was propagated in the media. Sebbar has featured veiled girls in her fiction (see, for instance, the short stories "Vierge folle, vierge sage" and "La fille au hijeb"), but here I am focusing on non-fictional texts.

41. "D'où viennent les foulards islamiques de Creil? Comment ont-ils pénétré dans les écoles françaises?" (9).

42. See also Bourdieu, Bouamama, Gaspard and Khosrokhavar. One of the Lévy sisters recalls how the agreement their father had reached with their high school principal to let them wear their scarves was an exception: "Un jour, je discutais dans le couloir avec une fille qui portait un foulard laissant apparaître la racine des cheveux, les oreilles et le cou, quand le proviseur est arrivé vers nous et l'a sommée de le retirer à l'instant même. . . . La fille était dégoûtée, et plusieurs comme elle, des Françaises d'origine maghrébine, sont allées se plaindre et demander des explications. Le proviseur ou des professeurs, je ne me rappelle plus, leur ont donné deux justifications: la première était que mon père était juif et la seconde, qu'il était avocat! On cumulait à la discrimination religieuse une discrimination sociale et professionnelle!" 'One day, I was talking in the hallway with a girl who was wearing a scarf showing her hairline, her ears, and her neck, when the principal arrived and demanded that she take it off right away. . . . The girl was disgusted, and several like her, French girls of Maghrebian origin, went to complain and ask for explanations. The principal or some teachers, I can't remember, gave them two justifications: the first one was that my father was Jewish and the second that he was a lawyer! Social and occupational discrimination were added to religious discrimination!' (27)

43. I am grateful to Siobhán Shilton for showing that picture during her talk on visual arts works and for helping me locate the picture, and to the http://theatrumbelli.hautetfort.com website owners for giving me the reference of the article in which it appeared.

Chapter 6

Portrait of a Terrorist: Slimane Benaïssa and Salim Bachi's 9/11 Novels

9/11 has already given rise to a genre of its own: the 9/11 fiction. Kristiaan Versluys rightly notes that three of the most interesting novels dealing with 9/11 were written by outsiders, and specifically Europeans, whose link with 9/11 is "more tangential than tangible" (69). But he does not mention Francophone Arab writers, who have directly engaged this event in essays (such as the works of Ben Jelloun and Meddeb discussed in the previous chapter) and works of fiction. Two of them, Slimane Benaïssa in *La dernière nuit d'un damné* (2003) and Salim Bachi in *Tuez-les tous* (2006), have made it the sole focus of a novel. Contrary to the 9/11 novels written by American and French writers,[1] these Francophone Arab writers have endeavored to portray the time leading up to the attacks, rather than their aftermath, and from the point of view of a hijacker instead of a victim's or a witness's. They are the only authors, to the best of my knowledge, to have done so in a novel.[2]

While providing a very different reading experience, these two novels have several resemblances: they are both creative attempts to imagine the indoctrination and thoughts of a 9/11 hijacker just before the attacks, and they both feature extensive quotations from the Qur'an, which are clearly marked and identified in Benaïssa's narrative but not in Bachi's. Both authors are Algerians exiled from their country in the 1990s because of the civil war that pitted Islamists against the army. However, neither pretends to offer a realistic reconstitution: elements in both novels depart from what we know about the 9/11 hijackers.[3] The most salient of these divergences are the following: Benaïssa's protagonist is Arab-American, and he does not board the plane; Bachi's protagonist is an Algerian who does go through with the attack but knows that his action will not earn him Paradise.

In this chapter, I sketch the various interpretations that have been given as explanations for 9/11, in order to examine where one can situate these novels in this debate. I analyze and compare the function of the intertext in both novels, with particular attention to religious references, and its effect on the representation of the role played by Islam in terrorism.

9/11, Islam, and Terrorism

9/11 has been a watershed event in many aspects, one of them being to bring religion back on the Humanities' radar screen. Scholars in the *PMLA*[4] issue of May 2005 noted that literary scholars had not taken notice that colleagues in the social sciences had been "debunking the illusion of the secularization thesis for some time" (Brown 884), and seemed to discover their "own intellectual impotence, [their] insistent refusal to recognize religion as part of the *current* (rather than past or primitive) state of humanity" (Chow 875).

9/11 has also given new currency to the theory of the clash of civilizations, and thus prompted numerous inquiries into the link between terrorism and Islam. The most prominent scholars who champion that theory, Bernard Lewis and Samuel Huntington, assert that Islam is by its very essence hostile to Western values (Qureshi and Sells 2-9). According to them, this antagonism rather than specific historical processes explains the current conflict between the West and Islam (a view also held, incidentally, by Islamic extremists). They question the Left's tendency to explain Islamic fundamentalism as a religious cloak for economic and political grievances.[5] This theory enjoys broad appeal, even with some postcolonial writers (such as Naipaul,[6] who has taken on and propagated that view as well, and Soyinka[7]). This view shows little recognition of the fact that had colonial policies been different, there might have been less sense of urgency by such newly independent states as Morocco, Algeria, and Tunisia to affirm Islam as the state religion. As underlined by Qureshi and Sells,

> If such identities, in the words of Edward Said, are constructed and inherently conflictual, then the claim of a clash of civilization is true, in the philosophically trivial sense of tautology: generalized identities that have been constructed in opposition to one another [as was the case in colonial contexts] are in opposition to one another. Said also points out that colonization justified by conflictually constructed ideologies generated reactive, conflictually constructed politics of identity among the colonized. (27)

As Stephen Morton noted, the equation of terrorism with Islam "is precisely a form of orientalism, which obfuscates the political dimension of resistance against western imperialism" (40). Scholars in fields ranging from philosophy (Baudrillard, Derrida) to political science have debunked the theory of the clash of civilizations. Jean Baudrillard's *The Spirit of Terrorism* and Slavoj Žižek's *Welcome to the Desert of the Real,* both essays on 9/11, dedicate considerable space to emphasizing the importance of socio-political factors. Žižek, recalling that Bin Laden was funded by the CIA, stresses that the USA is fighting "its own excess" (27).[8]

While it has become commonplace in the media and (popular) culture to explain suicide attacks through reference to Islamic fundamentalism, membership in Islam alone is not a prerequisite, since the vast majority of Muslims do not engage in such acts. Indeed, in a talk with the provocative title "Radical Sheik and the Missing Martyrs: Why Are There So Few Islamic Terrorists?" Charles Kurzman debunked the idea that terrorism is intrinsic to Islamic fundamentalism by addressing the question from the following angle: "If a considerable proportion of the world's billion Muslims believes in armed jihad and the joys of martyrdom, why don't we see terrorist attacks around the world every day?"

An alternative has emerged to both those who assert that religion serves only as a means to an end to redress socio-eco-political grievances and those who see it as an end in itself. In the field of International Relations, Scott Thomas argues that religion makes a difference because "religious terrorism seeks a cosmic or transcendent justification rather than only political, social or economic objectives" (147).

A close look at the history of suicide terrorism and ethnographic studies on the issue yields a more complex picture. Several studies on terrorism have demonstrated that suicide bombings are not the exclusive resort of Islamic groups: they have also been used by secular groups. The first wave of suicide missions in the twentieth century was conducted by Russian anarchists, and was followed by the second wave of Japanese Kamikaze[9] during World War II (Gambetta 285). The Tamil Tigers is a non-Muslim group that commits suicide missions. In *Making Sense of Suicide Missions*, scholars of political science show that suicide missions inspired by an Islamic rhetoric account for about a third of the suicide missions that took place between 1981 and 2003 (Gambetta 261). Indeed, their studies demonstrate that Islam is "neither a necessary nor a sufficient condition for SMs" (Kalyvas and Sánchez-Cuenca 216), since non-Muslim groups have resorted to it, while many Islamist groups who have resorted to violence (as in Algeria for instance) have not.

Similarly, Christoph Reuter shows that various explanations offered in the media do not stand scrutiny; he makes a strong case for looking at the specifics of each context (9-13). He states that "Islam as such is not the cause of terrorism and suicide attacks. Particular aspects of Islam do, however, lend themselves to being interpreted to justify a declaration of outright war against the West and against any opponents among their own peoples. They can equally be used to construct a democratic society" (Reuter 32).

However, religion can play a role in fostering and creating a receptive environment for terrorism, notably by promoting a cult of martyrdom. Stephen Holmes demonstrates that the grievances articulated by Atta and Bin Laden are almost entirely secular. Gambetta answers the question of how we can decide which of the religious or non-religious motives was predominant in the 9/11 attacks by concluding that they are intertwined: "While the real sources of the conflicts in which SMs [suicide missions] emerge are ultimately social and political, and secular groups can resort to these attacks too, those organizations that can bank on the 'right' religious beliefs can more easily summon the energy to enter into or … to continue, fighting against all odds" (293, see also Pedahzur).[10] This intertwining has been pointed out by an earlier study on the secularization theory that examined the revival of religions in countries ranging from Iran to the U.S. It concludes that religions "were not the principal causes of the radicalization of the conflicts, but rather conflict radicalization found symbolic resources in religion to further certain social and political causes" (Ricolfi 112). Holmes notes that Atta's grievances against the U.S. and the Muslim regimes it supports were "almost entirely secular" (139), as are Al-Qaeda's main objectives (164), and Bin Laden's (166); he concludes that "such a blurring of personal frustration, political protest, and religious convictions makes it very difficult, if not impossible, to demonstrate the specifically *religious* roots of Atta's commitment to jihadist violence" (140). It is therefore clear that grievances grounded in the here and now (specifically the presence and/or occupation of Arab countries by American soldiers and Israel) are necessary to spur Islamic terrorism.

Slimane Benaïssa's *La dernière nuit d'un damné*

Benaïssa has been primarily a playwright[11] who had already explored the issue of violence and religion on the stage. His novel *La dernière nuit d'un damné* is told in the first person by Raouf, an Arab American software engineer whose father is Egyptian and mother Lebanese. His father's death less than a year prior to the beginning of the story is a key event that marks the beginning of Raouf's questioning about life (20). His coworker Athmane, a Palestinian trained in France, introduces him to Djamel, a rich Kuweiti who grew up in London, led a life of debauchery before repenting, and broke ties with his family because of the Gulf War. After three months of Islamic theology lessons with Djamel, Raouf converts to Islam, and is recruited as a martyr for a mission. We see Raouf abandoning his ordinary life (starting with his separation from Jenny, his long-time girlfriend), undergoing his training, and planning for the mission. On the morning of the attack, Raouf decides to not take the pills he was given, and at the last minute does not board the plane. He is arrested shortly thereafter. The novel ends with a letter written by his mother on her deathbed, which Raouf reads in prison.

In his foreword, Benaïssa aligns himself with Victor Hugo's and Alexandre Solzhenitsyn's writings. He explains that Hugo's *Le dernier jour d'un condamné* and Solzhenitsyn's *Une journée d'Ivan Denissovitch* can be credited for being catalysts for change (9). Benaïssa feels compelled to follow in their footsteps for two reasons: because he is a Muslim and because of his "histoire personnelle face à l'intégrisme" 'personal experience with religious extremism' (9, Gross vii), which alludes to the death threats that forced Benaïssa to leave Algeria in 1993 (as indicated in the short biographical notice on the back cover) during the civil war. The title *La dernière nuit d'un damné* modifies the title of Hugo's text, a plea against capital punishment, to reflect a different situation: Benaïssa refutes the doctrine that a suicide attack will earn his character a place in paradise. In a striking move, he apologizes to the families of victims of fundamentalism: "*en tant que musulman, je demande pardon à toutes les familles*

des victimes de l'intégrisme international, quelle que soit leur confession"
'*speaking as a Muslim, I ask for forgiveness from all of the families who have
been victims of religious extremism across the globe, regardless of their faith*'
(11, Gross ix). This statement is set off typographically: it is a paragraph in itself
and is the only passage that is italicized. Benaïssa's reaction emblematizes what
Arab and/or Muslim writers and intellectuals have been feeling in the last decades, and more intensely since 9/11. Said sadly recalled in 1996 that after the
Oklahoma City bombing his office received numerous phone calls from journalists,

> all of them acting on the assumption that since I was from and had written
> about the Middle East that I must know something more than most other peo-
> ple. The entirely factitious connection between Arabs, Muslims, and terrorism
> was never more forcefully made evident to me, the sense of guilty involvement
> which, despite myself, I was made to feel struck me as precisely the feeling I
> was meant to have. The media had assaulted me, in short, and Islam—or rather
> my connection with Islam—was the cause. (*Covering* xiv)

Just as Said, it seems that Benaïssa felt guilty from the loose association, all the
more prevalent since 9/11, between terrorism and Arabs and Muslims, possibly
made all the more acute by the criticism levied both in France and in the U.S.
that Muslims had not spoken out forcefully enough against the attacks. Unfortunately, Benaïssa's apology has the (most probably unintended) consequence of
validating the perception that Muslims are guilty by association.

In addition to asking for forgiveness, Benaïssa apologizes for "la dureté de
certains propos dans ce roman. Car tout au long de cette écriture, je me suis de-
mandé si je devais dire ce que je crois être l'éclairage d'une vérité précise ou
ménager la douleur des familles des victimes" 'some of the harsh sections [re-
marks] in this novel. Throughout the entire time of writing, I wondered whether
I should say what I felt to be the most illuminating truth, or take into consideration the pain it might bring to the victims' families' (11, Gross ix). By this I assume he means the criticism of the West, and Unites States foreign policy,
which is put in the mouth of the terrorists, and which actually takes up very little
space in the novel. Benaïssa appears to be writing defensively, in an immediate
post-9/11 climate of binary rhetoric that left no place between "us" and "them"
and for critical discourse. As Judith Butler points out, "the binarism that Bush
proposes in which only two positions are possible—'Either you're with us or
you're with the terrorists'—makes it untenable to hold a position in which one
opposes both and queries the terms in which the opposition is framed" (2). Any
criticism of U.S. foreign policy can be easily dismissed by a chauvinistic American reader on the assumption that it is uttered by the terrorists or their sympa-
thizers, although it is grounded in various political claims that have widespread
support in the Arab world (such as the Palestinian cause), and are recognized as
legitimate by scholars worldwide.

Athmane and Raouf have disparate motivations for becoming martyrs.
Athmane is the most politicized of the two: through his mouth comes much of

the criticism of the West, and particularly of America's injustices in the world. Thus, while Raouf becomes indignant about the political dimension of the sermon of the clandestine imam, Athmane insists that since the Crusades, the West has had imperial designs on the East (135). The first planning meeting of the future hijackers is inaugurated by a speech that first presents grievances against the U.S. and the West: non-recognition of the contributions of Arab-Muslim civilization to Western civilization and wars of Western aggression that are plaguing the Muslim world; this political situation is given as the reason why they should strike the West to humiliate it in order to restore God's honor, thus mixing a political with a religious motive in a murky way (192-95). Athmane and the rest of the hijackers use Islam to address political issues of dispossession.

As for Raouf's motivation for participating, he mentions that he hopes to atone for his father's sins, while making Americans pay for refusing to acknowledge that his father's death was a work accident (190-91). Raouf has been shaken by his father's death, the mention of which recurs at key moments throughout the narrative to signal it as the event that marks Raouf's vulnerability to fundamentalist discourse (see pages 20, 93, 103, 110, 156, 165, 188, 217, 233). The insistence on a psychological motif has been explained as such by Butler: "That kind of story [what Mohammed Atta's family life was like, Bin Laden's break with his family] is interesting to a degree, because it suggests that there is a personal pathology at work" (5). Butler argues that this kind of story, with its emphasis on personal responsibility and agency, is easier for us to accept than a narrative with a global political and historical framework (5-8). Benaïssa's depiction of Raouf's indoctrination follows the brainwashing methods that psychologists have reconstructed based on their experience with Western sects (Reuter 8). However, Reuter points out that these "individual psychological models of interpretation . . . can't function as the complete explanation" (9).

Raouf obviously knows little about Islam. During some of his conversations with Athmane about religious issues, Raouf perceives that something is wrong with Athmane's arguments, though he does not have the tools to contradict him. The first such conversation occurs at the very beginning of the novel, during which Athmane uses the story of Abraham, Sarah, Hagar, Isaac, and Ishmaël to argue that Judaïsm exists thanks to Islam and not the other way around (28-29). In a rather unpersuasive section at the end, Raouf explains that, unconvinced by the guide's argument, he stopped taking the pills he was prescribed to help him go through with the attack, and did not board the plane.

According to the translators' statement preceding the English version, Benaïssa turned to the novel to treat this subject matter because fiction would allow him greater ease in introducing complex matters: "We acknowledge his [Benaïssa's] courage in turning to the novel as a way of introducing complex perspectives on Islam to a broad reading public, both Muslim and non-Muslim" (Gross, "Translators' Notes" xiv). The translators of the English edition have noted that "to demonstrate how Islamic teachings were used to shape the thinking of the main character, Slimane Benaïssa's novel makes use of extensive quotations from three types of religious writing" (Gross, "Translators' Notes" xiii). The reader is informed in a "note de l'éditeur" 'Publisher's Note' of the convention that was added to make the religious intertext easily identifiable (with different typographical conventions to distinguish the Qur'anic quotes from the Hadiths (sayings of the Prophet) and supplications, as well as a glossary at the end of the novel. There is a recurrent opposition between "l'ici-bas" 'Here and Now' and "l'au-delà" 'Hereafter,' the only words that are in bold font throughout the novel (in the original, not maintained in the English translation). The bold font is meant to attract the reader's attention to the opposition between the two notions (which indeed are part of monotheist faiths); they stress that worldly life is only a test and will determine one's fate in the afterlife (see for instance page 37). Despite these efforts to make the novel more legible to a readership that might not know much about Islam, nothing in the novel points out the different status of these religious writings in Islamic theology. Contrary to the translators' statement, my analysis demonstrates that Benaïssa's text falls short of presenting the complexity of Islam. In fact, I argue that his novel not only fails to counter stereotypes, it in fact perpetuates them.

Benaïssa's intertext is overwhelmingly Islamic. Most of the Qur'anic quotes are interspersed in sermons that each occupy several pages, and contribute to making this novel a rather tedious reading. The sermons at the beginning of the novel treat general theological issues framed by Islamic beliefs. The first sermon deals with the reconciliation of predestination and free will (32-41); the verses quoted insist on God's omnipotence and omniscience, and recall that man accepted the gift of free will from God; it also contains injunctions not to get distracted by worldly riches. The second sermon (a recording that Raouf listens to) talks about worldly inequities and about God's supreme authority to judge (54-58). During Raouf's repentance ceremony, the verses quoted emphasize God's mercy (98-103). One of the sermons he goes to with Athmane is on the topic of "parole, acte et action" (117-24) 'speech, act, and action' (99), the verses insist that God will put the believers to the test, and exhorts them to be patient and steadfast in their faith.

Once Raouf becomes involved with the terrorists in training, the sermons become more political and deal with specific worldly topics. These sermons are preached in an underground network, as is underlined by the precautions that are taken when the terrorist plotters go to listen to a clandestine imam. Tellingly, that sermon starts with a verse (24:31) specifying women to whom they may show themselves without a head cover, and goes on to making a parallel with Judaism and Christianity since all three religions place restrictions on women (130). This choice of verse is not innocent: it underlines that Muslim fundamentalists in different countries have made the implementation of restrictions on women one of their first priorities, be it in Iran after the Islamic revolution, Afghanistan with the Taliban, or Algeria during the 1990s' civil war, but does not point out that men are also subjected to restrictions (albeit lesser ones) in the preceding verse. The verses that are quoted during that sermon (130-35) are very general but are inserted as if to confirm the main development, which concentrates on the disparity between the Western and the Muslim worlds, blames colonialism, accuses Jews and Christians of having teamed up against Islam, and scolds Arab leaders for their corruption.

The first sermon during the training is a long one on death, with verses focusing on death in different contexts (167-74). Its purpose is to stress the centrality of death to the believer. This sermon is followed almost immediately by one on purity. It only contains two brief quotations from the Qur'an (one stating that God loves those who purify themselves, the second that God does not change a people until they change themselves). There is a logical slippage from the verse about purification to its interpretation, according to which the acculturation that came with being educated or trained in the West, as were the trainees, is considered an element of impurity (175-79). It also includes advice on how to behave in the airport. The next sermon informs the participants that a fatwa has recognized their action as part of jihad; it is peppered with Qur'anic quotes and Hadiths on death in combat for the cause of God, the privileged status of martyrs, and a promise that God will not burden anyone beyond endurance (181-87). The next sermon treats angels and includes several Qur'anic verses (210-13). After emphasizing that the angels stand out by their unconditional obedience to God, the sermon concludes with a syllogistic argument that the one who decides to become a martyr will be equal to angels in his obedience to God (212). Although the verses' meanings are general, they are brought to bear on specific issues by being interspersed in the sermon to lend credence to various statements.

In addition to the sermons, the Islamic intertext appears in other occasions. The future hijackers' wills (214-18) contain general verses that insist on God's testing of believers, and on Islam as the last revealed religion. A recurrent verse associated with death emphasizes that mankind belongs to God and will return to him (2:156). The pledge of allegiance to God recited by the new recruits contains some short suras (or chapters) from the Qur'an (sura 112 on God's unicity, a truncated part of verse 5:106, and the Fatiha, on pages 209-10). When informing Raouf that he will volunteer to become a martyr, Athmane quotes a verse that stresses faith to give credence to his argument that people who have been educated in Western universities need to fight for the cause (126). An example of a Hadith is given by Athmane in the context of his argument that Raouf must get rid of his dog (16). The recommendations, clearly inspired by the "road map" that was found by the FBI and translated and published in various newspapers, including *Le Monde*, are sprinkled with supplications praising and trusting God and a few verses about God granting victory to the believers.

A few passages show the distortion effected by fundamentalist discourse: for instance, when Athmane argues about Judaism existing thanks to Islam, or during a sermon about America being discovered by accident, by a man who got lost, and forecasting its perdition (177). In the last speech, a parallel is established between the five phases of the terrorist action, the five daily prayers, and the five pillars of Islam, as if to better inscribe the terrorist act in the rituals required of the faithful (219-21). However, this mechanism is not made at all obvious when it comes to Qur'anic quotes, which are often taken out of context. The subtle shift between the sermons that Raouf hears at the mosque and the ones in the terrorist network might not be noticed by readers who have never read the Qur'an. The Qur'anic quotes add a touch of authenticity to the fundamentalist discourse, but do not prompt a reflection on the faith or on alternate interpretations. When Athmane urges Raouf to break up with his girlfriend on the grounds that she is not a Muslim, Raouf wonders if there is an exception for the "gens du Livre" (142) 'people of the Book,'[12] which indeed there is, although nothing in the narrative hints at it except for Raouf's question, which remains unanswered since the terrorists consider no counter discourse to the fundamentalists' interpretation. And most importantly, there is no commentary whatsoever about practices not sanctioned by contemporary Islam, such as the fact that Djamel has slaves, or that an imam has the authority to recognize Raouf's repentance.

In the foreword, Benaïssa laments that "il y a certainement des milliers de façons de vivre l'islam. Malheureusement, aujourd'hui, il n'en apparaît que deux: celle d'un islam qui s'exprime et qui utilise toutes sortes de violences, et celle d'un islam qui se tait et dont le silence est plus qu'une absence" 'there are certainly thousands of ways to live as a Muslim. Unfortunately, in today's world there seem to be only two: one is an Islam that is expressed through all manner of violence, the other is an Islam that is silent and whose silence amounts to more than just an absence of words' (10, Gross viii). Indeed, these are the only two Islams that are featured in his book: that which uses the religion to justify terrorist attacks, and that of Raouf's parents (and more specifically of his mother), which is actually hidden and nonexistent, as exemplified by the scene when his mother refuses to bury his father according to Islamic rites. The novel ends with the mother's letter, which strongly advocates Western modernity as a solution to the Arab world's problems, a modernity where Islam does not seem to have much place. And yet, there is much evidence to the contrary throughout the Muslim world, as seen in the opinions of Muslims for whom Islam and modernity are not incompatible and who have spoken strongly against their faith being used as a justification for 9/11.[13]

The intertext seems to reinforce the idea of a clash of civilizations. Most of it is Islamic, with the exception of the mention of the film *Fureur de vivre* when describing Djamel's dissolute life style (73) and of the *Cantique des cantiques* as Jenny's reference (51), with an excerpt quoted (52). The intertext generally reinforces the dichotomy that is posited between East and West, Christianity and Islam. Most of the Qur'anic quotes in Benaïssa's novel function only to inscribe the hijackers' act in the Islamic faith. There are no Qur'anic quotations when Raouf recalls how he did not go through with the action; in fact, at that point in the story, he cannot recall any of the verses beyond the initial formula "in the name of God" that starts all the suras. The author could have quoted some well-known verses that condemn the killing of innocents (Bachi does so, as we shall see later). Similarly, his mother's letter, written on her death bed, does not contain a single Qur'anic quote. If her way of life is another path for Islam, then it is one that has eliminated all religious reference. The text's objections to the terrorist act are not grounded in the Islamic faith. The political grievances behind 9/11 are given very minimal space, whereas the sermons and Islamic material predominate in the narrative, thereby confirming the stereotype that there is something intrinsic to Islam that spurs terrorism, or at least, that devout believers are likely to be fanatical.

The Multicultural Intertext of Salim Bachi's *Tuez-les tous*

Told in the third person by an omniscient narrator, Bachi's novel presents the last hours of one of the pilots up to the moment when he crashed a plane into the World Trade Center. The protagonist, whose real name is never disclosed, is an Algerian who went on to France to pursue his education, and fell in love with a French woman, who aborted their child. This abortion is the symbol of his failed integration into French society and one of the key reasons why he joined a terrorist organization which he found via a Parisian mosque and a trip to Afghanistan, where he was given the name Seyf el Islam. Although the character tries a few times to back out of his mission (he tries to drown himself, to turn himself in to the police), he is saved every time, and the ineluctability of the tragedy of 9/11 looms constantly over the narrative through prolepses.

Contrary to Benaïssa, Bachi has no qualms when it comes to writing pointed criticism about the West, and more specifically the U.S. and France. The phrase "Paris, ville lumières éteintes" 'Paris, city of lights out' recurs like a leitmotiv through the course of the narration, and emphasizes the failure of the Enlightenment. Strident passages and allusions strongly chastise American politics, both domestic and foreign, indicting the CIA, the plight of the Blacks and the poor (20). In general, the Western world is accused of being responsible for numerous conflicts in various geographical areas. It is designated as "les adorateurs du veau d'or noir" 'the worshippers of the black golden calf' (21) adapting a Biblical (and Qur'anic) reference to the oil-dependent economies of the twentieth century. Several prolepses function as indirect criticism of the attention granted to 9/11 by the media: "tous verraient que leurs victimes [celles de l'Occident] avaient plus de poids que celles du monde entier" 'all would see that their victims carried more weight that those of the entire world' (17). This sentence refers to the U.S.'s "reputation as a militaristic power with no respect for lives outside of the First World" (Butler 17). There is also an ironic allusion to *Le Monde*'s article entitled "nous sommes tous américains" 'we are all Americans' (20), which was published two days after the attacks.[14]

The title of the book *Tuez-les tous* alludes to one of the darkest pages in French Medieval history: the Albigensian Crusade in the thirteenth century, indirectly recalling that Christianity has had its share of religious fanaticism. Arnaud Amaury (Arnold Amalric), abbot of Cîteaux, before the massacre at Bé-ziers in 1209, when asked how to distinguish the Cathars, considered heretics, from the other inhabitants of the town, infamously answered: "Tuez-les tous, Dieu reconnaîtra les siens." (Roquebert 245-61).[15] Bachi's title significantly omits the second part, which is a reference to the Bible: "The Lord knows those who are his" (2 Timothy 2:19). According to Michel Roquebert, the crusaders massacred the inhabitants of Béziers, including women and children, "parce que les croisés voulaient faire un exemple, propre à semer la terreur" 'because the crusaders wanted to make an example that would spread terror' (263). This event can thus be seen as an example of pre-modern terrorism in the name of religion. In modern times, that phrase (kill them all, let God sort them out) was used by American military during the Vietnam War. The title thus bridges French medieval and twentieth-century American histories, reflecting the recur-rent criticism of both countries in the novel. The title is also used in Hitchcock's film *The Birds*, one of Bachi's intertextual references, when one of the charac-ters argues for the destruction of the whole species following attacks by birds in the small town.

The terrorist "Organisation" sent Seyf to spend a month in Granada before flying him to Portland, Maine to accomplish his mission. His stay in Granada is an important detail that gives rise to several remarks by the character about the coinciding dates of the fall of the last Muslim ruler in Spain with the date that marks Columbus' journey to America. Granada was the last bastion of Muslim Spain, or al-Andalus, to fall. As Majid emphasizes, al-Andalus was character-ized for the mutual tolerance between the three monotheistic faiths (*Freedom* 23), although he cautions that "the myth of a golden era of multicultural rela-tions or of Islamic tolerance should not lead us into believing that there were no tensions among religious communities" (*Freedom* 24). For Seyf el Islam, the new world is "cette nouvelle saloperie, extension de l'Europe des lumières étein-tes" (55). His journey seems to mirror Columbus' journey, since he spends time in Cadix before going to Portland, and takes on a Spanish name, San Juan, as a pseudonym to accomplish his mission. The name San Juan evokes the town founded in 1521 by Spanish colonists in Puerto Rico, the oldest European set-tlement in the United States territory. The historian Fernand Braudel singles out 1492 as the date that marks the beginning of modern European colonialism. Ma-jid states that "the defeat of Islam and the 'conquest' of America in 1492 were interrelated events that culminated a long process of increasingly strident Chris-tian missionary wars against Islam in Spain" (*Freedom* 23). By calling attention to Columbus' journey, Seyf el Islam seems to incarnate the revenge of the West's Other by mimicking the path of the beginning of colonialism. This allu-sion to Columbus, going back in history well before our current era, shows that globalization started well before our century.

As in Benaïssa's novel, the Qur'an is the salient intertext (although the quotes are unidentified), but it is more than a device to legitimize fundamentalist discourse. The quotations and allusions to the Muslim scriptures fall into several categories. First, the Qur'an is evoked to stress the discrepancy between what the religious text advocates and the reality on the ground, particularly when it comes to women. Verse 2:187, which describes the (sexual) relations between husband and wife ("elles sont un vêtement pour vous, vous êtes, pour elles, un vêtement" 'They are your garments / And ye are their garments') is followed by the observation that Seyf El Islam had not seen anything like this in the world, and stresses that instead he has seen "des femmes dénudées offertes à l'assouvissement des bêtes" 'women stripped bare and offered to gratify the lusts of beasts' (31). This verse is repeated twice more (68, 85), again to emphasize the distance between what the verse evokes and his experience. This verse is again alluded to when hijackers are faulted for being "incapables d'être un vêtement pour une quelconque femme, mais prêts à piloter un Boeing pour faire sauter la planète" 'incapable of being a garment to any woman, but ready to pilot a Boeing to blow up the planet' (84). The Qur'an is also evoked when the character reflects about the gap between the world without women of Kandahar and what the Holy book says (61).[16] Likewise, two quotations (78 and 123) compare the Islamic terrorists he joins to the hypocrites who are persistent opponents of the Prophet in the Qur'an (verse 4:63 and 9:56-7).[17]

In the same vein as the first category, the second use of the Muslim scriptures features verses that are quoted to highlight Seyf's straying from Islam and its precepts, and most importantly his awareness of doing so. For instance, he remembers verse 2:154 ("Ne dites pas de ceux qui sont tués dans le Chemin de Dieu: 'ils sont morts!' Non! Ils sont vivants" 'Say not of those who are slain in the way of God: 'They are dead.' Nay, they are alive'), to better reflect that he himself "avait conscience d'être mort et de ne plus être sur le chemin de Dieu" 'was aware of being dead and no longer on God's path' (23, again on pages 108, 112, 132, with slight modifications). When alluding to verse 5:35 ("Celui qui a tué un homme qui lui-même n'a pas tué, ou qui n'a pas commis de violence sur la terre, est considéré comme s'il avait tué tous les hommes" 'if anyone slew a person—unless it be for murder or for spreading mischief in the land—it would be as if he slew the whole people'), he adds that "je vais tuer des innocents, sortir de la communauté des hommes" 'I'm going to kill innocents, leave the community of human beings' (25). Verse 5:35 is repeated during a dialogue between Seyf and Khalid in Kandahar in the presence of "le Saoudien" 'the Saudi' (Bin Laden, never named in the novel) (pages 58 and 118).[18] These verses and the character's reflections on them emphasize that Seyf el Islam knows his terrorist act is counter to Islamic religious precepts. Additional examples are as follows: verse 2:161 is quoted to emphasize that Seyf counts himself as a non-believer (34). Verse 4:74, about the reward awaiting those who fight in the way of God, is followed by "il allait être tué mais sans pardon sans victoire car Dieu rejetterait son acte" 'he was going to be killed but without forgiveness nor victory because God would reject his act' (54). Verse 24:35, which ends in "Dieu guide, vers sa lumière, qui il veut" 'God doth guide whom He will to His Light' is followed in the novel by "et Il l'avait oublié" 'and He had forgotten him' (70), the same with the quote from 5:41 ("tu ne peux rien faire contre Dieu pour protéger celui que Dieu veut exciter à la révolte" 79),[19] thereby inscribing his straying from the religion as something inscribed in it. In the same vein, verses 14:4 and 4:76 are juxtaposed to stress that his going astray is part of God's will (117).

Third, the Qur'an is also invoked to draw parallelisms between events recounted in it and the 9/11 attacks. Part of verse 2:50 about the Pharaoh being drowned to allow Moses to flee Egypt forecasts in Seyf el Islam's mind the abyss he will fall into the next day. Bachi modifies slightly the translation of verse 2:35 when God enjoins Adam to eat from the garden with the exception of one tree, and puts "tree" in the plural, for a slip in Seyf's mind assimilates the tree with the twin towers, with the acknowledgment that he will be "au nombre des injustes" 'among the unjust' (32). This verse and parallelism between the trees and the towers recurs on pages 69 and 123. Similarly, when he is in the elevator, and his ascent is compared to the Prophet Mohammed's *mi'raj* or ascent to heaven, his act is paralleled with 7:24 (121). Seyf remembers the following verse: "ils jurent par Dieu qu'ils sont des vôtres, alors qu'ils n'en sont pas, amis ce sont des gens qui ont peur, s'ils trouvaient un asile, des cavernes ou des souterrains, ils s'y précipiteraient en toute hâte"[20] followed by "et cela était bien ce qu'avait fait le Saoudien" 'and that was exactly what the Saudi had done' (123), recalling Bin Laden's flight to the caves during the U.S. invasion of Afghanistan.

The Qur'an is cited out of context to apply to a variety of situations. For instance, verse 8:5 ("c'est au nom de la Vérité . . . que ton Seigneur t'a fait sortir de ta demeure" 'Just as thy Lord ordered thee out of thy house in truth') is recited by Seyf during the takeoff, as if to sanction the act he is about to commit (130). When Seyf is in the plane, he keeps reciting Qur'anic verses that seem to announce what is about to happen, such as verse 7:4-5 about the destruction of cities, verse 17:1 about the Prophet's ascension (the original "de nuit" 'by night' is changed into "de jour" 'by day'), as if Seyf were a new prophet (131). Verses 17:16 and 16:112 are quoted as if they followed each other, with an indented passage to stress how the description fits New York and the World Trade Center towers. The change in the verb tense in 16:112 (in the past tense in the original and in the future in Bachi's quotation page 132) highlights the distortion caused by applying a verse that describes a past event to something yet to happen.

As in Benaïssa's novel, the Qur'anic quotes inscribe Bachi's narrative in the Arab cultural tradition and give it an authentic, legitimate touch. But in Bachi's text, they also highlight the discrepancy between Islamic ideals and reality in parts of the Muslim world. These quotes also emphasize the complexity of the character: a believer on the one hand, who sees some parallels between his terrorist act and stories recounted in the Qur'an, he knows his action is condemned by the religion, and yet rationalizes it through the theological tenet of destiny: he goes through with it since it is the will of God.

Contrary to Benaïssa's text, Bachi's novel features a rich multicultural intertext. It makes frequent allusions not only to the Qur'an and *The Conference of the Birds*, but also to *Hamlet*, *The Birds*, and *Hiroshima mon amour*. The Qur'an and *The Conference of the Birds* can be categorized as belonging to the Muslim religious tradition: one is a Holy book and the other a classic of Sufi (mystic) poetry. *Hamlet*, *The Birds*, and *Hiroshima mon amour* belong to the Western tradition and are more preoccupied with worldly issues than with spiritual questions.

Several citations from *Hamlet* appear in the novel; they draw a parallel between Seyf el Islam and Hamlet, his French girlfriend and Ophelia. Hamlet is called on by his father's ghost to avenge his wrongful death; to do so he has to fight the dominant power of the usurper king, his uncle. The spirit of Seyf's father comes to visit him as Hamlet's father's specter appears, but contrary to *Hamlet*, Seyf's father enjoins him to dissociate himself from the terrorists and their "unjust war" (63). Like Hamlet in the eponymous play, Bachi's protagonist wreaks havoc in the process of seeking revenge, and ends up dead.

The numerous mentions of the film *Hiroshima mon amour* are negative; it is described as "un sale titre de film vu dans une salle obscure à Paris" 'a nasty film title seen in a dark theater in Paris' (14, 49, 97) and is associated with the period when Seyf was trying to assimilate to French society. On a formal level, *Tuez-les tous* recalls *Hiroshima mon amour* with constant analepses and prolepses intertwining the past and the present, and not clearly indicated (sometimes happening within a single sentence). In *Hiroshima mon amour,* the French woman's love affair with the Japanese man brings back her love story with the German officer in Nevers. Similarly, Seyf's encounter with the American woman recalls memories of his French wife. In addition, repetitions of several passages blur the time sequence and can be quite disorienting for the reader.

Mentions of the film and pictures of Holocaust victims in a long sentence that intertwines the descriptions of bodies burnt by the atomic bomb and gassed in the concentration camp explain why the epithet of "sale" precedes the title: "*Hiroshima mon amour*, Auschwitz mon amour, brûlés, irradiés" '*Hiroshima my love*, Auschwitz my love, burnt, irradiated' (49).[21] The character's rejection of the title, expressed by always referring to it as a "sale" title, refuses the intent inscribed by Duras with her oxymoronic juxtaposition of love and the mass murder of civilians. Or rather, this rejection points out what Higgins formulated as follows: the film knows "that the desire to represent horror through a love story must be counterbalanced by an awareness of the danger of forgetting the horror entirely" (*New Novel* 22).

One passage highlights the misunderstandings that can result from referring to different traditions. When Seyf starts telling the story of the king of the birds, the well-known Sufi tale written by Farid Addin Attar in the twelfth century, the American woman he picked up in the Portland club thinks he is referring to Hitchcock's film (72). Birds are a constant reference in the novel, starting with the American woman he keeps referring to as a bird (recalling British slang), but more importantly through the Sufi tale. Attar's epic poem is a famous piece that tells the story of birds and their quest for the Simorgh (God); their journey exemplifies the different stages of the Sufi path, until at the end, only thirty birds reach the desired destination, only to realize that the Simorgh (which means thirty birds) is in themselves. The tale ends with the birds' fusion with the Simorgh, reflecting the Sufi doctrine that God is not external to or separate from the universe. In Bachi's text, the gist of the tale is recounted in the middle of the novel (72-74) and again at the end with slight modifications in the details. At the end of Bachi's novel, the plane flying into the World Trade Center is described as a bird and the tower as the mirrors. Although at the beginning the intertextual references to birds are a token of intercultural miscommunication, the final pages of the novel synthesize both references: the plane is compared to a bird that sees its image reflected in the windows of the tower (as in Attar's Sufi tale, except that Seyf merges with nothingness instead of with God). At the same time, the plane is attacking innocent people (as are the birds in Hitchcock's film). Žižek has compared the shot of the plane crashing into the second tower with the scene when Melanie is hit by a bird while on the boat in *The Birds* (14).

This merging of cultural references seems to highlight the destructiveness that acculturation can entail. At the beginning of the novel, Seyf invokes the Bible as well as Qur'anic scriptures when he quotes verses from Psalm 22 addressing God ("Mon Dieu. Pourquoi m'as-tu abandonné" 'my God, why have you forsaken me?' 31). Majid notes:

> That Muslims were in the throes of a maddening identity crisis should have been obvious to readers of novels by Muslim writers in the last four decades. Whether the writer hails from Senegal, Sudan, Morocco, Saudi Arabia, or India, the story is always the same: Islam's encounter with the West, whether at home or abroad, provokes terrible confusions that are often resolved through some violent, and often self-destructive, act. ("The Failure")

As Majid points out, there is a darker side to the positive effects of hybridity, touted by postcolonial studies ("The Failure"), and that is encapsulated by 9/11 in Bachi's narrative. *The Birds*, released the year after the Cuban Missile Crisis of October 1962, has been read as an allegory of the human condition during the height of the Cold War between the U.S. and the Soviet Union, and the birds as a symbol of the nuclear war threat (Hare 279-91). The allusions to Hitchcock's film by Bachi, whereby the plane that crashes in the WTC is compared to a bird, replaces the Cold War threat with that of Islamic fundamentalism, as occurs in Huntington's theory of the clash of civilizations.

Bachi's protagonist seems to conform to Khosrokhavar's portrait of Al Qaeda's members, whom he describes as "des êtres en mal d'identité" 'beings short of/longing for identity' (*Les nouveaux* 111). Khosrokhavar noted that although the Al Qaeda's martyrs are multicultural (they have lived in the West and master its language and cultural code), they still reject Western culture and civilization (*Les nouveaux* 241), and this rejection follows a feeling of betrayal (*Les nouveaux* 242). This sequence of experiences describes Seyf's itinerary very well. The following quote describes the main character: "il . . . s'apprêtait à devenir un des leurs, un sale type sans histoires et sans Histoire, un intégré en voie de désintégration, mais il avait préféré l'intégrisme" 'he was getting ready to become one of them, a nasty character with no story and no history, an integrated person in the process of disintegrating, but who had prefered fundamentalism' (14). The core of this quote comes back in other passages of free indirect speech, with some slight modifications (14, 36). Derrida's interpretation of 9/11 as a symptom of an autoimmune crisis argues that the 9/11 hijackers were trained by people who themselves were trained by the U.S. during the Cold War: the mechanism that was set up to protect the West against Soviet advances turned against what it was supposed to defend (Borradori 140). The terrorists are, in some sense, not an absolute other, but a reflection of ourselves (Borradori 115), as in Bachi's novel when the hijacker sees his reflection in the towers: the religious reference gives way to the symbolism of the West's horrible creations as consequences of its imperial policies.

Tuez-les tous also contains allusions to Conrad, the Bible, *L'éternel retour*, *Casablanca* (1942), *Le Faucon Maltais* (*The Maltese Falcon* 1941), and *Le grand sommeil* (*The Big Sleep* 1946). These last three films, all starring Humphrey Bogart, are labeled as "mauvais film[s]" 'bad movie[s]'(124). Since the narrator talks about destroying Hollywood, these films stand for the popularity and hegemony of American popular cultural production. The last two sentences of Conrad's *Heart of Darkness* serve as an epigraph to the book. Conrad's novel is set during the most somber period of Belgian imperialism in the Congo. As Said pointed out about the darkness to which the title refers, "They [Marlow and Kurtz] (and of course Conrad) are ahead of their time in understanding that what they call 'the darkness' has an autonomy of its own, and can reinvade and reclaim what imperialism had taken for *its* own" (*Culture* 30). Said continues stressing that these characters along with the author are unaware that what they label 'darkness' is a resistance to European imperialism: "As a creature of his time, Conrad could not grant the natives their freedom, despite his severe critique of the imperialism that enslaved them" (*Culture* 30). But taken from its original context, "le cœur même d'infinies ténèbres" 'the very heart of infinite darkness' that ends the sentence can in the context of a novel on 9/11 connote the evil motivation of the kamikazes.

The first part of the book is entitled "L'éternel retour" and can evoke two things: Nietzsche's idea of eternal return, and the film of the same title (1943), partially inspired by Nietszche's thought, for which Jean Cocteau wrote the screenplay. Although the plot is set in the twentieth century, there is no reference to historical events or socio-political issues. Nevertheless, the plot has been interpreted as an allegory of France during the Occupation (Tarr). According to Carrie Tarr, "In *L'Eternel retour*, Cocteau aimed to 'elevate a modern story to the status of myth' (*Art of Cinema* 189) by proving that Nietzsche's notion of 'eternal return' could be applied to the fate of the doomed lovers whose story is relived by others, without their even realizing it" (55).

Conclusion

These novels show that religious motivation is not an end in itself in suicidal terrorism, since socio-political grievances play a role. Both novels do in different ways point to a middle ground between the two interpretive grids that have

been used to understand 9/11. Between attributing the attacks to Islamic fundamentalism or to sociopolitical factors, Bachi and Benaïssa point out that both
factors are present. They also emphasize that, as Derrida phrased it, "Those
called 'terrorists' are not, in this context, 'others,' absolute others whom we, as
'Westerners,' can no longer understand. We must not forget that they were often
recruited, trained, and even armed, and for a long time, in various Western ways
by a Western world that itself, in the course of its ancient as well as very recent
history, invented the word, the techniques, and the 'politics' of 'terrorism'"
(cited in Borradori, 115).

Although Benaïssa's novel can be interpreted as demonstrating that 9/11
was triggered by socio-political claims, and that religion supplies the means to
get attention to those claims, the prominent Qur'anic intertext overwhelms any
such argument. The imbalance present in Benaïssa's novel will only confirm the
average Western reader in the stereotypes perpetuated in the media, and which
have only worsened since 9/11 and the subsequent invasion of Iraq. These
stereotypes have contributed to strengthening the association between Islam and
terrorism, with Islamic fundamentalism being conveniently and constantly brandished as an easy explanation for any bombing that happens in the Middle East.
Indeed, the predominance of the Islamic intertext in Benaïssa's novel seems to
confirm the belief that Islam (or a particular interpretation of it) is to blame for
terrorism, and that Western policies in the Middle East have nothing to do with
it (contrary to what many political scientists say, see Fuller 83-96).

Bachi's text, which traces the complexity of contemporary problems to historical events of the last six hundred centuries, offers a counter narrative to the
simplistic reductions of "us versus them" or "the axis of evil" that flourished
after 9/11 in official American discourses.[22] Bachi's novel is more apt than
Benaïssa's to prod the reader to do what Butler advocates. Butler distinguishes
between the conditions that foster terrorism and its causes, and urges that we
"take collective responsibility for a thorough understanding of the history that
brings us to this juncture," instead of becoming paralyzed by the faulty argument that to understand is to exculpate (10). As Derrida explains: "one can thus
condemn *unconditionally*, as I do here, the attack of September 11 without having to ignore the real or alleged conditions that made it possible" (qtd. in Borradori, 107).

Martin Amis and John Updike's works show that one does not need to be
Arab, or Muslim, or both, to write a fictive portrayal of a Muslim terrorist complete with Qur'anic quotes (if one needed such proof). That Francophone Arab
writers, contrary to other 9/11 novelists, have so far restricted their narratives to
depicting the itinerary of a 9/11 hijacker seems to imply that a syndrome of guilt
by association has been at work. While Benaïssa's apology gives fodder to that
association, Bachi's novel, with his critique of the West, complex narration, and
multicultural intertext, prompts the reader to go beyond such simplistic views.

That these writers decided to depart from what we know about the hijackers, I would argue, constitutes one of the strengths of these novels: they make us
see 9/11 not just through the eyes of the actual hijackers (as Amis does in his

short story), but through those of other potential hijackers as well, thereby drawing attention to the social conditions that breed terrorism. Khosrokhavar distinguishes two different kinds of martyr: on the one hand the ones who are linked to defense and/or establishment of the nation (such as the Iranian, Palestinian, and Lebanese cases), and on the other hand the one exemplified by Al Qaeda, which "revendique la réalisation d'une communauté mondiale incarnée par l'universalisme islamique en brisant la puissance du Mal qui s'y oppose: l'Occident" 'claims the realization of a world community incarnating Islamic universalism by smashing the Evil that opposes it: the West' (329). In addition to an identity crisis, Khosrokhavar (and others) emphasizes that Al Qaeda members represent the globalization of martyrdom (111). Reuter points out that "What makes this relatively new, clandestine network so dangerous is its recipe for combining two formidable elements so as to create a uniquely deadly form of militant group: an uncompromising, seductive, Manichean worldview that attracts a cult-like following, and a set of real, local grievances and ethnic and/or religious conflicts waiting to be enflamed. Like a parasite, al-Qaeda moves among the conflicts in the Islamic world, deriving sustenance from genuine, often well-founded local anger and grievances" (Reuter 153). According to Holmes, "What hit the United States on 11 September was not religion . . . Instead, the 9/11 terrorists represented the *pooled insurgencies* of the Arab Middle East. The fusing of these local insurgencies took place largely among diaspora Arabs outside the Middle East itself, in Afghanistan and Europe" (168).[23] By giving a different nationality to their hijacker, Benaïssa and Bachi seem to stress how local grievances can become global.

Notes

1. Novels by French authors include Luc Lang's *11 septembre mon amour* (Stock, 2003) and Frédéric Beigbeder's *Windows on the World* (Gallimard, 2005).
2. See also Tahar Ben Jelloun and Martin Amis, who each wrote a short story in the same vein.
3. See Terry McDermott's *Perfect Soldiers* for a reconstitution of the historical events of 9/11.
4. The publication of the leading association for scholars of literature in the U.S. (Modern Language Association).
5. See Brown's critique of Žižek (Brown 746). Brown points out that the distinction in the argument by Žižek (Islamic fundamentalism explained as "the sacralization of proper (economic) politics") depends on "an a priori distinction between religion and politics and on the separation of church and state" (747). Such a distinction, he adds, is not in operation in other parts of the world. Brown's assumption betrays an Orientalist mode of thinking as well as blindness to the influence of religion in American politics.
6. See Nixon's article in *The New Crusades*.
7. Although Soyinka does not refer to the clash of civilizations, his branding Islam as an element foreign to African culture partakes of the same essentialist view of cultures.

8. Morton criticizes Baudrillard, Žižek, and others' recent essays on terrorism because they overlook "the imperialist interests that are served by the discourse of terrorism by focusing on the emotional and aesthetic connotation of terror instead of examining the geopolitical context of its production" (37). Such works "reinforce the aestheticisation of terror . . . rather than examining the geopolitical determinants of terrorism as a discourse" (Morton 37). I find this criticism is only partially warranted for Baudrillard, and definitely not for Žižek.

9. The Japanese Kamikazes represent the highest number of suicide missions organized by a single source (Gambetta viii).

10. Reflecting on the fact that certain groups, such as the Christian Maronites, did not resort to suicide missions, and that self-immolations are mostly confined to Hindu and Buddhist countries, Gambetta concludes that "Different sets of religious beliefs are enabling and disabling different forms of self-sacrifice" (293). This conclusion, however, does not seem to recall that an entire chapter of the book is dedicated to the Tamil Tigers, who are 90 percent Hindu with a small minority of Christians (Hopgood 47).

11. Despite Gross' excellent analysis of Benaïssa's plays, I concur with Micheline Servin that his theater is more like sketches than full-fledged productions (qtd. in Gross 387).

12. That is Christians and Jews.

13. See the list compiled by Kurzman at http://www.unc.edu/~kurzman/terror.htm.

14. The comparison of 9/11 to the attack on Pearl Harbor was a misleading one; as an attack on civilians in an urban area the comparison with the bombing of Hiroshima would have been more pertinent, though more controversial (see Versluys n.23).

15. There is some dispute about the veracity of this story. See Sibly and Sibly (289-93).

16. Most of these allusions are to the advantage of women, with one exception. An allusion to a Hadith works the other way around: "ce n'était pas le paradis aux pieds de sa mère" 'it was not paradise at his mother's feet' is followed by a virulent critique of Maghrebian mothers (82).

17. "Il croyait parce qu'il n'était pas seulement un de ces hypocrites, ceux-là Dieu connaissait le contenu de leurs coeurs 'écarte-toi d'eux' il ne l'avait pas fait" (78) alludes to "These are they, the secrets of whose hearts Allah knows; so turn aside from them and admonish them" (4:63).

18. To which Khalid answers with another verse (2:216): "Fighting is prescribed for you, and ye dislike it. But it is possible that ye dislike a thing which is good for you, and that ye love a thing which is bad for you."

19. "And he for whom Allah intends temptation, thou controllest naught for him against Allah" (5:41).

20. "And they swear by Allah that they are truly of you. And they are not of you, but they are a people who are afraid. If they could find a refuge or caves or a place to enter, they would certainly have turned thereto, running away in all haste" (9:56-57).

21. Duras did not want to depict the horror of Hiroshima as had already been done by showing the actual devastating and horrific effects of the bomb; she wanted to "make this horror rise again from its ashes by [inscribing] it in a love [story]" (qtd. in Higgins 21-22).

22. See Butler's first chapter ("Explanation and Exoneration, or What We Can Hear") for a detailed analysis of the rise of censorship and anti-intellectualism that took

place in the U.S. after 9/11 to disparage anyone who tried to understand the reasons why the attacks had taken place.

23. This analysis seems to me more accurate than Khosrokhavar's statement that the Al-Qaeda martyr struggles for a transnational Umma (233). Khosrokhavar also points out that Al Qaeda is a product of globalization, the Muslim diaspora in the West, and crisis in Muslim society (233), and of course the issue of humiliation by proxy (239). However, Khosrokhavar's affirmation that this is a terrorism that has no specific territorial claim contradicts what has been demonstrated by Holmes: that is, that Bin Laden had very specific grievances regarding the presence of American troops on Saudi soil.

Conclusion

The Politics of Translation: Francophone Literature from the Arab World in the U.S.

In conclusion, I turn to the impact that international news has had on the translation of some of the texts treated in this study, as emblematic of Francophone literature from the Arab world. Two factors play in the translation, packaging, and reception of these texts: the U.S.' unconditional support of Israeli policies towards Palestinians, and 9/11 and the subsequent invasion of Afghanistan and Iraq. Reflecting on the spike of American interest in the cultural production of the Arab and Muslim world in general, this chapter offers a critical evaluation of this trend's implications in general and for Francophone Studies in particular.

Well-established writers usually see their work automatically translated into English. Given that Ben Jelloun, winner of the prestigious Goncourt prize in 1987, is one of the most prominent Francophone Maghrebian writers (and one whose creative work has been translated into numerous languages), it should be no surprise that his essay on Islam was promptly translated into English in 2002.[1] However, his book promises more than it delivers, since it contains several statements that are not representative of mainstream practitioners of Islam in France or elsewhere, and fails to account for the complexity of issues tied to the affair of the scarf (as demonstrated in chapter five). Maalouf, another Goncourt prize winner (in 1993), also enjoys international recognition since his work has been widely translated into many languages. The English translation of his essay *Identités meurtrières* came out in England in 2000; the 2003 Penguin North American edition consists of the very same English version, but repackaged in light of 9/11. The paratext, in the form of excerpts from book reviews that appear on the front cover and first page, casts the essay as shedding light on why 9/11 happened. As an example, the cover features a quote from the *Los Angeles Times* that states: "This striking and pungent polemic is so searingly pertinent, it confirms that . . . the mass murder of September 11, while indelibly shocking, is not wholly surprising."

9/11 has had sizeable repercussions not only on the packaging, but especially on the publication of translations of texts from the Arab world in the United

States, as evidenced by the following cases. Although Myriam Antaki has published four novels in French since 1985, she is unknown in the field of Francophone literature. *Les versets du pardon*, published in 1999 in France, was her first (and only book to date) to be translated into English (New York: Other Press, 2002). The subject matter of the Arab-Israeli conflict and the novel's setting in historical Palestine are not commonly thought of as being within the realm of Francophone studies, despite the fact that events in the Middle East have been having repercussions in France on the relations between the French Muslim and Jewish communities and on the Jewish minorities in the Maghreb, as elaborated on in chapter two.

Although Benaïssa is a relative newcomer as a novelist, *La dernière nuit d'un damné* (2003) appeared in English the next year after its French publication, and is his only novel and second book to have been translated into English. Despite being a rather unremarkable novel by a minor writer, it enjoys a relatively wide distribution, if one can judge by the number of libraries that own it (over 600 according to the WorldCat database), and was reprinted in 2005. Novelists such as Antaki and Benaïssa are minor writers, yet they have in common that one of their works has made it quickly on the U.S. market post 9/11 thanks to their subject matter linked to "Arab-Muslim" terrorism.

In contrast, Meddeb is a well-established writer who has been publishing since 1979, yet none of his creative work, which has long engaged with Islam,[2] has been translated into English. However, the English version of his essay *La maladie de l'islam* was published promptly in 2003. This is an example of an established writer's work receiving selective translation, a fact that can be explained on several accounts. First and foremost, the subject matter linked to 9/11 made it a timely and relevant publication. Second, its title confirms from the start the horizon of expectations of readers fed with prejudiced media accounts that something is inherently wrong with Islam (while Meddeb's other works offer a more complex picture).

In any event, the availability of Francophone authors to an Anglophone readership should provide cause for rejoicing for scholars, all the more so when the former offer perspectives not widely presented in the mainstream American media, particularly the criticism of the double standards of American foreign policy and the Palestinians' plight. For instance, Antaki's novel, which features Zionist terrorist acts by Irgoun and Stern in 1948 and subsequent displacement of Palestinian refugees, does offer a historical perspective and a point of view that are usually absent from contemporary media coverage of the Arab-Israeli conflict. This novel helps humanize Palestinians by showing the suffering that Marie goes through and linking it directly with the tragedy of the Holocaust. In the United States, Palestinians' suffering is considered too politically charged to even be mentioned. Butler has demonstrated that when it comes to the Middle East, Israeli and Palestinian deaths do not entail the same reaction in the U.S., that there is "a hierarchy of grief" (32) at work.[3] Popular culture in the U.S. frequently associates Palestinians with terrorist violence, suicide bombings, and Islamic extremism. These associations have only been reinforced by the 9/11 attacks, after which Israel banked on the U.S.'s "War on Terror" to justify its policies in the Occupied Territories. Said observed that public discourse always occults the fact that "Israeli violence against Palestinians has *always* been *incomparably* greater in scale and damage" than the reverse (Said, "The Essential" 153), a fact that still rings true twenty years after he made that remark (witness the December 2008 massive bombing of Gaza).

However, I would like to express a reservation concerning this recent phenomenon of craze for translating such works in general. Different contexts affect how works are read and received. Antaki writes in Syria (she is one of the few writers treated in this study who still lives in the Arab world), but her work is in French and is published in Paris. The cultural production of the second half of the twentieth century in France and in French has given its due attention to World War II and the Holocaust, but the harm of colonization, such as Arabs' plight during the Algerian war for instance, has lagged behind. In fact, the third and fourth phase of the Vichy syndrome (the return of the repressed and obsession, respectively), as defined by historian Henri Rousso, "may have been precipitated by the desire to cover up the double loss caused by the Algerian trauma" (Donadey, *Recasting* 7).

Antaki's novel was not well received in the Middle East[4] for two reasons. First, it features the Holocaust, a fact that was not well received in an area where there is widespread downplaying of the suffering endured by Jews under Nazism because of the crucial role played by Western nations' guilt about it in the establishment of the state of Israel. Second, because it uses the word "terrorist" to describe Ahmed (E-mail to the author, January 22, 2007). Various scholars have insisted on the exploitation of the term "terrorist" by powers suppressing independence movements; Butler (among others) insists that, "The term 'terrorist' is used, for instance, by the Israeli state to describe any and all Palestinian acts of resistance, but none of its own practices of state violence" (4). I believe that Antaki's use of the term terrorist, juxtaposed to "dreamer," serves to highlight the fact that terrorism is not an end in itself, but only a tactic. But as Antaki's book travels to other readerships, particularly in the U.S., it might reinforce the image of the Palestinian as "the essential terrorist" (to borrow Said's phrase).

Similarly, as previously noted, Meddeb's essay was promptly translated into English because it directly addressed issues of immediate concern to the U.S. Shohat and Stam rightly point out that "in the current situation, U.S. power is global, yet the knowledge of too many of its citizens is local and monoperspectival" (5). Hence, people are unable to make a connection between resentment about the U.S.'s foreign policy of support for dictators and attacks on American interests.[5] On the one hand, Meddeb, who chastises the double standard of American foreign policy in the Middle East, does offer a perspective on the world that is rarely presented in mainstream American media. However, since less than five pages are dedicated to a brief recapitulation of U.S. interference in the politics of the Arab world, this book will add to what has become a pervasive problem:

> Much of what one reads and sees in the media about Islam represents the aggression as coming from Islam because that is what "Islam" is. Local and concrete circumstances are thus obliterated. In other words, covering Islam is a one-sided activity that obscures what "we" *do*, and highlights instead what Muslims and Arabs by their very flawed nature *are*. (Said, *Covering*: xxii)

The emphasis on Islamic fundamentalism (for which Meddeb's title, *La maladie de l'islam*, is a periphrasis) relegates external interferences and influences to the background, and foregrounds Islam as the main source of terrorism. As S. Sayyid points out, "Islamist challenges to the prevailing order can only be represented as acts of terrorism, because there is no space for challenges to the prevailing political order. Thus, the legitimacy of the Islamist struggle against repression is denied as the protestors are labeled as terrorists, while those who staff and command the repression machines of the state are presented as reasonable and moderate members of the international community" (xii). Meddeb's uneven-handed account of the internal and external reasons for Islam's so–called disease might not be what his readership is most in need of.

The same reservation applies to Benaïssa's novel. Unfortunately, since few pages are dedicated to the disastrous legacy of colonialism and current imperialist foreign policies, while the Muslim scriptures are given ample space, this book will do little to redress the pervasive popular view that violence is intrinsic to Islam. As already detailed in chapter six, Benaïssa's and Bachi's 9/11 novels have a lot in common. Bachi is also an emerging novelist, but his work has already earned several literary prizes, most notably the Goncourt for a first novel (*Le chien d'Ulysse* in 2001). Nevertheless, there is no sign of *Tuez-les tous* being considered for an English translation. According to Bachi, "Il semblerait que le sujet du livre dérange les éditeurs outre-Manche et outre-Atlantique" 'it seems that the topic of the book disturbs British and American publishers' according to the person in charge of foreign rights at Gallimard (E-mail to the author, March 29, 2007). Although *Tuez-les tous* was only recently published, the translation of Benaïssa's *La dernière nuit* shows that it is not the subject matter that is in dispute, on the contrary. I can only surmise that the way the subject is treated is the culprit (in addition to its narrative structure and elaborate intertext which both contribute to making this a challenging read), in the sense that it questions stereotypes and commonplace ideas that mainstream America might not be ready, or willing to reconsider.

The impact of 9/11 on what is made available in American bookstores is not without implications. In the case of Francophone literature published in the U.S. post 9/11, the recent translations discussed above seem to indicate that the spike of American interest in the literary production of that region is limited to whatever can be linked to the traumatic event of 9/11, and not literary recognition already established by the original publication, as is customarily the case. For instance, the English translation of Antaki's novel makes no mention of her previous novels, as if knowing about her untranslated work was superfluous and of no value to an American readership. Thus, the American public does not acknowledge that the cultural production of these countries is worthy of interest regardless of their centrality to U.S.'s interests, and not because they have been defined by public discourse as potential enemies. As Mary Louise Pratt aptly states in the context of language learning and national security imperatives, "It is critical that . . . linguistic others not be defined from the start as potential enemies" (115), and that we not become interested in foreign cultural production only when it is too late.

Some of the texts treated in this study perpetuate uncalled-for stereotypes about Islam and Muslims. While texts such as *L'excisée* and *La dernière nuit d'un damné* do mention socio-political factors that play a role in fomenting and perpetuating various conflicts, their religious intertexts, and specifically Qur'anic quotations, contribute to marking Islam as the culprit and thus downplay essential triggers.

In *L'excisée*, religious sources are quoted in such a way as to suggest that Islam, which is the source of subjugation of these women, requires excision, which the women perpetuate in a ruthless manner, with no hope of change and progress coming from the inside (as demonstrated in chapter 3). Despite a few passages critical of Christian theology, the allegorical reading supported by the novel inscribes it within a Christian framework that subscribes to the values of sacrifice, redemption, and salvation.

Given this, it should not be viewed as a coincidence, therefore, that *L'excisée*, in addition to being featured in various anthologies,[6] has found a new readership, if one can judge by the fact that the French original was reedited in 1992 and its English translation in 1994 (and reprinted in 2005),[7] during a period when Islam made notorious headlines, both domestically in France (with the issue of the veil in public schools for instance) and internationally.[8] In addition, *L'excisée* (and Accad's work in general) is starting to receive more attention from scholars.[9]

The implications of the new interest generated by this novel in the contemporary socio-political U.S. climate can be serious. As a teacher in the United States, I would think twice before assigning *L'excisée* for a general education course, for the same reasons reported by an unnamed Middle Eastern scholar, who

> wanted no part of the tendency in the West to focus on this image of Middle Eastern and African women. In her experience, many people know little about the Middle East except the topics of veils and circumcision. We should be writing about many other topics . . . , lest unflattering North American and European stereotypes of Arabs, Muslims, and Africans be reinforced and allowed to fuel hostile political and economic policies. (qtd. in Gruenbaum 204)

This concern is particularly valid in the post-9/11 climate. A recent example of women's oppression being used for political purposes would be the plight of Afghani women under the Taliban's regime, which became a concern of the Bush administration only after September 11, 2001, and was then used as an additional validation to gain support for invading Afghanistan. More recently, critics have analyzed why the success of Azar Nafisi's memoir *Reading Lolita in*

Tehran is highly problematic, with its criticism of the Iranian Islamic revolution and government without sufficient contextualization happening concurrently with increased threats from the Bush administration against Iran, therefore leading itself to being recuperated for conservative political purposes (see Donadey and Ahmed-Ghosh). A similar conclusion could be reached about the success of Marjane Satrapi's animated film *Persepolis* (2007), although the film, with its criticism of European racism, and the English translation of the graphic novel, with an introduction giving a brief historical background that focuses on Western intervention in Iran, lend themselves less easily to such a reappropriation.

While this certainly does not mean that one should only present positive aspects of a culture, I fear that in the current political climate, a novel such as *L'excisée* only reinforces stereotypes. A teacher would have to nudge students into a critical self-reflection, relating how some Western cultural practices can be paralleled to Female Genital Cutting, such as fraternity hazing in the U.S. as a form of ritualized violence and the corset[10] as an "ideal of femininity . . . mediated by *pain*" (Lionnet 133),[11] the "neotribal" practices that have gained some popularity in Western countries among the "modern primitives" (Zabus, *Between Rites* 269-73), or unnecessary hysterectomies, procedures that also involve the removal of an organ, still being performed in the U.S. despite the potential loss of libido and health consequences they entail. Otherwise, students whose understanding of African and Middle Eastern cultures is often too scanty and prejudiced, all the more so when it comes to Muslim cultures in a post-September 11, 2001 period, would only feel comforted in their view of this threatening Other.

In light of post 9/11 events, the following question is very pointed: "To what extent have Arab peoples, predominantly practitioners of Islam, fallen outside the 'human' as it has been naturalized in its 'Western' mold by the contemporary workings of humanism?" (Butler 32). One could easily replace the adjective "Arab" with "Muslim" in the previous quote, and extend Butler's question about the nameless Palestinian dead to Afghani and Iraqi civilians. The U.S. news memorializes daily the U.S. military that have died in Afghanistan and Iraq by showing their pictures and their names on the news, while the Afghan and Iraqi civilians remain bundled into some abstract numbers whose accuracy is impossible to determine.

Some of the texts treated in this study, while written well before 9/11, have found a renewed relevance. I have already mentioned the repackaging of Maalouf's *Identités meurtrières*. Reading Maalouf's *Les croisades vues par les Arabes* in the United States in the context of post-September 11, 2001 and after the Iraq invasion of 2003, where a widespread discourse of the clash of civilizations among policy makers influences American public opinion, it is evident that Maalouf's essay is as timely now as it was when it was published twenty years ago. Witness the outcry that followed the use of the word "crusade" by George W. Bush to describe the military campaign against terrorism in Afghanistan. While Maalouf's epilogue is colored by the Middle Eastern politics of the twentieth century up to the early 1980s (as detailed in chapter 1), reading this text in the United States in the post-September 11, 2001, post-Iraq invasion era, I cannot help lamenting the total lack of impact that his essay, which was translated into many languages (and into English as early as 1984) has had in the political sphere.[12] For had George W. Bush read Maalouf, he might have at the very least avoided making such a blunder as to characterize the American invasion of Afghanistan, a Muslim country, as a "crusade," and rethought the terms in which his foreign policy is clad.

Maalouf's historical essay, despite its shortcomings, exemplifies the form of political engagement that Said and Bourdieu advocated for public intellectuals. As Said put it, "we need to think about breaking out of the disciplinary ghettos in which as intellectuals we have been confined, to reopen the blocked social processes ceding objective representation (hence power) of the world to a small coterie of experts and their clients, to consider that the audience for literacy is not a closed circle of three thousand professional critics but the community of human beings living in society" ("Opponents" 146).[13] One only wishes that their voices had been heard, and their words taken to heart.

Instead, postcolonial theory (and Said's *Orientalism* as emblematic of it) found itself at the center of a controversy about the alleged bias of Title VI-funded programs in Middle Eastern Studies (Kurtz). The House Committee on Education had approved H.R. 3077, which creates an Advisory Board to supervise Title VI programs.[14] Had that bill passed, *The Crusades through Arab Eyes* might be declared by the proposed advisory board unfit to be taught by faculty affiliated with Title VI centers, since its title easily identifies it as a work giving a one-sided approach. Such a measure would silence an Arab perspective on a crucial page of history at a time when it has been made extremely relevant by public discourse and foreign policy. As Said reminds us in his posthumous work, "At least since Nietzsche, the writing of history and the accumulations of memory have been regarded in many ways as one of the essential foundations of power, guiding its strategies, charting its progress" (*Humanism* 141). And Maalouf's 1983 revisiting of the Crusades resonates in uncannily relevant ways twenty years later.

One of the most depressing insights gained from this study was to note that even scholars of Said's stature seem to have had little impact, witness the current debacle of American foreign policy in the Middle East. Scholars working on the Middle East have been particularly scrutinized and under fire lately. There has been some progress since Hassan lamented in his article that "given the U.S.'s imperial role in the region, notably its unconditional economic and military commitments to Israel, there is not more criticism of Israel in those quarters of academic study that claim to oppose colonialism in all its forms" (33). However, Barghouti's piece about the dehumanization of Palestinians in Israeli society published in *PMLA*, the journal of the leading association for scholars and teachers of language and literature in the U.S., elicited two negative letters (see the Forum section of the March 2007 issue), demonstrating that scholars of literature will not be immune to their peers wrongly equating criticism of Israel with anti-Semitism. Indeed, young scholars critical of Israel in various fields in the United States have seen their bid for tenure denied or generating intense campaigns,[15] while preeminent scholars such as John J. Mearsheimer and Stephen M. Walt have had their invitation to lecture cancelled (Jaschik). As Butler points out, the distinction between Israel and Jews needs to be clearly maintained, so that criticism of Israeli policy not be automatically branded as anti-Semitism, and vice versa, to not reduce Jews and Judaity to Israeli concerns (125).

JuifsArabes, Boudjellal's best selling comic book, has been translated into German and Italian, but not English (personal interview, July 2, 2008), while Albou's film is available on DVD in the U.S. Memmi's writings, both fictional and non-fictional, have been translated into English and are widely available.[16] His stance on Arabs and Jews, which recuperates the colonial ideology of separation between the two groups, has become the dominant one. In a series of interviews with Marie Redonnet, El Maleh deplores that his books did not get any recognition in France.[17] His work, which offers a different perspective, remains marginalized, despite the increased recognition and critical attention that it has been getting in recent years. El Maleh started writing later than Memmi, which partially explains why he is less well-known. Another factor is that his writings have not easily found publishers, partially because they did not correspond to the horizon of expectation of readers. El Maleh recalls that one of the publishers he submitted his manuscript to could not understand why he had linked his story to the events taking place in Lebanon, and would rather have seen him talk about his "enfance juive, entre deux cultures: l'origine traditionnelle, l'acculturation, la découverte et l'entrée dans la culture française" 'Jewish childhood, between two cultures: the traditional origin, acculturation, discovery and entrance into French culture' (Redonnet 75). Contrary to Memmi's writings, which correspond to the description given by El Maleh of French publishers' expectations, El Maleh's texts challenge these expectations and current political agendas. None of El Maleh's books have been translated into English. Given his strong stance on Israeli policies towards Palestinians, and his comparisons between them and Nazi crimes, I would surmise that this will not be remedied any time soon in the United States.

Given the stature of some of the writers treated in this study, essays such as Ben Jelloun's and Meddeb's exacerbate the distortion that the field of Francophone studies creates, in that, as Richard Serrano stated in a provocative study entitled *Against the Postcolonial*, "the Francophone Studies model promotes a tiny sliver of literary and cultural production as representative" of the Francophone world (1), although its cultural output is expressed in many languages. As this study has shown, several books by well-known writers are not helping to bring a full picture about what is going on in the Arab world and its diaspora, particularly when Islam is concerned.[18] In fact, many of them just give us a skylight rather than a window on those issues.

Unfortunately, in the current political climate, such texts, with their downplaying of the legacy of colonialism and neo-colonialism, and emphasis on Islam as a fundamentalist religion opposed to the democratic West as the source of all problems, participate, even if unwillingly, in manufacturing consent (as Herman and Chomsky demonstrated for the mass media) to justify military intervention against other nations. In addition, these writers fail to render the fact that Islam does have a certain appeal, as attested by its growth. In his analysis of the global resurgence of religion, Thomas presumes that this phenomenon may indicate that there are other ways of being modern than Westernization (45). Majid makes a persuasive case for non-Western peoples, including Muslims, to reconnect with their religious traditions, and sees "the insistence on secular solutions in profoundly religious cultures" as "yet another sign of Eurocentrism" (*Freedom* 212-21). In the same vein, Graham Fuller points out that "efforts in the Muslim world to advance political and social thought *totally independent of the framework of Islamic culture* is doomed to be fractured, unintegrated, rootless, and alienated" (201). As Majid emphasizes after persuasively recapitulating the destructiveness and impoverishment (both culturally and materially) brought about by capitalism worldwide, there are other ways of being in the world than the one promoted by the West.[19] Increased translation might be seen as transparently helpful in a post-9/11 world, but given that it tends to disseminate the least critical writings that come from the Arab world, it only serves to assuage the liberal conscience.

Notes

1. Another edition of the French text with activities targeted at learners of the French language also appeared in 2002 in Italy.

2. *Phantasia* for instance is replete with literary allusions and references from the Qur'an and Arab poets (among others); this intertext contributes to his work not being easily accessible.

3. Butler tells about the case of obituaries and memorials of Palestinians killed by the Israeli army that were rejected by a U.S. newspaper on the ground that "the newspaper did not wish to offend anyone" (35). Butler then proceeds to ask pointed questions about the implications of this incident, among some: "What is the relation between the violence by which these ungrievable lives were lost and the prohibition on their public grievability? . . . Does the prohibition on discourse relate to the dehumanization of the deaths—and the lives?" (36).

4. Carol Corm states in a brief interview that it "stirred strong reactions in the Middle East" (15); similarly, Nathalie Galesne states that "des débats houleux ont eu lieu à l'occasion des présentations de l'ouvrage, notamment en Jordanie" 'stormy debates took place during presentations of the book, notably in Jordan' (157), but neither specifies any further.

5. See for instance Said's discussion of then President Carter's reaction to the hostage crisis in Tehran as symptomatic of this in *Covering Islam* (xiv-xvi).

6. See Mary Ann Caws' and Margot Badran and Miriam Cooke's anthologies.

7. Boulder, London: Lynne Rienner, 2005.

8. See the new introduction to Said's revised edition of *Covering Islam*, especially xii-xiv for an abbreviated list for events between 1983 and 1996.

9. When I first started working on this book, a search in the MLA International Bibliography only yielded four entries (see Heistad 2000, Marie, Mudimbe-Boyi, and Zahnd; see also Zabus' 1999 article). Since then, a volume of essays on Accad's work has been published in France (see Heistad 2005) and another one in English just appeared (see Toman), both edited by former students of Accad.

10. Cosmetic surgery such as breast implants would be a contemporary equivalent of the now defunct corset. Here is an example of how culture determines our choice of words: cosmetic surgery (most of which is not performed to heal) is never thought of as mutilation; in a similar vein see Lionnet for a provocative discussion of abortion as mutilation (160-61).

11. Richard Shweder reports how a proposal developed by a Seattle hospital to accommodate an immigrant Somali family was discarded, although "from a medical point of view, the proposed procedure (a small cut in the prepuce that covers the clitoris) was less severe than a typical American male circumcision" (234).

12. After Operation Enduring Freedom in Iraq, the same can be said of *Orientalism*, where Said, after quoting Chateaubriand, comments: "Already in 1810 we have a European talking like Cromer in 1910, arguing that Orientals require conquest, and finding it no paradox that a Western conquest of the Orient was no conquest after all, but liberty" (172).

13. See also Bourdieu's *Contre-feux 2*. Here is what he advocated in his 1999 intervention at the MLA convention entitled "A scholarship with commitment" ["Pour un savoir engagé"], later published in *Contre-feux 2*: "Les écrivains, les artistes et surtout les chercheurs . . . doivent transcender la *frontière sacrée*, qui est inscrite aussi dans leur cerveau, plus ou moins profondément selon les traditions nationales, entre le *scholarship* et le *commitment*, pour sortir résolument du microcosme académique, entrer en interaction avec le monde extérieur . . . au lieu de se contenter des conflits 'politiques' à la fois intimes et ultimes, et toujours un peu irréels, du monde scolastique" (39-49).

14. The American Council on Education reports concerns from the higher education community that such a board might interfere with the curriculum ("Controversial Graduate and International Education Bills Pass House Committee" *Higher Education and National Affairs* 52.18 (10/6/03). 14 December 2003 <http://www.acenet.edu/hena/ >.

15. Norman Finkelstein, a political scientist, and Nadia Abu El-Haj, an anthropologist (see Jaschik's "Middle East Tensions Flare Again in U.S. (Update)."

16. Incidentally, the translation of *Portrait du décolonisé arabo-musulman et de quelques autres* received financial assistance from the French Ministry of Culture.

17. "Je n'ai pas trouvé ma place en tant qu'écrivain en France, malgré la réédition de mes livres et l'illusion qu'elle allait pouvoir amorcer une relance" 'I did not find my place as a writer in France, despite the new edition of my books and the illusion that it would begin an upturn' (Redonnet 13). Later on, he indicates being awarded the title of Chevalier de la légion d'honneur (for which he was nominated by the French embassy): "Paradoxalement, il m'a fallu revenir au Maroc pour qu'une reconnaissance officielle me consacre en tant qu'écrivain ayant une place particulière dans la littérature de langue française" 'paradoxically, I had to go back to Morocco before an official recognition consecrated me as a writer having a special place in literature in French' (Redonnet 14).

18. Francophone writers are not the only ones downplaying colonialism when it comes to better accusing Islam (see Nixon's article).

19. Taking the example of Islamic cultures, he contends that "By stating that Allah has deliberately divided humanity into many nations and tribes, then challenged us to know one another, the Qur'an clearly revealed that God's design is for a world of diversi-

ties competing in pious deeds. There is no reason to believe that such a divine intent is less inspiring than the one that champions a brave new world of interest-seeking individuals whose collective endeavors, we are told, automatically add up to the coveted blessings of happiness and social harmony" (*Unveiling* 21).

Bibliography

Abul-Husn, Latif. *The Lebanese Conflict. Looking Inward.* Boulder & London: Lynne Rienner, 1998.

Accad, Evelyne. "Author's Preface. Ectomy." *The Excised.* Trans. David K. Bruner. Revised and augmented ed. Colorado Springs, CO: Three Continents Press, 1994. ix-xvii.

———. *L'excisée.* Paris: L'Harmattan, 1982. Trans. as *The Excised*, by David K. Bruner. Washington, DC: Three Continents Press, 1989.

———. *Sexuality and War: Literary Masks of the Middle East.* New York: New York University Press, 1990.

———. *Veil of Shame. The Role of Women in the Contemporary Fiction of North Africa and the Arab World.* Sherbrooke, Canada: Naaman, 1978.

———. "Writing One's Life: Arab Francophone Women." *Contemporary French Civilization* 26.1 (Winter/Spring 2002): 46-62.

Ahmadu, Fuambai. "Rites and Wrongs: An Insider/Outsider Reflects on Power and Excision." *Female "Circumcision" in Africa: Culture, Controversy, and Change.* Ed. Bettina Shell-Duncan and Ylva Hernlund. Boulder & London: Lynne Rienner, 2000. 283-312.

Ahmed, Leila. *Women and Gender in Islam: Historical Roots of a Modern Debate.* New Haven & London: Yale UP, 1992.

Aït-Embarek, Moussa. *L'Algérie en murmure. Un cahier sur la torture.* Plan-Les-Ouates, Switzerland: Hoggar, 1996.

Albou, Karin, dir. *La petite Jérusalem.* DVD. Océan Films Distribution, 2005.

Alcalay, Ammiel. *After Jews and Arabs: Remaking Levantine Culture.* Minneapolis: University of Minnesota Press, 1993.

Alloula, Malek. "Mes enfances exotiques." *Une enfance algérienne.* Ed. Leïla Sebbar. Paris: Gallimard, 1999 [1997]. 7-23.

Amis, Martin. "The Last Day of Muhammad Atta." *Observer* Sunday September 3, 2006. http://www.martinamisweb.com/documents/lastdays_one.pdf.

Antaki, Myriam. *Les versets du pardon.* Paris: Actes Sud, 1999. Trans. as *Verses of Forgiveness*, by Marjolijn de Jager. New York: Other Press, 2002.

Armstrong, Karen. *Holy War.* London: Macmillan, 1988.

Ashcroft, Bill, Gareth Griffiths, and Helen Tiffin. *Key Concepts in Post-Colonial Studies.* London & New York: Routledge, 1998.

Attar, Farid Ud-Din. *The Conference of the Birds.* Trans. S. C. Nott. London & New York: Continuum, 2000.

Aubrac, Lucie. *La résistance expliquée à mes petits-enfants.* Paris: Seuil, 2000.

Auger, Marie. *L'excision.* Montréal: XYZ, 2003.

Azria, Régine. "Achkénazes et Séfarades en France, une rencontre difficile." *Contemporary French and Francophone Studies* 11.2 (2007): 207-16.

Bachi, Salim. *Le chien d'Ulysse*. Paris: Gallimard, 2001.

———. *La Kahéna*. Paris: Gallimard, 2003.

———. *Tuez-les tous*. Paris: Gallimard, 2006.

Badran, Margot, and Miriam Cooke, eds. *Opening the Gates*. Bloomington: Indiana University Press, 1990.

Balibar, Etienne. *Droit de cité*. Paris: PUF, 2002 [1998].

Barghouti, Omar. "Relative Humanity: Identity, Rights, and Ethics—Israel as a Case Study." *PMLA* 121.5 (October 2006): 1536-43.

Barthes, Roland. *La chambre claire: Note sur la photographie*. Paris: Cahiers du cinéma, 1980.

Baubérot, Jean. *Histoire de la laïcité française*. Paris: PUF, 2000.

Baudrillard, Jean. *The Spirit of Terrorism and Other Essays*. Trans. Chris Turner. New Edition. London & New York: Verso, 2003. [2002]

Benaïssa, Slimane. *La dernière nuit d'un damné*. Paris: Plon, 2003. Trans. as *The Last Night of a Damned Soul*, by Janice and Daniel Gross. New York: Grove Press, 2004.

Benbassa, Esther. "Jewish-Moslem Relations in Contemporary France." *Contemporary French and Francophone Studies* 11.2 (2007): 189-94.

Bencheikh, Jamel Eddine. "Tlemcen la haute." *Une enfance algérienne*. Ed. Leïla Sebbar. Paris: Gallimard, 1999 [1997]. 25-39.

Benguigui, Yamina. *Mémoires d'immigrés. L'héritage maghrébin*. Paris: Canal +, 1997.

———, dir. *Mémoires d'immigrés. L'héritage maghrébin*. Canal & Bandits, 1997.

Ben Jelloun, Tahar. "Contamination." *Le Monde* 27 Jan. 2004. Web. 3 Aug. 2006 <http://www.lemonde.fr>.

———. "L'enfant trahi." *Amours sorcières*. Paris: Seuil, 2003. 248-53.

———. *Hospitalité française: Racisme et immigration maghrébine*. Paris: Seuil, 1984.

———. *L'Islam expliqué aux enfants*. Paris: Seuil, 2002. Trans. as *Islam explained*. New York: New Press, 2002.

———. *La nuit sacrée*. Paris: Seuil, 1987.

———. *Le racisme expliqué à ma fille*. Paris: Seuil, 1998.

Bensmaïa, Réda. "The Phantom Mediators: Reflections on the Nature of the Violence in Algeria." *Diacritics* 27.2 (1997): 85-97.

Bensoussan, Albert. "L'enfant perdu." *Une enfance algérienne*. Ed. Leïla Sebbar. Paris: Gallimard, 1999 [1997]. 41-54.

Berger, John. *Ways of Seeing*. London & New York: BBC & Penguin, 1977. [1972]

Borradori, Giovanna. *Philosophy in a Time of Terror. Dialogues with Jürgen Habermas and Jacques Derrida*. Chicago & London: University of Chicago Press, 2003.

Bouamama, Saïd. *L'affaire du foulard islamique. La production d'un racisme respectable*. Le Geai bleu, 2004.

Boudjedra, Rachid. *Le FIS de la haine*. Paris: Denoël, 1992.

———. "Postface." *Le FIS de la haine*. 2nd edition. Paris: Denoël, 1994. 115-35.

Boudjellal, Farid. *Le beurgeois*. Toulon: Soleil, 1997.

———. *Le gourbi*. Paris: Futuropolis, 1985.

———. *JuifsArabes*. Paris: Futuropolis, 2006.

———. *L'oud*. Paris: Futuropolis, 1983.

———. *Ramadân*. Paris: Futuropolis, 1988.

Boudjellal, Farid, and Martine Legardette. *Jambon-beur: Les couples mixtes*. Toulon: Soleil, 1995.

Bourdieu, Pierre. *Contre-feux 2: Pour un mouvement social européen*. Paris: Raisons D'Agir, 2001.

————. "Un problème peut en cacher un autre." *Le foulard islamique en questions*. Ed. Charlotte Nordmann. Paris: Editions Amsterdam, 2004. 45-46.

Bourget, Carine. *Coran et tradition islamique dans la littérature maghrébine*. Paris: Karthala, 2002.

————. "A l'écrit sans images: Le foulard islamique dans des oeuvres de Leïla Sebbar et Yamina Benguigui." *Expressions maghrébines* 6.1 (Summer 2007): 19-35.

Bouzar, Dounia. "Françaises et musulmanes, entre réappropriation et remise en question des normes." *Le foulard islamique en questions*. Ed. Charlotte Nordmann. Paris: Editions Amsterdam, 2004. 54-63.

Bouzar, Dounia, and Saïda Kada. *L'une voilée, l'autre pas. Le témoignage de deux musulmanes françaises*. Paris: Albin Michel, 2003.

Bowen, John. *Why the French Don't Like Headscarves: Islam, the State, and Public Space*. Princeton: Princeton University Press, 2007.

Boyle, Elizabeth Heger. *Female Genital Cutting. Cultural Conflict in the Global Community*. Baltimore and London: Johns Hopkins University Press, 2002.

Brown, Bill. "The Dark Wood of Postmodernity (Space, Faith, Allegory)." *PMLA* 120.3 (May 2005): 734-50.

Burgat, François. *The Islamic Movement in North Africa*. Translation of an updated version of *L'Islamisme au Maghreb*. Trans. William Dowell. 2nd edition. Austin: Center for Middle Eastern Studies at The University of Texas at Austin, 1997.

Butler, Judith. *Precarious Life. The Powers of Mourning and Violence*. London, New York: Verso, 2004.

Carlier, Omar. "Violence(s)." *La guerre d'Algérie: 1954-2004, la fin de l'amnésie*. Ed. Benjamin Stora and Mohammed Harbi. Paris: R. Laffont, 2004. 347-79.

Carrard, Philippe. *Poetics of the New History. French Historical Discourse from Braudel to Chartier*. Baltimore and London: John Hopkins University Press, 1992.

Caws, Mary Ann, ed. *Ecritures de femmes: Nouvelles cartographies*. New Haven: Yale University Press, 1996.

Cesari, Jocelyne. *Etre musulman en France*. Paris: Karthala, 1994.

————. "Islam in France: The Shaping of a Religious Minority." *Muslims in the West: From Sojourners to Citizens*. Ed. Yvonne Haddad. New York: Oxford University Press, 2002. 35-51.

Chédid, Andrée. *La maison sans racines*. Paris: Flammarion, 1985. Trans. as *The Return to Beirut*, by Ros Schwartz. London: Serpent's Tail, 1989.

Chomsky, Noam. "Middle East Terrorism and the American Ideological System." *Blaming the Victims: Spurious Scholarship and the Palestinian Question*. Ed. Edward Said and Christopher Hitchens. London & New York: Verso, 2001 [1988]. 97-147.

Chow, Rey. "Forum: Responses to Bill Brown's 'The Dark Wood of Postmodernity (Space, Faith, Allegory).'" *PMLA* 120.3 (May 2005): 874-85.

Chraïbi, Driss. *L'homme du livre*. Paris: Balland, 1995.

Cixous, Hélène. "Mon algériance." *Les inrockuptibles* 115 (20 août-2 septembre) 1997: 71-74.

————. "My Algeriance, in Other Words: To Depart Not to Arrive from Algeria." Trans. Eric Prenowitz. *Stigmata: Escaping Texts*. London, UK: Routledge, 1998. 153-72.

————. "Pieds nus." *Une enfance algérienne*. Ed. Leïla Sebbar. Paris: Gallimard, 1999 [1997]. 55-66.

Cocteau, Jean. *Three Screenplays. L'éternel retour, Orphée, la Belle et la Bête*. Trans. Carol Martin-Sperry. New York: Grossman Publishers, 1972.

Cohen, Annie. "Viridiana mon amour." *Une enfance algérienne*. Ed. Leïla Sebbar. Paris: Gallimard, 1999 [1997]. 67-81.

Cohen, William. "Pied-noir Memory, History, and the Algerian War." *Europe's Invisible Migrants*. Ed. Andrea Smith. Amsterdam: Amsterdam University Press, 2002. 129-44.

Colombani, Jean-Marie. "Nous sommes tous Américains." *Le Monde* 13 Sept. 2001. Web. 26 Jan. 2006 <http://www.lemonde.fr>.

Conan, Eric, and Christian Makaria. "Enquête sur la montée de l'islam en Europe." *L'Express* 26 Jan. 2006.

Constable, Giles. "The Historiography of the Crusades." *The Crusades from the Perspective of Byzantium and the Muslim World*. Ed. Angeliki Laiou & Roy Mottahedeh. Washington, DC: Dumbarton Oaks Research Library and Collection, 2001. 1-22.

Cooke, Miriam. "Dying to Be Free: Wilderness Writing from Lebanon, Arabia, and Libya." Ed. Cheryl Toman. *On Evelyne Accad: Essays in Literature, Feminism, and Cultural Studies*. Birmingham, AL: Summa, 2007. 13-31.

———. *War's Other Voices. Women Writers on the Lebanese Civil War*. Cambridge: Cambridge University Press, 1988.

Corm, Carol. "Definitions and Dialects of the Novel. Interview with Myriam Antaki." *Aljadid* 9.45 (Fall 2003): 15-16.

Crépon, Marc. *L'Imposture du choc des civilisations*. Nantes: Pleins Feux, 2002.

Culler, Jonathan. *On Deconstruction. Theory and Criticism after Structuralism*. Ithaca, NY: Cornell University Press, 1982.

Dadoun, Roger. "Hammam." *Une enfance algérienne*. Ed. Leïla Sebbar. Paris: Gallimard, 1999 [1997]. 83-98.

Daniel, Jean. "Arrêts sur images." *Une enfance algérienne*. Ed. Leïla Sebbar. Paris: Gallimard, 1999 [1997]. 99-114.

Dareer, Asma El. *Woman, Why Do You Weep? Circumcision and Its Consequences*. London: Zed Press, 1982.

De Certeau, Michel. *L'écriture de l'histoire*. Paris: Gallimard, 1975. Trans. as *The Writing of History*, by Tom Conley. New York: Columbia University Press, 1988.

———. "History: Science and Fiction." *Heterologies: Discourse on the Other*. Minneapolis: University of Minnesota Press, 1986. 199-221.

De Goncourt, Edmond, and Jules de Goncourt. *Germinie Lacerteux*. Paris: Flammarion, n. d. Trans. as *Germinie Lacerteux*, by John Chestershire. Philadelphia: George Barrie & Sons, 1897.

Deleuze, Gilles, and Félix Guattari. *Mille plateaux*. Paris: Minuit, 1980.

Delphy, Christine. "Une affaire française." *Le foulard islamique en questions*. Ed. Charlotte Nordmann. Paris: Editions Amsterdam, 2004. 64-71.

Desai, Gaurav. In "Editor's Column: The End of Postcolonial Theory? A Roundtable with Sunil Agnani, Fernando Coronil, Gaurav Desai, Mamadou Diouf, Simon Gikandi, Susie Tharu, and Jennifer Wenzel." *PMLA* 122.3 (May 2007): 641-42.

Dib, Mohammed. "Rencontres." *Une enfance algérienne*. Ed. Leïla Sebbar. Paris: Gallimard, 1999 [1997]. 115-26.

Dirlik, Arif. "History without a Center? Reflections on Eurocentrism." In *Across Cultural Borders: Historiography in Global Perspective*. Ed. E. Fuchs & B. Stuchtey. Lanham, MD: Rowman & Littlefield, 2002. 247-60.

Djebar, Assia. *Loin de Médine*. Paris: Albin Michel, 1991.

Donadey, Anne. "Foreword." *An Algerian Childhood*. Ed. Leïla Sebbar. Trans. Marjolijn de Jager. St. Paul, MN : Ruminator Books, 2001. vii-xvii.

———. *Recasting Postcolonialism: Women Writing between Worlds*. Portsmouth, NH: Heinemann, 2001.

Donadey, Anne, and Huma Ahmed-Ghosh. "Why Americans Love Azar Nafisi's *Reading Lolita in Tehran.*" *Signs: Journal of Women in Culture and Society* 33.3 (2008): 623-46.

Donadey, Anne, and Adlai Murdoch. *Postcolonial Theory and Francophone Literary Studies.* Gainesville, FL: University Press of Florida, 2005.

Douglas, Allen, and Fedwa Malti-Douglas. *Arab Comic Strips: Politics of an Emerging Mass Culture.* Bloomington & Indianapolis: Indiana University Press, 1994.

Drake, David. *Intellectuals and Politics in Post-War France.* New York: Palgrave, 2002.

Durmelat, Sylvie. "L'Algérie est à réinventer ou Femmes d'Alger hors de leur appartement dans *Viva Laldjérie* de Nadir Moknèche." *Expressions maghrébines* 6.1 (Summer 2007): 93-112.

———. "Transmission and Mourning in *Mémoires d'immigrés: L'héritage maghrébin*: Yamina Benguigui as 'Memory Entrepreneuse.'" *Women, Immigration and Identities in France.* Ed. Carrie Tarr and Jane Freedman. Oxford, NY: Berg, 2000. 171-90.

Eaglestone, Robert. "The Age of Reason Is Over . . . an Age of Fury Was Dawning." *Wasafiri* 22.2 (2007): 19-22.

El-Khoury, Barbara. "La fonction du voile et de l'excision chez Evelyne Accad." *Evelyne Accad: Explorations.* Ed. Deirdre Heistad. Paris: L'Harmattan, 2005. 123-46.

El Maleh, Edmond Amran. "Au seuil de l'interdit : Interrogations." *Revue d'études palestiniennes* 2.2 (Winter 1982): 18-34.

———. *Mille ans, un jour.* Marseille: André Dimanche, 2002. [1986]

———. "Le visage d'une négation." *Revue d'études palestiniennes* 5 (Automne 1982): 17-24.

El-Solh, Camillia Fawzi, and Judy Mabro, eds. *Muslim Women's Choices: Religious Belief and Social Reality.* Providence, RI: Berg, 1994.

Entelis, John. "Islamist Politics and the Democratic Imperative: Comparative Lessons from the Algerian Experience." *The Journal of North African Studies* 9.2 (Summer 2004): 202-15.

Esposito, John. "Religion and Global Affairs: Political Challenges." *SAIS Review* 18.2 (1998): 19-24.

Euben, Roxanne. *Enemy in the Mirror: Islamic Fundamentalism and the Limits of Modern Rationalism.* Princeton, NJ: Princeton University Press, 1999.

Farès, Nabile. "La mémoire des autres." *Une enfance algérienne.* Ed. Leïla Sebbar. Paris: Gallimard, 1999 [1997]. 127-42.

Fernea, Robert. Foreword. *The Islamic Movement in North Africa.* By François Burgat. Translation of an updated version of *L'Islamisme au Maghreb.* Trans. William Dowell. 2nd edition. Austin: Center for Middle Eastern Studies at The University of Texas at Austin, 1997. ix-xi.

Forsdick, Charles, and David Murphy. *Francophone Postcolonial Studies: A Critical Introduction.* London: Arnold, 2003.

Fuller, Graham. *The Future of Political Islam.* New York: Palgrave Macmillan, 2003.

Gafaïti, Hafid, ed. *Rachid Boudjedra: Une poétique de la subversion.* Paris: L'Harmattan, 1999.

Galesne, Nathalie. "*Les versets du pardon,* ou ' le livre de la paix'." *La pensée de midi*: 157-59.

Gallaire, Fatima. "Baï." *Une enfance algérienne.* Ed. Leïla Sebbar. Paris: Gallimard, 1999 [1997]. 143-58.

Gambetta, Diego. "Can We Make Sense of Suicide Missions?" *Making Sense of Suicide Missions.* Ed. Diego Gambetta. Oxford: Oxford University Press, 2005. 259-99.

———, ed. *Making Sense of Suicide Missions.* Oxford: Oxford University Press, 2005.

Gaspard, Françoise, and Farhad Khosrokhavar. *Le foulard et la République*. Paris: La Découverte, 1995.

———. "The Headscarf and the Republic." *Beyond French Feminisms: Debates on Women, Politics, and Culture in France, 1981-2001*. Ed. Roger Célestin, Eliane Dalmolin, and Isabelle de Courtivron. New York: Palgrave Macmillan, 2003. 61-67.

Gaumer, Patrick, and Claude Moliterni. *Dictionnaire mondial de la bande dessinée*. 2nd ed. Paris: Larousse, 2001.

Genette, Gérard. *Figures III*. Paris: Seuil, 1972.

———. *Paratexts: Thresholds of Interpretation*. Trans. Jane Lewin. Cambridge: Cambridge University Press, 1997.

Giraud, Véronique, Yves Sintomer, and Alma and Lila Lévy. *Des filles comme les autres: Au-delà du foulard*. Entretiens. Paris: La Découverte, 2004.

Gopin, Marc. "Forgiveness as an Element of Conflict Resolution in Religious Cultures: Walking the Tightrope of Reconciliation and Justice." *Reconciliation, Justice, and Coexistence: Theory and Practice*. Ed. Mohammed Abu-Nimer. Lanham, MD: Lexington Books, 2001. 87-99.

———. *Holy War, Holy Peace: How Religion Can Bring Peace to the Middle East*. New York: Oxford University Press, 2002.

Gossman, Lionel. *Between History and Literature*. Cambridge, MA: Harvard University Press, 1990.

Gravdal, Kathryn. *Ravishing Maidens: Writing Rape in Medieval French Literature and Law*. Philadelphia: University of Pennsylvania Press, 1991.

Grewal, Inderpal, and Caren Kaplan. "Warrior Marks: Global Womanism's Neo-Colonial Discourse in a Multicultural Context." *Camera Obscura: A Journal of Feminism and Film Theory* 39 (1996): 5-33.

Groensteen, Thierry. *The System of Comics*. Trans. Bart Beaty and Nick Nguyen. Jackson: University Press of Mississippi, 2007.

Gross, Janice. "The Tragedy of Algeria: Slimane Benaïssa's Drama of Terrorism." *Theatre Journal* 54 (2002): 369-87.

Gross, Janice, and Daniel Gross. "Translators' Notes." *The Last Night of a Damned Soul*. By Slimane Benaïssa. Trans. Janice and Daniel Gross. New York: Grove Press, 2004.

Grosser, Paul, and Edwin Halperin. *Anti-Semitism: Causes and Effects*. New York: Philosophical Library, 1983.

Grousset, René. *Les croisades*. Paris: PUF, 1960.

———. *Histoire des croisades*. 3 vol. Paris: Plon, 1934-1936.

Gruenbaum, Ellen. *The Female Circumcision Controversy. An Anthropological Perspective*. Philadelphia: The University of Pennsylvania Press, 2001.

Guénoun, Solange. "Accueils et écueils identitaires-communautaires en France postcoloniale: 'Ils disent que je suis sépharade . . . .' " *Contemporary French and Francophone Studies* 11.2 (April 2007): 217-30.

Haarscher, Guy. *La Laïcité*. Paris: PUF, 1996.

Hallam, Elizabeth, ed. *Chronicles of the Crusades. Eye-Witness Accounts of the Wars between Christianity and Islam*. London: Weidenfeld & Nicolson, 1989.

Harbi, Mohammed. "L'Algérie en perspectives." *La guerre d'Algérie: 1954-2004, la fin de l'amnésie*. Ed. Benjamin Stora and Mohammed Harbi. Paris: R. Laffont, 2004. 27-45.

Harbi, Mohammed, and Benjamin Stora, eds. *La guerre d'Algérie: 1954-2004, la fin de l'amnésie*. Paris: R. Laffont, 2004.

Hare, William. *Hitchcock and the Methods of Suspense*. Jefferson, NC & London: McFarland, 2007.

Hargreaves, Alec. "The Challenges of Multiculturalism: Regional and Religious Differences in France Today." *Contemporary French Cultural Studies.* Ed. William Kidd and Siân Reynolds. London: Arnold, 2000. 95-110.

Harrison, Nicholas. "Learning from Experience: Hélène Cixous's 'Pieds nus.'" *Paragraph: A Journal of Modern Critical Theory* 27.1 (March 2004): 21-32.

Hartman, Michelle. "Multiple Identities, Multiple Voices: Reading Andrée Chédid's *La maison sans racines.*" *French Studies* 54.1 (2000): 54-66.

Hasenclever, Andreas, and Volker Rittberger. "Does Religion Make a Difference? Theoretical Approaches to the Impact of Faith on Political Conflict." *Religion in International Relations. The Return from Exile.* Ed. Hatzopoulos, Pavlos and Fabio Petito. New York: Palgrave Macmillan, 2003. 107-45.

Hassan, Salah. "Undertaking Partition: Palestine and Postcolonial Studies." *Journal X* 6.1 (Autumn 2001): 19-45.

Hatzopoulos, Pavlos, and Fabio Petito, eds. *Religion in International Relations. The Return from Exile.* New York: Palgrave Macmillan, 2003.

Heistad, Deirdre, ed. *Evelyne Accad: Explorations.* Paris: L'Harmattan, 2005.

———. "Writings from the Borderzone: Tales of Recuperation and Transgression in the Works of Malika Mokeddem, Calixthe Beyala, and Evelyne Accad." Diss. University of Illinois at Urbana, 2000.

Herman, Edward S., and Noam Chomsky. *Manufacturing Consent: The Political Economy of the Mass Media.* New York: Pantheon Books, 1988.

Higgins, Lynn. *New Novel, New Wave, New Politics: Fiction and the Representation of History in Postwar France.* Lincoln: University of Nebraska Press, 1996.

———. "Screen/Memory: Rape and Its Alibis in *Last Year at Marienbad.*" *Rape and Representation.* Ed. Lynn Higgins and Brenda Silver. New York: Columbia University Press, 1991. 303-21.

Hochberg, Gil. *In Spite of Partition: Jews, Arabs, and the Limits of Separatist Imagination.* Princeton & Oxford: Princeton University Press, 2007.

Holmes, Stephen. "Al-Qaeda, September 11, 2001." *Making Sense of Suicide Missions.* Ed. Diego Gambetta. Oxford: Oxford University Press, 2005. 131-72.

The Holy Qur'an. Trans. Abdullah Yusuf Ali. Washington, DC: Khalil Al-Rawaf, 1946. [1934]

Hopgood, Stephen. "Tamil Tigers, 1987-2002." *Making Sense of Suicide Missions.* Ed. Diego Gambetta. Oxford: Oxford University Press, 2005. 43-76.

Hosken, Fran. *Stop Female Genital Mutilation. Women Speak. Facts and Actions.* Lexington, MA: Women's International Network News, 1995.

Hottell, Ruth. "A Poetics of Pain: Evelyne Accad's Critical and Fictional World." *World Literature Today* 71.3 (Summer 1997): 511-17.

Houen, Alex. "Novel Spaces and Taking Place(s) in the Wake of September 11." *Studies in the Novel* 36.3 (Fall 2004): 419-37.

Huston, Nancy, and Leïla Sebbar, eds. *Une enfance d'ailleurs.* Paris: Belfond, 1993.

Hutcheon, Linda. *A Poetics of Postmodernism.* London & New York: Routledge, 1988.

———. *The Politics of Postmodernism.* London & New York: Routledge, 1989.

Ibn Munqidh, Usamah. *An Arab-Syrian Gentleman and Warrior in the Period of the Crusades.* Trans. Philip K. Hitti. New York: Columbia University Press, 1929.

Imache, Djedjiga, and Inès Nour. *Algériennes entre Islam et islamisme.* Aix-en-Provence: Edisud, 1994.

Issa, Amira. "Révolte et image christique dans *L'excisée* d'Evelyne Accad." *Evelyne Accad: Explorations.* Ed. Deirdre Heistad. Paris: L'Harmattan, 2005. 163-72.

Jadla, Ibrahim. "Les juifs en Ifriqiya à l'époque hafside." *Histoire communautaire, histoire plurielle: La communauté juive de Tunisie.* Tunis: Centre de Publication Universitaire, 1999. 145-51.

Jaschik, Scott. "Middle East Tensions Flare Again in U.S. (Update)." *Inside Higher Ed* 5 Sept. 2007. Web. 28 March 2008. <http://www.insidehighered.com>.

Kacimi-El-Hassani, Mohamed. "A la claire indépendance." *Une enfance algérienne.* Ed. Leïla Sebbar. Paris: Gallimard, 1999 [1997]. 159-74.

Kalyvas, Stathis, and Ignacio Sánchez-Cuenca. "Killing without Dying: The Absence of Suicide Missions." *Making Sense of Suicide Missions.* Ed. Diego Gambetta. Oxford: Oxford University Press, 2005. 209-32.

Kandiyoti, Deniz. "Identity and Its Discontents: Women and the Nation." *Colonial Discourse and Post-Colonial Theory: A Reader.* Ed. Patrick Williams and Laura Chrisman. New York: Columbia University Press, 1994. 376-91.

Karnoub, Elisabeth. "Du sacrifice au sacrilège: le suicide d'une femme enceinte." *Evelyne Accad: Explorations.* Ed. Deirdre Heistad. Paris: L'Harmattan, 2005. 105-22.

Kenbib, Mohammed. *Juifs et musulmans au Maroc: 1859-1948.* Rabat: Faculté des lettres et des sciences humaines, 1994.

Kepel, Gilles. *Les banlieues de l'islam. Naissance d'une religion en France.* Paris: Seuil, 1987.

————. *Jihad. Expansion et déclin de l'islamisme.* Paris: Gallimard, 2000.

Khosrokhavar, Farhad. *Les nouveaux martyrs d'Allah.* Rev. ed. Paris: Flammarion, 2003. [2002]

Kinoshita, Sharon. "The Romance of MiscegeNation: Negotiating Identities in *La fille du comte de Pontieu.*" *Postcolonial Moves: Medieval through Modern.* Ed. Patricia Ingham and Michelle Warren. New York: Palgrace Macmillan, 2003. 111-31.

Koso-Thomas, Olayinka. *The Circumcision of Women. A Strategy for Eradication.* London & New Jersey: Zed Books Ltd., 1987.

Kurtz, Stanley. "Testimony before the Subcommittee on Select Education, Committee on Education and the Workforce, U.S. House of Representatives, June 19, 2003." Web. 14 December 2003. <http://edworkforce.house.gov/hearings/108th/sed/titlevi61903/kurtz.htm>.

Kurzman, Charles. "Radical Sheik and the Missing Martyrs: Why Are There So Few Islamic Terrorists?" Center for Middle Eastern Studies. University of Arizona. 12 Feb. 2006.

Larguèche, Abdelhamid. "La communauté juive de Tunis à l'époque husseïnite: Unité, contrastes et relations intercommunautaires." *Histoire communautaire, histoire plurielle: La communauté juive de Tunisie.* Tunis: Centre de Publication Universitaire, 1999. 165-80.

Laronche, Martine. "La loi sur le voile a conduit à deux premières exclusions." *Le Monde* 21 Octobre 2004.

Laroussi, Farid. "When Francophone Means National: The Case of the Maghreb." *Yale French Studies* 103 (2003): 81-90.

Laskier, Michael M. *North African Jewry in the Twentieth Century: The Jews of Morocco, Tunisia, and Algeria.* New York: New York University Press, 1994.

Layachi, Azzedine. "Political Liberalisation and the Islamist Movement in Algeria." *The Journal of North African Studies* 9.2 (Summer 2004): 46-67.

"'Le dernier soir' avant le 11 septembre." *Le Monde* 2 Oct. 2001. Web. 3 August 2007 <http://www.lemonde.fr>.

Lévy, Simon. *Essais d'histoire et de civilisation judéo-marocaine.* Rabat: Centre Tarik Ibn Zyad, 2001.

Lewis, Bernard. *Histoire du Moyen-Orient*. Trans. J. Arnaud and J. Lahana. Paris: Albin Michel, 1997.

Lionnet, Françoise. "Dissymmetry Embodied: Nawal El Saadawi's *Woman at Point Zero* and the Practice of Excision." Chapter 6. *Postcolonial Representations: Women, Literature, Identity*. Ithaca & London: Cornell University Press, 1995. 129-53.

Lloyd, Simon. "The Crusading Movement 1096-1274." *The Oxford Illustrated History of the Crusades*. Ed. J. Riley-Smith. Oxford: Oxford University Press, 1995. 34-65.

Maalouf, Amin. *Les croisades vues par les Arabes*. Paris: Lattès, 1983. Trans. as *The Crusades through Arab Eyes*, by Jon Rothschild. London: Al Saqi Books, 1984.

———. *Les échelles du Levant*. Paris: Grasset, 1996. Trans. as *Ports of Call*, by Alberto Manguel. London: The Harvill Press, 1999.

———. *Les identités meurtrières*. Paris: Grasset, 1998. Trans. as *In the Name of Identity: Violence and the Need to Belong*, by Barbara Bray. New York: Arcade Publishing, 2000.

Mackie, Gerry. "Female Genital Cutting: The Beginning of the End." *Female "Circumcision" in Africa: Culture, Controversy, and Change*. Ed. Bettina Shell-Duncan and Ylva Hernlund. Boulder & London: Lynne Rienner, 2000. 253-81.

Majid, Anouar. "The Failure of Postcolonial Theory after 9/11." *Chronicle of Higher Education* 1 Nov. 2002: B11-12.

———. *Freedom and Orthodoxy: Islam and Difference in the Post-Andalusian Age*. Stanford, CA: Stanford University Press, 2004.

———. "Islam and the Literature of Controversy." *The Postcolonial Crescent: Islam's Impact on Contemporary Literature*. Ed. John C. Hawley. New York: Peter Lang, 1998. 84-91.

———. *Unveiling Traditions: Postcolonial Islam in a Polycentric World*. Durham, NC; London: Duke University Press, 2000.

Marie, Elisabeth Anne. "Sacrifice, sacrifiée, sacrificatrice: L'étrange triptyque. Sacrifices au féminin dans trois romans francophones libanais." Diss. The University of North Carolina at Chapel Hill, 2002.

Martinez, Louis. *The Algerian Civil War 1990-1998*. Trans. Jonathan Derrick. London: Hurst & Company, 2000.

———. "Why the Violence in Algeria?" *Journal of North African Studies* 9.2 (Summer 2004): 14-27.

Marx-Scouras, Danielle. "The Poetics of Maghrebine Illegitimacy." *L'esprit créateur* 26.1 (Spring 1986): 3-10.

Masson, Pierre. *Lire la bande dessinée*. Lyon: Presses universitaires de Lyon, 1985.

McDermott, Terry. *Perfect Soldiers: The Hijackers. Who They Were, Why They Did It*. New York: HarperCollins, 2005.

McKinney, Mark. "*Métissage* in Post-Colonial Comics." *Post-Colonial Cultures in France*. Ed. Alec Hargreaves and Mark McKinney. London & New York: Routledge, 1997. 169-88.

McQuillan, Libbie. "The Francophone Bande Dessinée: An Introduction." *The Francophone Bande Dessinée*. Ed. Charles Forsdick, Laurence Grove, and Libbie McQuillan. Amsterdam, NY: Rodopi, 2005. 7-13.

Mearsheimer, John, and Stephen Walt. *The Israel Lobby and U.S. Foreign Policy*. New York: Farrar, Straus and Giroux, 2007.

Meddeb, Abdelwahab. *Face à l'islam*. Paris: Textuel, 2004.

———. *La maladie de l'islam*. Paris: Seuil, 2002. Trans. as *The Malady of Islam*, by Pierre Joris and Ann Reid. New York: Basic Books, 2003, and *Islam and Its Discontents*. London: William Heinemann, 2003.

Mekay, Emad. "Female Genital Mutilation Continues, Says Report." *Inter Press Service* 7 February 2004. <http://www.commondreams.org/headlines04/0207-06.htm>

Memmi, Albert. "La folie intégriste." *Le magazine littéraire* 323 (1994) : 31-32.

———. *Juifs et Arabes*. Paris: Gallimard, 1974. Trans. as *Jews and Arabs*, by Eleanor Levieux. Chicago: J. P. O'Hara, 1975.

———. *Portrait du décolonisé arabo-musulman et de quelques autres*. Paris: Gallimard, 2004. Trans. as *Decolonization and the Decolonized*, by Robert Bononno. Minneapolis: University of Minnesota Press, 2006.

———. *La statue de sel*. Paris: Gallimard, 1966. Trans. as *The Pillar of Salt* by Edouard Roditi. Boston, MA: Beacon Press, 1992. [1955]

Mernissi, Fatima. *Dreams of Trespass*. Cambridge, MA: Perseus Books, 1994.

———. *Le harem politique*. Paris: Albin Michel, 1987.

———. "Palace Fundamentalism and Liberal Democracy." *The New Crusades: Constructing the Muslim Enemy*. Ed. Emran Qureshi and Michael Sells. New York: Columbia University Press, 2003. 51-67.

———. *Sultanes oubliées*. Casablanca: Le Fennec, Paris: Albin Michel, 1990. Trans. as *Forgotten Queens of Islam,* by Mary Jo Lakeland. Cambridge: Polity Press, 1993.

Michaud, Joseph François. *Bibliothèque des croisades*. New York: AMS Press, 1978. [reprint of the 1829 ed. published by A. J. Ducollet, Paris]. 4 vol.

Millecam, Jean-Pierre. "Apocalypses." *Une enfance algérienne*. Ed. Leïla Sebbar. Paris: Gallimard, 1999 [1997]. 175-90.

Mimouni, Rachid. *De la barbarie en général et de l'intégrisme en particulier*. Tunis: Cérès Productions, 1992.

Miraglia, Anne-Marie. "Le temps et ses reflets dans *La maison sans racines* d'Andrée Chédid." *Francophonia* 35 (Fall 1998): 17-33.

Mitchell, W.J.T. *What Do Pictures Want?* Chicago & London: University of Chicago Press, 2005.

Mohanty, Chandra Talpade. "Under Western Eyes: Feminist Scholarship and Colonial Discourses." *Third World Women and the Politics of Feminism*. Ed. Chandra Talpade Mohanty, Ann Russo, Lourdes Torres. Bloomington: Indiana University Press, 1991. 51-80.

Mortimer, Robert. "Islamists, Soldiers, and Democrats: The Second Algerian War." *Middle East Journal* 50.1 (Winter 1996): 18-39.

Morton, Stephen. "Terrorism, Orientalism and Imperialism." *Wasafiri* 22.2 (July 2007): 36-42.

Mudimbe-Boyi, Elisabeth. "Enfermer et contrôler: Lieu social et espace textuel dans *L'excisée* de Evelyne Accad." *Francofonia: Studi e ricerche sulle letterature di lingua francese* 23 (Fall 1992): 3-19.

Navarro, Mireya. "The Most Private of Makeovers." *New York Times* 28 November 2004. Web. 12 March 2009. <http://www.nytimes.com>.

Naylor, Philip. *France and Algeria: A History of Decolonization and Transformation*. Gainesville: University Press of Florida, 2000.

The New Oxford Annotated Bible. Ed. Bruce Metzger and Roland Murphy. New Revised Standard Edition. New York: Oxford University Press, 1991.

Nixon, Rob. "Among the Mimics and Parasites: V. S. Naipaul's Islam." *The New Crusades: Constructing the Muslim Enemy*. Ed. Emran Qureshi and Michael A. Sells. New York; Chichester [England]: Columbia University Press, 2003. 152-69.

Noiriel, Gérard. *Les fils maudits de la République. L'avenir des intellectuels en France*. Paris: Fayard, 2005.

Nordmann, Charlotte, ed. *Le foulard islamique en questions*. Paris: Editions Amsterdam, 2004.

Nordmann, Charlotte, and Jérôme Vidal. "La République à l'épreuve des discriminations." *Le foulard islamique en questions.* Ed. Charlotte Nordmann. Paris: Editions Amsterdam, 2004. 5-14.

Noudelmann, François. "Introduction." *Politique et filiation.* Ed. R. Harvey, E. Ann Kaplan, and François Noudelmann. Paris: Kimé, 2004. 9-12.

———. *Pour en finir avec la généalogie.* Paris: Léo Scheer, 2004.

———. "Pour une pensée archipélique, Edouard Glissant." *Politique et filiation.* Ed. R. Harvey, E. Ann Kaplan, and François Noudelmann. Paris: Kimé, 2004. 194-205.

Oldenbourg, Zoé. *Les croisades.* Paris: Gallimard, 1965.

Pappé, Ilan. *A History of Modern Palestine.* 2nd Edition. Cambridge: Cambridge University Press, 2006. [2004]

Pedahzur, Ami. *Suicide Terrorism.* Cambridge, UK: Polity Press, 2005.

Pélégri, Jean. "Quand les oiseaux se taisent..." *Une enfance algérienne.* Ed. Leïla Sebbar. Paris: Gallimard, 1999 [1997]. 191-202.

Podselver, Laurence. "Le pèlerinage d'El Hamma à Sarcelles." *Histoire communautaire, histoire plurielle: La communauté juive de Tunisie.* Tunis: Centre de Publication Universitaire, 1999. 275-86.

Pratt, Mary Louise. "Building a New Public Idea about Language." *Profession* 2003: 110-19.

Qureshi, Emran, and Michael A. Sells. "Introduction: Constructing the Muslim Enemy." *The New Crusades: Constructing the Muslim Enemy.* Ed. Emran Qureshi and Michael A. Sells. New York: Columbia University Press, 2003. 1-47.

Redonnet, Marie. *Entretiens avec Edmond Amran El Maleh.* Rabat: La pensée sauvage, 2005.

Reuter, Christoph. *My Life Is a Weapon. A Modern History of Suicide Bombing.* Trans. Helena Ragg-Kirkby. Princeton: Princeton University Press, 2004. [2002]

Ricolfi, Luca. "Palestinians, 1981-2003." *Making Sense of Suicide Missions.* Ed. Diego Gambetta. Oxford: Oxford University Press, 2005. 77-129.

Riley-Smith, Jonathan. "The Crusading Movement and Historians." *The Oxford Illustrated History of the Crusades.* Ed. J. Riley-Smith. Oxford: Oxford University Press, 1995. 1-12.

Roquebert, Michel. *L'épopée cathare. 1198-1212: L'invasion.* Toulouse: Privat, 1970.

Rosello, Mireille. *Declining the Stereotype: Ethnicity and Representation in French Cultures.* Hanover & London: University Press of New England, 1998.

———. "Michèle Maillet's *L'étoile noire*: Historian's Counter-History and Translator's Counter-Silence." *Callaloo* 16.1 (Winter 1993): 192-212.

———. "Tactical Universalism and New Multiculturalist Claims in Postcolonial France." *Francophone Postcolonial Studies. A Critical Introduction.* Ed. Charles Forsdick and David Murphy. London: Arnold, 2003. 135-44.

Rosenthal, Franz. *A History of Muslim Historiography.* Leiden: E.J. Brill, 1968.

Roy, Olivier. *Globalised Islam. The Search for a New Ummah.* London: Hurst & Co., 2004. Revised and updated translation of *L'islam mondialisé* (Paris: Seuil, 2002).

Runciman, Steven. *A History of the Crusades.* 3 vol. Cambridge: Cambridge University Press, 1951-54.

Said, Edward. "The Clash of Definitions." *Reflections on Exile and Other Essays.* Cambridge, MA: Harvard University Press, 2000. 569-90.

———. *Covering Islam. How the Media and the Experts Determine How We See the Rest of the World.* Revised Edition. New York: Vintage Books, 1997. [1981]

———. *Culture and Imperialism.* New York: Vintage Books, 1994.

———. *The End of the Peace Process. Oslo and After.* New York: Pantheon Books, 2000.

———. "The Essential Terrorist." *Blaming the Victims: Spurious Scholarship and the Palestinian Question*. Ed. Edward Said and Christopher Hitchens. London & New York: Verso, 2001 [1988]. 149-58.

———. *Humanism and Democratic Criticism*. New York: Columbia University Press, 2004.

———. "Introduction." *Blaming the Victims: Spurious Scholarship and the Palestinian Question*. Ed. Edward Said and Christopher Hitchens. London & New York: Verso, 2001 [1988]. 1-19.

———. "Opponents, Audiences, Constituencies, and Community." *Reflections on Exile and Other Essays*. Cambridge, MA: Harvard University Press, 2000. 118-47.

———. *Orientalism*. New York: Vintage Books, 1979. [1978]

———. *The World, the Text, and the Critic*. Cambridge, Mass.: Harvard University Press, 1983.

Salem, Elise. *Constructing Lebanon: A Century of Literary Narratives*. Gainesville: University Press of Florida, 2003.

Salibi, Kamal. *Crossroads to Civil War. Lebanon 1958-1976*. Delmar, NY: Caravan Books, 1976.

———. *A House of Many Mansions: The History of Lebanon Reconsidered*. London: I.B. Tauris, 1988.

Sassine, Antoine. "Entretien avec Amin Maalouf: L'homme a ses racines dans le ciel." *Etudes francophones* 14.2 (Fall 1999): 25-36.

Satrapi, Marjane. *Persepolis*. New York: Pantheon Books, 2003. [2000]

Sayyid, Salman. *A Fundamental Fear: Eurocentrism and the Emergence of Islamism*. 2nd edition. London & New York: Zed Books, 2003.

Scharfman, Ronnie. "Narratives of Internal Exile. Cixous, Derrida, and the Vichy Years in Algeria." *Postcolonial Theory and Francophone Literary Studies*. Ed. H. Adlai Murdoch and Anne Donadey. Gainesville: University Press of Florida, 2005. 87-101.

———. "The Other's Other: The Moroccan-Jewish Trajectory of Edmond Amran El Maleh." *Yale French Studies* 82 (1993): 135-45.

Screech, Matthew. *Masters of the Ninth Art: Bandes dessinées and Franco-Belgian Identity*. Liverpool: Liverpool University Press, 2005.

Sebag, Paul. *Histoire des Juifs de Tunisie: Des origines à nos jours*. Paris: L'Harmattan, 1991.

Sebbar, Leïla, ed. *Une enfance algérienne*. Paris: Gallimard, 1997. Trans. as *An Algerian Childhood*, by Marjolijn de Jager. St. Paul, MN: Ruminator Books, 2001.

———, ed. *Une enfance outremer*. Paris: Seuil, 2001.

———. "La fille au hijeb." *Sept filles: nouvelles*. Paris: T. Magnier, 2003. 79-89.

———. *Journal de mes Algéries en France*. St-Pourçain-sur-Sioule [France]: Bleu autour, 2005.

———. *Mes Algéries en France*. St-Pourçain-sur-Sioule [France]: Bleu autour, 2004.

———. "On tue des instituteurs." *Une enfance algérienne*. Ed. Leïla Sebbar. Paris: Gallimard, 1999 [1997]. 203-14.

———. "Pourquoi cette peur?" *Le Monde* 24 Oct. 1989.

———. "Vierge folle, vierge sage." *La jeune fille au balcon*. Paris: Seuil, 1996. 107-24.

Serrano, Richard. *Against the Postcolonial: "Francophone" Writers at the Ends of French Empire*. Lanham, MD: Lexington Books, 2005.

Shell-Duncan, Bettina, and Ylva Hernlund. "Female 'Circumcision' in Africa: Dimensions of the Practice and Debates." *Female "Circumcision" in Africa: Culture, Controversy, and Change*. Ed. Bettina Shell-Duncan and Ylva Hernlund. Boulder & London: Lynne Rienner, 2000. 283-312.

Shih, Shu-Mei. "Global Literature and the Technologies of Recognition." *PMLA* 119.1 (January 2004): 16-30.

Shilton, Siobhán. "Negotiating Female Identities: 'Franco-Maghrebi' Journeys in the Visual Arts." Maghreb, Visual Arts and the French Exception. The 20th and 21st Century French and Francophone Studies International Colloquium. Hilton Hotel and Conference Center, College Station, TX, 23 March 2007.

Shohat, Ella. "Rupture and Return: Zionist Discourse and the Study of Arab Jews." *Social Text* 21.2 (Summer 2003): 49-74.

——. "Sephardism in Israel: Zionism from the Standpoint of Its Jewish Victims." *Dangerous Liaisons: Gender, Nation, and Postcolonial Perspectives.* Ed. Anne McClintock, Aamir Mufti, and Ella Shohat. Minneapolis: University of Minnesota Press, 1997. 39-68.

Shohat, Ella, and Robert Stam. *Multiculturalism, Postcoloniality, and Transnational Media.* New Brunswick: Rutgers University Press, 2003.

Shumway, David. "Disciplinary Identities." *Affiliations: Identity in Academic Culture.* Ed. Jeffrey Di Leo. Lincoln; London: University of Nebraska Press, 2003. 89-100.

Shweder, Richard. "'What about Female Genital Mutilation?' and Why Understanding Culture Matters in the First Place." *Engaging Cultural Differences. The Multicultural Challenge in Liberal Democracies.* Ed. R. Shweder, M. Minow, and H.R. Markus. New York: Russell Sage Foundation, 2002. 216-51.

Siberry, Elizabeth. "Images of the Crusades in the Nineteenth and Twentieth Centuries." *The Oxford Illustrated History of the Crusades.* Ed. Jonathan Riley-Smith. Oxford: Oxford University Press, 1995. 365-85.

——. *The New Crusaders. Images of the Crusades in the Nineteenth and Early Twentieth Centuries.* Aldershot, England: Ashgate Publishing, 2000.

Sibly, W.A., and M.D. Sibly, trans. and eds. *The History of the Albigensian Crusade. Peter of Les Vaux-de-Cernay's Historia Albigensis.* Woodbridge, UK: Boydell Press, 1998.

Sivan, E. *Modern Arab Historiography of the Crusades.* Kfar Chabad, Israel: Tel-Aviv University, 1973.

Smith, Charles. *Palestine and the Arab-Israeli Conflict.* 6th edition. New York: St. Martin's Press, 2007.

Solomon, Alisa. "Who Gets to Be Human on the Evening News?" *PMLA* 121.5 (October 2006): 1585-92.

Sontag, Susan. *On Photography.* New York: Farrar, Straus & Giroux, 1977.

Steel, James. "*Let's Party!* Astérix and the World Cup (France 1998)." *The Francophone Bande Dessinée.* Ed. Charles Forsdick, Laurence Grove, and Libbie McQuillan. Amsterdam, NY: Rodopi, 2005. 201-18.

Stora, Benjamin. *La guerre invisible: Algérie, années 90.* Paris: Presses de Sciences Po, 2001.

——. "L'impossible neutralité des Juifs d'Algérie." *La guerre d'Algérie: 1954-2004, la fin de l'amnésie.* Ed. Benjamin Stora and Mohammed Harbi. Paris: R. Laffont, 2004. 287-316.

——. *Les trois exils. Juifs d'Algérie.* Paris: Stock, 2006.

——. "1999-2003, guerre d'Algérie, les accélérations de la mémoire." *La guerre d'Algérie: 1954-2004, la fin de l'amnésie.* Ed. Benjamin Stora and Mohammed Harbi. Paris: R. Laffont, 2004. 501-14.

Stora, Benjamin and Mohammed Harbi, eds. *La guerre d'Algérie: 1954-2004, la fin de l'amnésie.* Paris: Laffont, 2004.

Sullivan, Zohreh. "The Body and the City: Evelyn Accad's and Etel Adnan's Beirut." *On Evelyne Accad: Essays in Literature, Feminism, and Cultural Studies.* Ed. Cheryl Toman. Birmingham, AL: Summa, 2007. 71-78.

Talbi, Mohamed. "Rénovation de la pensée musulmane, l'islam et les juifs: quelle relation?" *Histoire communautaire, histoire plurielle: La communauté juive de Tunisie.* Tunis: Centre de Publication Universitaire, 1999. 41-50.

Tarr, Carrie. "L'Eternel Retour: Reflection of the Occupation's Crisis in French Masculinity?" *SubStance* 27.3, Issue 87: Special Issue: The Occupation (1998): 55-72.

Tengour, Habib. "Enfance." *Une enfance algérienne.* Ed. Leïla Sebbar. Paris: Gallimard, 1999 [1997]. 215-28.

Ternisien, Xavier. "Des manifestations contre la loi sur le voile ont rassemblé quelques milliers de personnes." *Le Monde* 17 Feb. 2004.

Terray, Emmanuel. "L'hystérie politique." *Le foulard islamique en questions.* Ed. Charlotte Nordmann. Paris: Editions Amsterdam, 2004. 103-17.

Thieme, John. *Postcolonial Con-texts: Writing Back to the Canon.* London; New York: Continuum, 2001.

Thomas, Scott. *The Global Resurgence of Religion and the Transformation of International Relations: The Struggle for the Soul of the Twenty-First Century.* New York, N.Y.: Palgrave Macmillan, 2005.

Toman, Cheryl, ed. *On Evelyne Accad: Essays in Literature, Feminism, and Cultural Studies.* Birmingham, AL: Summa, 2007.

Tramson, Jacques. "La bande dessinée du Maghreb: L'Arlésienne de l'autre côté de la Méditerranée." Jean Foucault. *Imaginaire du jeune méditerranéen.* Itinéraires et contacts de cultures, v. 31. Paris: L'Harmattan, 2002. 33-49.

Tyerman, Christopher. *The Invention of the Crusades.* Toronto: University of Toronto Press, 1998.

Updike, John. *Terrorist.* New York: Alfred A. Knopf, 2006.

Valensi, Lucette. "Une Histoire des juifs de Tunisie est-elle nécessaire? Est-elle possible?" *Histoire communautaire, histoire plurielle: la communauté juive de Tunisie.* Tunis: Centre de Publication Universitaire, 1999. 51-63.

Versluys, Kristiaan. "9/11 as a European Event: The Novel." *The European Review* 15.1 (2007): 65-79.

Verthuy, Maïr. "Evelyne Accad, or the Hijacking of Sexuality." *On Evelyne Accad: Essays in Literature, Feminism, and Cultural Studies.* Ed. Cheryl Toman. Birmingham, AL: Summa, 2007. 157-70.

Vircondelet, Alain. "Le retour des sources." *Une enfance algérienne.* Ed. Leïla Sebbar. Paris: Gallimard, 1999 [1997]. 229-43.

Volpi, Frédéric. *Islam and Democracy: The Failure of Dialogue in Algeria.* London; Sterling, VA: Pluto Press, 2003.

Voltaire. *Dictionnaire philosophique, ou la raison par alphabet.* 7th edition. Londres, 1770. Vol. 1.

Watt, Stephen. "It Seems (Af)Filiation Is to Blame." *Affiliations: Identity in Academic Culture.* Ed. Jeffrey Di Leo. Lincoln; London: University of Nebraska Press, 2003. 115-30.

Wieviorka, Annette. *Auschwitz expliqué à ma fille.* Paris: Seuil, 1999.

Willis, Michael. *The Islamist Challenge in Algeria: A Political History.* New York: New York University Press, 1996.

Women's Caucus of the African Studies Association. "Position Paper on Clitoridectomy and Infibulation." *Genital Cutting and Transnational Sisterhood. Disputing U.S. Polemics.* Ed. Stanlie M. James and Claire Robertson. Urbana & Chicago: University of Illinois Press, 2002. 1-3.

Zabus, Chantal. *Between Rites and Rights: Excision in Women's Experiential Texts and Human Contexts*. Stanford, CA: Stanford University Press, 2007.

———. "Bouches cousues: l'autobiographie de l'excisée." *L'animal autobiographique: Autour de Jacques Derrida*. Ed. Marie-Louise Mallet. Paris: Editions Galilée, 1999. 331-52 .

Zafrani, Haïm. *Mille ans de vie juive au Maroc: Histoire et culture, religion et magie*. Paris: Maisonneuve et Larose, 1983.

Zahnd, Elizabeth. "Two Eyes for an Eye: Women, Violence, and Modernity in Two Lebanese Novels." *Literature and Cruelty/Littérature et cruauté*. Proc. of the 6th Annual Graduate Conf. in French, Francophone and Comparative Lit., Columbia Univ., March 1, 1996. Ed. Vincent Desroches. New York: Columbia University, 1996.

Zainaba. "Lecture on Clitoridectomy to the Midwives of Touil, Mauritania." Introduced and translated by Elizabeth Oram. *Opening the Gates*. Ed. Margot Badran and Miriam Cooke. 63-71.

Žižek, Slavoj. *Welcome to the Desert of the Real! Five Essays on September 11 and Related Dates*. London & New York: Verso, 2002.

Index

About the Author

Carine Bourget is associate professor of French and Francophone studies in the French and Italian Department at the University of Arizona, and holds a courtesy appointment with the Near Eastern Studies Department. Her research focuses on the cultural production from the Francophone Arab world, with special interests in Islam in literature, Islam in France, politics and literature, and history and literature. She is the author of *Coran et tradition islamique dans la littérature maghrébine* (Paris: Karthala, 2002), a study that analyzes the religious intertext in works by Tahar Ben Jelloun, Driss Chraïbi, Assia Djebar, and Fatima Mernissi. Her most recent articles have appeared in *L'Esprit Créateur, The French Review, Research in African Literatures, Studies in 20th and 21st Century Literature, Expressions maghrébines*, and *French Cultural Studies*.

Breinigsville, PA USA
09 February 2011
255225BV00002B/10/P